# The Craft of Criticism

# The Craft of Criticism

ALLAN RODWAY

*Reader in English, University of Nottingham*

## Cambridge University Press

*Cambridge*
*London   New York   New Rochelle*
*Melbourne   Sydney*

Published by the Press Syndicate of the University of Cambridge
The Pitt Building, Trumpington Street, Cambridge CB2 1RP
32 East 57th Street, New York, NY 10022, USA
296 Beaconsfield Parade, Middle Park, Melbourne 3206, Australia

First published 1982

Printed in Great Britain at the University Press, Cambridge


Library of Congress catalogue card number: 82–4499

*British Library cataloguing in publication data*
Rodway, Allan
The craft of criticism.
1. English poetry – Explication
I. Title
821'.009    PR502
ISBN 0 521 23320 8 hard covers
ISBN 0 521 29909 8 paperback

# Contents

# Contents

# Preface

Students of literature are not short of expositions of principle and examples of practice. What they *are* short of is the sort of thing a craft apprentice gets: specific aid in bridging the gap between the theory and the practice. On the one hand, books of critical theory are available — but such works were never easy and are now becoming both more abstruse and more remote from literary appreciation. On the other hand, there are books of practical criticism — but such works never spell out the principles, if any, underpinning their practice. What seems to be needed, then, is neither more abstract theorising nor more take-it-or-leave it exemplification but rather explanations given whilst the critical job is in progress — that is to say, in the form of guidance, of appropriate tips.

This book attempts to provide some such combination of principle and practice, as a guide towards what is fundamental to any kind of literary criticism claiming some validity (and what other kind warrants attention?): namely, a *justifiable* appreciation of the words on the page. The bulk of the book consists of practical critiques of poems of various kinds from various periods, all being of interest in their own right, but also illustrating *a variety of critical methods* (for in this area no standard bridge exists for all crossings). But there is no question of matching each poem with one method so as to give a neat simple 'line' on the poem and, eventually, a rota of distinguishable methods (formal, historical, social, psychological, and so on). On the contrary, most methods are likely to be applicable to most poems, *though in very different degrees.* In so far as poems themselves are many-sided so far must an adequate critique be — the craft of criticism often resembling nothing so much as a difficult juggling act in which several objects of different sizes and weights have to be kept in play. Each poem, therefore, is given as full and rich a practical criticism as seems necessary, and relevant points of critical principle underpinning the practice are elucidated, as briefly and plainly as possible, during the process.

Only in the introduction, then, is theory to be found in separation from practice, and even there a number of examples are used. Moreover, all concepts that might present difficulty owing to the necessary brevity of an introduction are more fully explained in the glossary at the end. In any event, they should, of course, become gradually clearer and subtler as they crop up in different contexts during the critiques that form the body of the work.

Chronological order in the arrangement of these critiques has been deliberately avoided in order not to deflect attention from critical to historical concerns (though the fact that historical scholarship is often relevant to practical criticism is not overlooked).

Verse has been preferred to prose, firstly, because it more easily yields a variety of complete works of suitable length, and secondly, because while involving no theoretical difference in critical approach (if narrative verse is included) in practice it tends to a greater concentration of literary effects.

Allan Rodway
University of Nottingham

# Acknowledgements

The author and publisher would like to make acknowledgements as
follows with regard to the quotation of copyright material: 'Poem in
October' from *Collected Poems* by Dylan Thomas, reprinted by permission
of J.M. Dent; 'Piazza Piece' from *Selected Poems* (third edition, revised
and enlarged) by John Crowe Ransom, reprinted by permission of
Laurence Pollinger Ltd and Alfred A. Knopf, Inc., copyright 1927 by
Alfred A. Knopf, Inc., renewed 1955 by John Crowe Ransom; 'Two X'
from *Complete Poems 1913–1962* by e.e. cummings, reprinted by permission of Granada Publishing Ltd, and from *IS 5* by e.e. cummings,
reprinted by permission of Liveright Publishing Corporation, copyright
1926 by Boni and Liveright, renewed 1953 by e.e. cummings; 'To A Steam
Roller' from *The Complete Poems of Marianne Moore*, reprinted by permission of Faber and Faber Ltd and Macmillan Publishing Co., Inc., copyright 1935 by Marianne Moore, renewed 1963 by Marianne Moore and
T.S. Eliot; 'Thistles' from *Wodwo* by Ted Hughes, reprinted by permission
of Faber and Faber Ltd, and from *New Selected Poems* (1982) by Ted
Hughes, reprinted by permission of Harper and Row, Publishers, Inc., ©
1961 by Ted Hughes; 'Deceptions' from *The Less Deceived* by Philip
Larkin, reprinted by permission of The Marvell Press; 'Snow' from *The
Collected Poems of Louis MacNeice*, reprinted by permission of Faber and
Faber Ltd; 'A Martian Sends a Postcard Home' from *A Martian Sends a
Postcard Home* by Craig Raine, reprinted by permission of Oxford Univer-
sity Press, © Craig Raine 1979; 'The Draft Horse' from *The Poetry of
Robert Frost*, ed. Edward Connery Lathem, reprinted by permission of the
Estate of Robert Frost, Jonathan Cape Ltd and Holt, Rinehart and
Winston, Publishers, © 1962 by Robert Frost, © 1969 by Holt, Rinehart
and Winston; 'An Irish Airman Foresees His Death' from *Collected Poems*
by W.B. Yeats, reprinted by permission of M.B. and Anne Yeats,
Macmillan (London) Ltd and Macmillan Publishing Co., Inc., copyright
1919 by Macmillan Publishing Co., Inc., renewed 1947 by Bertha Georgie
Yeats; Sebastian's sestina from *The Sea and the Mirror* from *Collected*

# Introduction

As this book is to move from the mainly theoretical, in the introduction, to the mainly practical, in the critiques forming the body of the work, it will be appropriate for this introduction itself to move from the more abstractly theoretical to the less. That is to say, from discussion of *Criticism* to discussion of the *Craft* by which critical principles are put to practical use. In each case some oversimplification will be unavoidable, since both topics are highly complex. But that may be no bad thing. As the end in view is a practical one (see the preface) this introduction can properly be used as a sort of scaffolding to be eventually discarded.

## I

What, then, is literary criticism? Why do we need it? And why is it so much concerned with *how* literature* means rather than *what* it means?

Too much ink, it may be objected, has already been spilt over such questions. But some answers must be given, however sketchy, if only that we may know what we are talking about and why it should be worth talking about.

However, fairly straightforward answers, commonsensical rather than metaphysical, will serve our turn, provided that three things — questioned by today's trendier theorists — are taken as given. The first is that the world and other people exist in their own right (not as mere fictions, unsuitable therefore as material for literary fictionalising); the second, that language can and does communicate meaning; the third (a logical consequence of the first and second), that works of literature carry meanings, even across the centuries, that can be communicated — and may well be worth the deciphering since, though perhaps fictional themselves, they bear some relation to some sort of reality.

*All words starred on their first appearance are commented upon — if necessary at some length — in the glossary. Often the glossary will also be found to provide material for further discussion.

If the first two assumptions were not granted, there would be little point in doing, saying, or studying *anything*; and if the third were not, it would be difficult indeed to account for the zeal with which authoritarians over the ages have banned or burned books (and sometimes their authors). Certainly, not to accept the first assumption in practice — as distinct from engaging in a purely theoretical exercise — would clearly lead to disaster. The second seems adequately justified by the everyday facts of existence (and those who argue against it *cannot* logically sustain their case since they must illogically exclude the language of their own argument from it). The third assumption, by this fact: that though much literature is *not* worthwhile, when the dross is sorted out (one good reason for criticism) what remains is a great cultural bank, so to speak, a publicly available hoard of non-monetary treasure. Literature is the most memorable means by which human perceptions, wisdom, experience, and feelings, from fields far more varied than any one individual could command, can be handed on. In this above all, we differ from other animals.

There is, then, good reason for the practice of a *literary* criticism: the deciphering, explanation, and critical appreciation of literary meaning* (including, of course, emotional meaning). A process normally to be followed — at any rate by those criticising for the benefit of others — by the discrimination of works more worth reading, on various grounds, from those less worth the trouble. The word 'criticism', however, is often used to cover very different activities related to literature: in particular, *scholarship* (a concern for the facts of literature), or *metacriticism** (a concern for the significance* of literature, e.g. how it impinges on morality or politics, what it unwittingly reveals of contemporary social attitudes, and so on).

These are clearly very different concerns, in principle, from those of *criticism* proper (or 'literary' or 'intrinsic'* criticism) whose concern is with the full meaning of the text itself, with its identity. To put it another way, criticism is concerned with what the work *is*, metacriticism with what it is (usually unwittingly) a *sign of*, and scholarship with *information about it*. To establish the correct text of a Shakespeare play would be scholarship. To use the play as a guide to the refinements of Elizabethan modes of feeling, thinking, or dressing, or to the personality of Shakespeare; or, as many Marxist critics would, to assess it in terms of its likely political effects — all these would be metacritical activities. To establish the meaning and qualities of the play itself and assess their literary value would be criticism.

In practice, there is some unavoidable overlapping. The scholarly editor, for instance often has to choose on literary-critical grounds alone between a reading in the Folio (the collected Shakespeare plays of 1623) and a reading in a Quarto (one of the smaller earlier volumes containing one play). On the other hand, the critic will be unable even to understand the text in its simplest sense, without the aid of some scholarly apparatus to explain obsolete words, references, and ideas. And clearly, when the meta-critic uses the play as a document to add some subtle extra to another subject — biography, sociology, morality, or whatever — he must at least have a correct text and a correct understanding of it, if his additions are to carry any weight.

To take an example, almost at random:

> THESEUS: Now fair Hippolyta, our nuptial hour
> Draws on apace. Four happy days bring in
> Another moon — but O, methinks how slow
> This old moon wanes! She lingers my desires,
> Like to a stepdame or a dowager
> Long withering out a young man's revenue.
> HIPPOLYTA: Four days will quickly steep themselves in night;
> Four nights will quickly dream away the time,
> And then the moon, like to a silver bow
> Now bent in heaven, shall behold the night
> Of our solemnities.

Here are the opening speeches of *A Midsummer Night's Dream*. We need editorial scholarship to tell us the contemporary meanings of several words: *lingers*, delays; *stepdame*, stepmother; *dowager*, widow with a jointure or dower; *withering out*, being a charge on, causing to decrease. It is generations of editors, too, who decided on the punctuation, since slavish acceptance of the antiquated punctuation of the Folio or Quarto texts would often positively obscure the sense for a modern audience. As further aid to comprehension, editors have divided the text into acts and scenes, for neither the Folio nor any Quarto records scene divisions, and only the Folio is divided into acts. The Folio and the first Quarto of *A Midsummer Night's Dream* are the chief authorities for the text. Here and there, though, they differ; and here and there neither makes good sense; so if an editor simply copied them he would not be giving literary critics the facts they need: those of a good text and the explanations of its contemporary references and shades of meaning. Most editors give line ten above as 'New-bent'; presumably assuming that 'Now bent' requires '*the* silver bow'. But 'Now bent' is what is given by both Folio and Quarto texts. That *may* be a repeated misprint, but it does not seem an impossible reading, if we imagine a bit of stage business, and re-punctuate:

> And then the moon, like to a silver bow [*pointing*]
> (Now bent in Heaven), shall behold . . .

But do not such decisions force the scholarly editor to be something of a literary critic as well? Indeed they do, as do decisions about what constitutes a scene and what is the better reading when Folio and Quarto differ.

The critic will be primarily concerned with such matters as the aptness of these lines as an opening gambit. Do they give necessary information, in a manner that the audience can take in while still settling down? Do they establish an appropriate mood? Is the language right for courtly rulers (as distinct from the fairies, rude mechanicals, and lovers, each of which groups has its own style)? He might point out how aptly, by means of long vowels and extra stresses, the language *enacts* as well as states its meaning in:

> Ó, mĕthínks hów slów
> Thĭs olď moón wánes!

And so on. Yet before he can start understanding the text in this deeper sense, he must understand it in the simplest sense of knowing what the words mean; and therefore, since some of the meanings are obsolete, must become a scholar, at any rate to the extent of absorbing what scholars have established.

The metacritic might be most interested in what lines five and six reveal of Elizabethan social attitudes to money or to the elderly, or in the type of personality that could so offhandedly unite, through this simile, monetary toughness with amorous tenderness, apparently without any sense of incongruity. But the latter interest — depending on a judgement of tone — surely has much in common with a critical interest in the character of Theseus (though the literary critic would be using this material to move inward, into the play; the metacritic to move outward, towards Elizabethan psychology in general). Clearly, any metacritical statements as to the extra-literary meaning (the significance) of the literary meaning have no chance of being valid unless they are based on a correct text and a correct literary understanding of it. They are the metacritic's *evidence* — and scholarship and criticism, whether his own or someone else's, are what provide it.

In such ways, then, distinctions clear enough in principle become blurred in practice, become a matter of different emphasis rather than absolute difference. Nevertheless, we can now restate, more fully, what 'criticism' is, so far as this book is concerned. It is what is left over when metacriticism and scholarship have been set aside.

What precisely is it that is left over? It is the endeavour to come to as full an understanding of a literary work as possible, an understanding that is both judicial and sympathetic — and justifiable: supportable, that is to say, by reasonable evidence, as against mere assertions of liking or disliking. It is, in short, an endeavour to get out of a work everything that is really there, and not to read into it anything that is not.

One more example, to sum up:

> The curfew tolls the knell of parting day
>> The lowing herd winds slowly o'er the lea,
> The ploughman homeward plods his weary way,
>> And leaves the world to darkness and to me.

> Now fades the glimmering landscape on the sight . . .

If we had a metacritical interest in social history we might be struck to find that the curfew — introduced and enforced in the early Middle Ages — was still being sounded, pointlessly, in the mid eighteenth century, when Gray's 'Elegy' was composed. If our interest were linguistic we might note that the original, literal meaning of the word, *couvre-feu* (cover-fire) still lingered, at least for Gray (but that noting would depend on a previous literary-critical perception, as we shall see). If our interest were historical or theological, we might recall that the ploughman in medieval writings and sermons was a symbolic figure, symbolising man as he ought to be, or even Christ (but that recollection would depend on a literary-critical sensitivity — to Gray's subtle hint at our medieval past through the word 'curfew'). As critics, our interest in these facts would not be historical or linguistic, but literary. We should be interested in what, for example, 'curfew' contributed to a finer understanding of the poem rather than in what it contributed to a finer understanding of eighteenth-century social customs. So we should start by noting that the phrase 'tolls the knell' gives a double sense to 'parting'; so that it means 'dying' as well as merely 'departing'. The dead march of the metre, we might then note, reinforces the solemnity imparted by 'tolls'. It is at this point that the bit of scholarly information about 'curfew' might come to seem relevant — if we had a literary sensibility sufficiently trained to be receptive to such relevances. Knowing that the curfew had long ceased to be enforced, we should see that to literate readers in Gray's age, as to us, the word must have carried its history with it, bearing the mind back through all the generations of the churchyard to the Dark Ages of a gothic past. A little biographical scholarship would assure us that Gray could hardly have been unaware of the original meaning, '*couvre-feu*'. And of course the poem supports this, for the personifying 'knell' suggests that a damper of darkness is putting out the fires of life as well as the fires of the day. Not surprisingly then, the opening of the second stanza, 'Now fades the glimmering landscape on the sight' takes on a doubly eerie quality: at once that of the day's death and of a human deathbed, as one might suppose it in cases of easy, 'natural' dying. All perfectly appropriate for an elegy in a country churchyard where 'the rude forefathers of the hamlet sleep'. And especially for such an elegy as this, which is to range widely over the current eighteenth-century world of great and humble and go far back in time, always moving between concrete examples and general musings on life and death. But there is more to it than this. The sense of pastness infused into the poem by 'curfew' is what makes 'the ploughman' — significantly not '*a* ploughman' — a little more than realistically meaningful. He is not a fully symbolic medieval figure; on the other hand he is not just any old country labourer. In so far as we are sensitive to the rhythms of lines two and three, which do wind slowly and plod wearily with the aid of long vowels, alliteration, and iambics* that are so often nearly spondees,* we incline to a realistic interpretation. In so far as we are sensitive to tone* (which also alerts us to the timeless quality of this scene — in the days before factory farming) we incline a little to the symbolic (so that later on we are prepared to accept general human conclusions drawn from the particular 'rude forefathers' mouldering in country graves). The ploughman is thus sensed as typical and timeless, silhouetted on the glimmering border of day and night, life and death. Like that 'curfew', and in part because of it, he carries the mind back through the ages of our history — the same history that is (symbolically) writ small in the churchyard, with its village Hampdens, little tyrants, mute inglorious Miltons, and petty Cromwells.

Scholarship, criticism, and metacriticism, then, are interdependent in practice though independent in principle. Scholarship, however, is merely a servant of criticism (and itself requires a trained critical sensibility). Metacriticism, of the best kind, is valuable in its own right, but depends on previous, just criticism; since obviously conclusions drawn from a falsely interpreted text cannot themselves claim any truth.

There are good logical reasons, then, for giving criticism priority, for trying first of all to sharpen and methodise whatever good sense and literary sensibility nature has provided us with. Hence the attempt, in the critiques to follow, to establish the full *meaning* of the poems themselves rather than their *significance* in relation to something else; to apprehend what they *are* in all their richness rather than what they may (unwittingly) be *signs of* — an attempt, however, that may sometimes require reference to relevant scholarly information or, more rarely, to apparent metacritical significances.

But there are other reasons for giving criticism priority. What is read becomes part of the reader's life, and in so far as it affects him by way of subtle personal change, we have a transfer from art to life that is not of a metacritical kind. Such transfers, however, do not normally — and never wholly — come through pure subject-matter or paraphrasable messages. The meaning of a work of literature will also be a matter of its *qualities*. As Shelley said in the *Defence of Poetry* the value of creative writing lies not only in the facts and messages it may offer to the mind, but in that it 'awakens and enlarges the mind itself'.

Language communicates far more than information. For instance pity, fear, indignation, irony, wit, tenderness, eroticism, humour — and it does so in many ways. So the mind is 'enlarged' by literature not only in the area of thinking but also in the areas of feeling, intuition, and sensing; it is 'awakened' when things dulled by habit are seen freshly, when the humdrum is made strange, when new contemplation (as in Gray's 'Elegy') is made to grow out of old facts. Literature, in short, is enlivening in a world where many factors conspire to deaden. That is why criticism is more concerned with *how* literature means than with *what* it means. And that brings us to the craft by which critical principle is put into practice.

## II

As we have delimited 'criticism', a work on the craft of it may be practicable and useful — though not easy; for no one method, no 'correct' approach appropriate for all literary work is to be found even for intrinsic criticism alone. Since writers, whether in verse* or prose,* may write about anything, in any mood, with any attitude to their audience, and in any style, it is obvious that flexibility and openness must combine with discrimination as prime requirements for a critic. The only indisputable principle of approach seems to be that of *pluralism*: the principle that there are more ways than one to the heart of works of creative literature — though certain works in practice do seem strongly to invite one approach more than others, according as the work itself is clearly, say, realistic or fantastic, comic or tragic, psychological or sociological. Most works, however, are many-sided, even if one side is considerably more prominent than others; so it is always desirable to look round before leaping to a conclusion — and therefore to cultivate ways of testing for other potentially profitable approaches.

It is for this reason that criticism seems to be better referred to as a 'craft' than anything else. Those who have claimed it as a science have usually been metacritics. The mode of being a literary work (which comes

7

to life only when read) is so intangible and has so many facets, that it has always been tempting to move prematurely from study of the work itself to study of its *causes* in the writer or society (criticism then becoming a metacritical form of amateur psychology, biography, or history) or else to study of its *effects* on the audience (a form of amateur sociology, anthropology, or mass-psychology), while imagining that by doing so one was obtaining insights into literature. Since these subjects are more amenable to scientific treatment than works of creative literature themselves which, unlike the material world, are not suitable for controlled experiment or mathematical quantification, there could be at least the illusion of a 'scientific' criticism.

Of course, causes and effects do have to be studied in criticism proper. The point is that there is a difference between examining *in the work* the cause of some effect in the reader and examining the cause of that cause in the writer or his society; between examining *in the work* some effect achieved by the writer and examining the effect of that effect on the reading public. Such examination of *literary* causes and effects cannot properly be described as scientific — for the reason given above — however precise the examination may be. Nor can it be considered an art,* since it is far more descriptive than creative.

Those who have claimed that criticism is, or can be, an art have done so on the grounds that just as creative literature organises the raw material of life into meaningful and pleasing patterns, so criticism may organise *its* raw material, literature. Now of course there is nothing to stop a writer using another writer's material as a springboard for a creative leap of his own, but in that case he will simply be producing a piece of parasitic art — itself inviting criticism. It will not fulfil the special task of criticism, as we define it: namely, the humble but useful one of bringing about a better understanding of someone else's creative work. Such a task requires sensibility, as science does not, but does not require original creativity, as art does, and seems therefore best described as a craft.

It is, however, a unique kind of craft, since its raw material is in fact *im*material — and this gives rise to the critic's special difficulty: the need to be subjectively objective,* or more accurately, objectively subjective.* These are points of such importance that they deserve further comment.

True enough, a literary work does have some sort of material existence, usually that of paper and printer's ink. But that material existence is trivial. It makes no difference to a poem, as such, whether it be printed in black or red, on thick paper or thin. It's real existence is what takes place in the mind when it is read or heard. So we can properly say that a literary work's material existence is insignificant, its significant existence

8

immaterial. This is where the critic's special difficulty comes in. If he reads into the work what is not really there, or fails to read out of it what really is there, then he is not himself getting, or giving his readers, whatever it is the work has to offer. Instead of sharing the inherited cultural treasure that literature represents he is distributing a false coinage of his own making. The result may be interesting or pleasurable but will not be educative. For this reason, the critic who is to be a craftsman rather than a parasitic, or second-order artist must be objective. That does not mean, as it might in a scientific context, that he must rely on machinery and mathematics rather than his own impressions. The immaterial nature of his material renders that an impossibility. What it does mean is that he must find ways of putting aside his prejudices and avoiding self-indulgence, must even find ways of perceiving the value of what he himself temperamentally dislikes. He must be objective in the sense of being as unbiassed as possible, of justifying rather than merely asserting. On the other hand, he cannot be coldly detached; analysing a poem is not like analysing a chemical compound. Much of its value lies in its qualities, and much of them lies in *how* it means, not in *what* it means. And these qualities only come into being, as we have just seen, in so far as they are recreated in the critic's mind as he reads. It follows that unless he has felt the bitterness, irony, longing, or humour of a piece, responded personally to its rhythms,* imagery, and implications, he is in no position to analyse; these human qualities *are* the elements of the analysis, and can properly be appreciated only by a human sensibility: that is to say personally, subjectively. The dilemma, then, is that, for different reasons, he will miss much that the work has to offer if he is *merely* subjective or *merely* objective. That is why a major part of the craft of criticism consists of finding aids for the difficult trick of being objectively subjective: fair, though personally involved.

This can be put another way. To say simply that a literary work can be judged by its effect is untenable. Is the effect on an idiot, an illiterate, a disturbed delinquent, a foreigner with an imperfect knowledge of the language to count equally with the effect on a sensible, sensitive, well-educated native speaker? Is the judgement of a passionately biassed reader likely to be as reliable as that of an unbiassed one? On the other hand, as we have seen, literary works significantly exist *only* as effects in the mind. Clearly, to count as criticism, rather than mere opinion, the effects must be *justifiable* effects; and the mind in which they come to life from previously dead print must be sensitive in its responses but at the same time able to discriminate among them: to be objectively subjective. That we are in fact able to do this depends on two things: firstly, that we share a

9

common language with the writer (though bits of it may need to be revived for us if he is of the past), so that ultimately poems mean what they do say, not what we would like them to; and secondly, that we share a common human nature, as conditioned by a common culture. (It may not be impossible for a Western reader eventually to appreciate, say, an eighteenth-century Chinese poem, but a just appreciation of an eighteenth-century English one will be much easier — and that of a twentieth-century one easier again, other things being equal.)

It follows that by *pluralism* — the principle that there are more ways than one to the heart of literary matters — we cannot mean that *any* approach will do. How pluralist, then, are we allowed to be? It is impossible to state a number; there are no seven roads to Seven Pillars of Wisdom. All depends on what the work itself suggests; so, though there are ways of testing for potentially profitable approaches, tips for going right, there are no fixed *rules* that will prevent those utterly unsuited to literary studies from going wrong (criticism not being a science). Anyone who takes *Macbeth*, on a first reading, to be a whodunnit, in which Macbeth is not really the murderer, or Gray's 'Elegy' to be a comedy, simply is not cut out for literature. Short of such extremes, though, a great deal can be done to improve native ability, despite the subtle and intangible nature of literature (it is, after all, also the most richly human of subjects).

Though the only valid principle of *approach* may be the principle that no one principle can be the only principle — an approach that imposes a considerable burden of choice — the principles of *assessment* can comfortingly be reduced to two: two standards by which one interpretation* may be deemed preferable to another. These are *unity* and *purport*.*

Without them, criticism as a common pursuit (as against a private, a *merely* subjective response) would be impossible, as there would be no grounds for choosing between rival interpretations of the meaning of any given part of a poem in relation to the whole. With them, however, we not only have grounds for such choices but also aid in choosing our principles of approach. Anyone undecided whether to approach *Macbeth* as a whodunnit or a psychological tragedy, for instance, would find by these two standards strong support for the latter approach.

It has to be taken as axiomatic, then, firstly, that the more inclusive interpretation is to be preferred, the one that leaves fewest loose ends, that most nearly, and with least straining, knots everything into a coherent whole; and secondly, that it is pointless to criticise a work as something it does not purport to be: that is to say, as something incompatible with its characteristics. *Macbeth* would be very bad as a murder mystery — even worse than *The Mousetrap* — but all its characteristics indicate to anyone

10

with the slightest literary sensibility that it is not setting out, does not purport, to be any such thing. Let us take the following seventeenth-century poem as an example:

To Phyllis

Phyllis, for shame, let us improve
    A thousand several ways
These few short minutes stol'n by love
    From many tedious days.

Whilst you want courage to despise
    The censure of the grave,
For all the tyrants in your eyes
    Your heart is but a slave.

My love is full of noble pride,
    And never will submit
To let that Fop, discretion, ride
    In triumph over wit.

False friends I have, as well as you,
    That daily counsel me
Vain frivolous trifles to pursue
    And leave off loving thee.

When I the least belief bestow
    On what such fools advise
May I be dull enough to grow
    Most miserably wise.

                                  *Sir Charles Sedley*

A minimal amount of scholarship may be necessary to clarify certain points. Simply to know the period of composition may be enough to send the reader to a good dictionary for the words 'fop' (now obsolete), and 'several', 'want', and 'wit' (clearly not used in quite their modern senses). For a careful reader, perhaps even this amount of outside information will not be necessary, since he will see that, for instance, 'want' interpreted in the usual modern way as 'desire', 'wish for', does not fit in with the general sense so well as its now rare interpretation as 'lack'; so that the principle of unity indicates that he should prefer the latter. To establish purport, however – namely, the sort of thing the poem seems to present itself as, or to be aiming at – it will certainly help to know that the period is that of the Restoration (*c.* 1660–1700), that the author was of the

Court not the City, and therefore was likely to have been anti-puritan (a likelihood confirmed by his biography), and that such courtly writers, recently returned from exile in France, were ambitious of Parisian sophistication as a life-style and Parisian cleverness and elegance for their literary style. With this in mind, the reader is less likely to leap in with censure of the poem for a lack of high seriousness or sincere passion. Rather he will assume that it very likely purports to be an amusing provocative work of an anti-puritan tendency, and will approach it as such. If he finds that such an approach leads to a more coherent and inclusive interpretation than any other, an interpretation that leaves no loose ends, no puzzling details that won't 'fit in', then he can be sure it is as 'correct' as possible (since it is justified by the literary facts of the words on the page and by the linguistic, biographical, and historical probabilities given by elementary scholarship). Certainly, this idea of the poem's purport will *help* in resolving one crucial point, which no amount of dictionary work or other scholarly effort, however, can prove. Does 'the grave' refer to a place of burial or to a type of person? Here the test of unity or coherence is conclusive. If 'the grave' is a burial-place, then there are serious discrepancies between tone and theme (and unity, of course, is not a matter solely of sense). Moreover, the techniques of provocation (paradox and the inversion of normal notions) are inept; and finally the obvious sense of many lines has to be *gravely* distorted in order to make continuous sense of the poem. On the other hand, as soon as 'the grave' is taken to mean sober respectable people, especially those of puritanical leanings, everything falls into place. The poem is seen to progress logically, if perhaps perversely, to the culmination of provocative paradoxes in the last stanza;* and certain difficulties clear up like magic. That 'shame', for instance. It makes better sense to be ashamed of not having the courage to flout respectable puritans than not having courage to flout death. A heart that is a slave to *religion* makes 'tyrants' difficult to account for (can eyes somehow express pretended atheism?). Anyway, on orthodox principles one *should* be slave to religion. Eyes, however, that express scorn and rejection tyrannise over the lover, but are the sign not of a virtuous personality but of a slave to *convention*, if 'the grave' is taken to mean 'the respectable'. Similarly, the provocative idea of the 'shame' of *not* making love in a thousand ways is quite compatible with shame at lacking courage to defy convention; but is not easily fitted in with shame at lacking courage to defy God, or the supernatural, or whatever post-mortal censorious authority 'the grave' as burial-place might be supposed to indicate. Again, if 'vain frivolous trifles' were to be interpreted religiously as, say, devotion, prayer, meditation, this stanza would be *seriously* ironical and thus quite out of keeping with the general

12

flippancy of the poem. Interpreted in terms of respectability as, say, prudence, work, money-making, the irony is light and elegant, quite of a piece with the general tone, and — adopting what now seems the obvious meaning of 'the grave' — theme* of the poem.

Neither *purport* nor *unity* is as simple as it seems at first. Practically nothing in literary criticism is. Just as scholarship, criticism, and metacriticism overlap, and principles of *approach* and *assessment* may interact instead of following neatly one after the other, so *purport* and *unity* are neither simple in themselves nor wholly separable from each other. None of this is really surprising; it simply reflects the make-up of literary works, in which one word or phrase will quite commonly be part of metre, imagery, paraphrasable sense, theme, rhyme-scheme, and story. Nor is it either surprising or deplorable that no principles, no method will automatically give right answers. Indeed, as a literary work is in part valuable for its pure qualities, for the way it 'awakens and enlarges the mind itself', the very concept of a right answer is irrelevant; there are only better or worse interpretations. A 'correct' interpretation must mean not a perfect one but only that for which the best justification has been offered. That is why criticism, though it needs some theory, needs practice more.

The idea of a work's purport — what in general it seems to be up to — is a hypothesis derived from an open-minded, quick preliminary reading, to be tested, and if necessary amended, by a more careful reading. But some works are not really what they purport to be. That is to say there lurks an implicit purport beneath the ostensible one: the real face is more or less masked (though not wholly, or we could not know it to be there). Ironic works are the simplest example of this. Here the plain purport is normally the opposite of the real one; but since such surface purports — usually a pretence of praise — are meant to be seen through, to be taken ironically, they rarely present problems to the perceptive reader. Suppose, though, the author intends to deceive, or is himself deceived by unacknowledged inner feelings at odds with his conscious beliefs? In these cases, the quick preliminary reading is likely to mislead — a fact, however, that should show up as an unacceptable degree of disunity, incoherence, or incompleteness in the consequent interpretation.

Alas, the idea of unity, too, has its complications. The most obvious test for it is that of story-line or argument. But not all prose works nowadays have either, and few poems do. Unity of mood,* then? Suppose, though, the writer was trying to convey a mixture of moods? How do we distinguish *that* purport, successfully realised, from failure and muddle in a work purporting to convey one rather complex mood? Such differences are, in fact, easier to demonstrate practically than to state abstractly —

though we can state that density of coherence will usually be relevant. A work in which argument, tone, theme, and form are all at one with themselves and each other would properly be labelled 'complex' rather than 'muddled', and therefore would properly be rated (whatever one's personal prejudices) above one in which there was less coherence.

Detecting complex purports and variegated unities (the chief source of esthetic* pleasure), and distinguishing them from muddled ones, however, is not easy, nor can it be done by rote. In fact, the principles of approach and of assessment often become inextricably entangled, in practice, with the various methods of detection and analysis, as well as with each other. Initially, to be truthful, criticism tends to be a matter of trial and error, tentative question and dubious answer, purport and unity being no more than phantasmal presences at the back of the mind, the critical 'methods' no more than tips to guard against self-deception, personal prejudices, or private and eccentric interpretation — until bit by bit perceptions become clearer and the phantasms take on form and substance.

In short, the craft of criticism is more akin to the practice of law than to the practice of either science or art. Poems — and equally novels and plays — are somewhat like criminals, given to breaking and entering into closed minds and locked and guarded personalities. They are commonly mixed-up, passionate, pleading, boasting, lying, or unpredictable. For their assessment, cross-examination and the accumulation of circumstantial evidence is what is appropriate. All that can properly be attempted is to put literary matters 'beyond reasonable doubt'. Like prisoners, they are not in the realm of irrefutable proof — and if they were, would not possess the uniquely human value they do possess.

Techniques of legal practice have, of course, been worked out over the centuries, from the days of trial by combat or by ordeal, to ensure as much objectivity as possible in the judgement of alleged criminals; neither strong intuitions of guilt on the part of accusers, nor any public desire to find a scapegoat, is allowed to deputise for valid evidence. And on the whole, though not invariably, they work. Similarly, techniques for minimising unsupported opinionation in literary judgements can be worked out — but with even more difficulty, and rather less certainty. For, unlike the judge, the critic is faced with the two facts discussed earlier, and the extra problems they involve.

Firstly, there is the fact that though literary judgements, if they are to have any legitimate claim on our attention, must not be *merely* subjective, they must *be* subjective in order to be properly *literary* judgements. This gives rise to the problem of distinguishing between subjectivity as bias or eccentricity and subjectivity as a true sensitive response — the response

that is a *re*creation of the poet's public poem as against the one that is
partially a private creation of the reader. Secondly, there is the fact that
literary works only come alive when read or heard, their interpretation
therefore being literally 'all in the mind'. This gives rise to the following
problem: if $x$ minds recreate a poem from a number of black squiggles on
white paper why do we not have $x$ different poems? Or, if you like, why
should not all different interpretations of the same squiggles be equally
valid? Those of the stupid and the clever, the sensitive and the crude, the
trained and the untrained? The bases for a solution, we said, lay in the
facts that we share a common humanity and a common language. Though
leading French structuralists* today deny the latter fact — or at any rate
deny that language communicates meaning — this basis seems much less
questionable than that of a common humanity (which they also deny).
For we may add to the remarks made towards the beginning of this introduction, the fact that a language is essentially, indeed by definition,
public; a matter of agreed and therefore shareable meanings. All the evidence, historical and contemporary, indicates that communication was the
job it was designed for — and therefore it does communicate, unless some
obstruction prevents its doing so or, as with some modernists, the writer
takes pains to prevent its doing so. Thus, certain interpretations can normally be ruled out as 'un-English', or as being based on a mistaken idea of
a word's accepted meaning — certainly if the more normal usage or normal
meaning accords better with the rest of the work. Common humanity,
however, seems less communal than a common language. Even within a
common culture there are deep divisions of class, and within any class,
divisions of individual temperament and psychological type. Nevertheless,
there is enough in common for us to be able, *with some effort*, to appreciate how others may think or feel even when we diverge from them —
especially if their thoughts and feelings are expressed in striking and
memorable language.

How then do we go about minimising all those problems, moving
towards criticism as the common pursuit of true judgement? Firstly,
obviously, by avoiding dogmatism, always offering reasons for an opinion,
making intuitions conscious and articulate. Secondly, by cultivating an
openness of approach, a readiness to approve what one may personally dis-
like, to the extent that there are grounds for approval (and conversely to
disapprove of what one may happen to like, to the extent that there are
grounds for disapproval). Perhaps this is the same thing as the cultivation
of self-awareness: knowledge of one's temperamental or ideological bias.
And, thirdly — to be less psychological and more literary — by adopting
devices that will encourage looking round, and into, the work before

leaping to conclusions. The chief among such devices (though others will crop up in the course of the following critiques) seem to be these: *triangulation*, *classification*, and *interrelation*.

By triangulation is meant simply checking one's position from time to time from two other points of view, as a safeguard against going too far wrong in any one direction. Thus an interpretation of form would be checked for coherence with tone and theme, an interpretation of sense with, say, purport and the probabilities indicated by scholarship.

By classification is meant, mainly, asking after: *type** (is the work lyric,* dramatic,* or narrative?*), *mode** (what sort of work do we finally count it as being in its most general aspects; e.g. is it fictional or factual? metaphoric or literal? tragic or comic? or, of course, some mixture of these?), or *kind** (what sort of work is it more specifically: pastoral ? elegy? moral fable?).

By interrelation is meant bearing in mind the principle of unity. How does everything 'fit in' with everything else? (In so far as this is not covered by triangulation, we can say, as a rule of thumb, that it could be covered by asking how far the actual performance in the end seems to tally with the purport assumed at the beginning of the critical process.)

All these devices of the craft of criticism, and more, are aids to basic good sense and sensibility, but cannot be a substitute for them — and all need to be used with some flexibility. Not all will be relevant to every case; to some cases none may be relevant. All, however, prove more enlightening in practice than in theory. It is high time to come to cases.

# Critiques

## 1. Dylan Thomas

'Poem in October'

It was my thirtieth year to heaven
Woke to my hearing from harbour and neighbour wood
    And the mussel pooled and the heron
        Priested shore
      The morning beckon
With water praying and call of seagull and rook
And the knock of sailing boats on the net webbed wall
      Myself to set foot
      That second
    In the still sleeping town and set forth.

My birthday began with the water-
Birds and the birds of the winged trees flying my name
    Above the farms and the white horses
        And I rose
      In a rainy autumn
And walked abroad in a shower of all my days
High tide and the heron dived when I took the road
      Over the border
      And the gates
    Of the town closed as the town awoke.

A springful of larks in a rolling
Cloud and the roadside bushes brimming with whistling
    Blackbirds and the sun of October
        Summery
      On the hill's shoulder,
Here were fond climates and sweet singers suddenly
Come in the morning where I wandered and listened
      To the rain wringing

Wind blow cold
In the wood faraway under me.

Pale rain over the dwindling harbour
And over the sea wet church the size of a snail
   With its horns through mist and the castle
      Brown as owls
     But all the gardens
Of spring and summer were blooming in the tall tales
Beyond the border and under the lark full cloud.
     There could I marvel
      My birthday
   Away but the weather turned around.

It turned away from the blithe country
And down the other air and the blue altered sky
   Streamed again a wonder of summer
      With apples
     Pears and red currants
And I saw in the turning so clearly a child's
Forgotten mornings when he walked with his mother
     Through the parables
      Of sunlight
   And the legends of the green chapels

And the twice told fields of infancy
That his tears burned my cheeks and his heart moved in mine.
   These were the woods the river and the sea
      Where a boy
     In the listening
Summertime of the dead whispered the truth of his joy
To the trees and the stones and the fish in the tide.
     And the mystery
      Sang alive
   Still in the water and singing birds.

And there could I marvel my birthday
Away but the weather turned around. And the true
   Joy of the long dead child sang burning
      In the sun.
     It was my thirtieth
Year to heaven stood there then in the summer noon
Though the town below lay leaved with October blood.

> O may my heart's truth
>   Still be sung
> On this high hill in a year's turning.

Ideally, ignorance of author, period, and background is desirable when starting on the criticism of an expressive poem like this one; for such ignorance makes easier a first reading without preconceptions. Later, some knowledge of all three may be desirable as a check on our tentative assessment. Not a logical check, for no outside information could *prove* that a particular work was not uncharacteristic of its author, age, and area; but a psychological check, giving either reassurance as to the rightness of our initial reactions, or a strong tip to re-read carefully, according as those reactions were consistent or inconsistent with the new information.

But how do we know this *is* an expressive poem and not a realistic or a didactic one, relying to some extent on presumed knowledge of a particular place or system of beliefs — perhaps an outmoded system from the past? In principle, we do not know; it is an assumption we might well make after an ignorant, innocent, responsive first reading. In practice, we know it is by a modern Welsh poet characteristically (though not invariably) given to non-intellectual self-expression; and therefore we are potentially biassed from the start — though in a good position to check our critical insights at the end against this mite of scholarly knowledge, if we can negate that potential bias. But how?

Well, first that quick reading, preferably aloud, presenting ourselves to the poem as a blank sensitised plate ready for impressions. Immediately, it is apparent that the weather is too rapidly changeable even for the British Isles; and moreover it is often used metaphorically: 'a shower of all my days', 'the listening / Summertime of the dead', and so on. Not obviously realistic, then. Didactic? Well, we have 'heaven', 'priested', 'praying', 'parables', and 'chapels', but if we are meant to get an orthodox moral message there is an awful lot of irrelevant verse obscuring it. It is not easy, either, to bring away any definite Christian doctrine or attitude. Indeed, on first reading, the poem is not easy at all. In spite of the appearance, indeed the fact, of regularity in stanza-structure, the poem soon makes evident its non-traditional, modernistic* nature.[1] Though strongly rhythmic it is not formally metrical.* And it does not rhyme — or more accurately it sets a typically modernist uncertainty against the feeling of definiteness set up by traditional rhymed* and metrical verse. The promise of assurance implied by the regular stanza-form remains unfulfilled. The

1. i.e. not necessarily contemporary; rather, typical of the experimentalism of the period *c.* 1910–50.

19

fifth line of each stanza usually half-rhymes (or less than half-rhymes) with the penultimate (or antepenultimate) line: *beckon – second, autumn – border, shoulder – cold, gardens – marvel*; but then we have a fourth line (*apples*) rhyming with an ultimate line (*chapels*), then a third *and* fifth line (*sea, listening*) echoing different syllables of the antepenultimate line (*mystery*), and finally a third line (*burning*) fully rhyming with the last line of the poem (*turning*) – a point we might bear at the back of our minds along with those odd religious words, since whatever is somewhat different from the general context may turn out to be significant. In addition, we have teasing consonances and assonances that never quite settle into a system. The first stanza has *heaven – heron, wood – rook, shore – forth, beckon – second*; the second stanza *water – horses, autumn – border, rose – road*, and *days – gates*. And so we could go on, noting now that we might have added the first line of each stanza to those that half-rhyme with the fifth. In short, shadowy regularities verge on materialisation and then dissolve, hints of system subliminally suggest themselves and disappear. What is the effect of this? Surely it conveys *formally* to the sensitive reader a sense of tentativeness, of reaching for something not easy to grasp – very apt for a poem expressive of intangible inner experiences,[2] most inept for a descriptive, informative, or didactic poem. As a preliminary hypothesis, then, we may reasonably say this purports to be an expressive, personal poem – a hypothesis gaining further support from the frequent use of personal pronouns, and the knowledge that such poetry is in no way untypical of modernist poetry in general or that of Dylan Thomas in particular. We might add, as a tentative value judgement, that the poet was wise to eschew both free verse and formal verse, an intangible inner content requiring such a regular structural form to prevent amorphousness, but also requiring such irregular rhymes and unexpected textural* features as we have already noticed ('shower of all *my days*', 'twice told *fields*') to prevent oversimplification. Put another way, this tension gives a sense of the sensory and semi-conscious being brought towards conscious focus, made graspable.

Before proceeding on this hypothesis to a closer reading, however, perhaps we ought to test it by one or two more general questions. Suppose we ask the most general *modal* question of all: is it fictional or non-fictional? Well, obviously if it is personally expressive it must be non-fictional! But wait, that 'if . . . ' is what we are testing – and anyway the poet might be deceiving himself, or attempting to deceive us, in which case

---

2. Contrast, for example, the more definite form and precise diction of relatively impersonal poems such as 'Deceptions' (critique 12) and 'An Irish Airman' (critique 19).

we should have to say that the ostensible purport was not the real one, that the non-fictional was infected by fictional implications;* showing up as little patches of textural mould, so to speak. Something to watch out for, but not immediately evident on first reading. What is evident — and it does tend to confirm our hypothesis — is that apparent statements of continuous physical fact (waking and walking) are couched in a most undocumentary manner: not exactly fictional but not what one would call factual either (we have already noted examples of metaphorical weather). If fiction proper is recalled by 'tall tales', 'marvel', 'parables', and 'legends' it may serve to show that the writer is trying not to deceive himself or us; at any rate he is not allowing the possibility of fictionalising experience to be overlooked.

What is the *type* of this poem? *Dramatic*? Clearly not. *Narrative*? Hardly; in a longish poem we have simply the action of getting up and going for a walk. That leaves *lyric* — and indeed it has all the characteristics normally associated with lyric: direct communication of poet (or persona*), a sense of overhearing something slightly private, and a predominance of mood over action, mind over matter. This too tends to confirm our assumption. So it is now time to read more closely, stanza by stanza, with this sense of the whole kept undogmatically in mind.

The first stanza notably lacks grammar and punctuation. What is more, no ingenuity of punctuation would put it into logical or grammatical order. Moreover, while 'the morning beckoned' or 'the morning beacon' are possible English, 'the morning beckon' is not; both meanings come to mind. Since the rest of the poem is more normal we must assume craft rather than incompetence in this stanza. And of course it is all appropriate enough for the expression of waking and feeling the outside world flood in, all at once; and richly, for there is implied an instantaneous awareness of this being a birthday. A particularly significant one, of course; for just as October is poised between summer and winter, so at thirty one is poised between youth and maturity; ambiguous both: happy in so far as they represent a peak, sad in so far as all is downhill thenceforth. So far, though, we have only the elated rush of sensations — unless 'heaven' gives a tiny hint of death as well as happiness. We might note that, though 'priested' and 'praying' are visually and sonically right for their referents,* those referents are natural not churchly. The lack of hyphens, however, has no potential significance. If we know Dylan Thomas's work we recognise it as simply a habit.

The second stanza begins with the only hyphen in the poem — perhaps because of the strong risk of misreading, otherwise. For, after all, the birthday did begin with the water (the first stanza clearly evoking a small port); a fact sufficiently indicated by the placing of 'water-'. But 'water-*birds*' is wanted as a parallel to the 'birds of the winged trees' – a parallel which not only associates the poet with sea and land (the whole world of nature) but also prepares us for his walk inland – to a different sphere. This latter phrase is richly, not confusedly, ambiguous, suggesting as it does both a plenitude of birds when roosting, and the tree itself taking wing in the wind and 'flying' his name like the birds. We know that it is windy from the brilliant ambiguity of the next line: the 'white horses', like the birds, being those of water and land.

In the context of 'a shower of all my days', which is clearly psychological as well as meteorological – and very fine as an expression (rather than statement) of innumerable hardly separable memories – the phrase 'In a rainy autumn' seems possibly to carry a hint of contrast to the general feeling of elation. At present there is no more than a possibility. More obvious is the symbolic character of the 'border' and 'the gates'. If there is still some town in Wales, or indeed in the United Kingdom, that has gates and closes them daily, it will certainly not do so in the early morning, but rather at nightfall. These, then, must be gates of experience, the border a psychological one. That being so, it is hardly possible to avoid the feeling that 'High tide' and 'the heron dived' also have symbolic* connotations* in addition to their denotatory* meaning. October and one's thirtieth birthday are high tides of the year and of life, and there seems to be a high tide of feeling hereabouts too. The heron goes from one element to another, just as the poet crosses a border from a 'town' state of mind – presumably the orthodox and humdrum – to a 'natural' one, a feeling of identification with the vital forces of nature.

The third stanza contains references to all four seasons, in 'springful', 'October', 'Summery', and 'cold', thus confirming that the weather is largely internal, a matter of moods embodied in nature. 'Springful of larks' also suggests the sound of a mountain stream – a water image picked up by 'brimming', normally used only of liquids, but again suggesting plenitude, fullness, the 'High tide'. 'Fond' is normally used of people not climates; and this too encourages an expressive reading. The 'rain wringing' cold wind therefore seems to indicate a bleak world escaped from – but clearly only for a time. One cannot stay on the sunlit peaks for ever. The sombre hint in 'heaven', and 'rainy autumn', and for that matter in the common idea of thirty being a watershed in life, is now considerably strengthened. And perhaps we may now remark that the very shape of the stanza, concertina'd in and out, sets up a rhythmic alternation that would not be out of keeping with a content of to-and-froing feelings.

Sure enough, in the next stanza 'the weather turned around', as it does again in the fifth stanza; and the poem ends on the strongly emphasised word 'turning' (one of the only two last lines of a stanza to be rhymed). But all this is preceded by some lines reminiscent of fairy-tale or legend. The church is seen as very far away, transmuted into a natural form, the castle takes on something of the mystery and sinisterness of the wise birds of prey it is likened to, and its unusual colour further removes it from reality. No wonder we pass to 'tall tales' and 'marvel'! Here the poet does seem to admit to a certain fictionalising or romanticising of his birthday experience. And with that implicit admission, inevitably comes a change of mood. Not, however, as one might have expected, to a wintry realism. At first sight, in fact, the weather seems not to have turned at all, since we go from 'the gardens of . . . summer' to 'a wonder of summer'.

On closer inspection, though, we see that it has turned from a possibly romanticised present to a real past, a vivid recapturing of 'forgotten mornings' when such rapturous union with nature was automatic and everyday. At this point we see that our original idea of purport must be amended somewhat, for it here becomes evident that the poem is to some degree religious — though not Christian. On the contrary, as well as being personally expressive it is *implicitly* making an anti-Christian statement. Christian terms are given a blatantly different reference — which deliberately flouts the normal upbringing of a child in Nonconformist Wales, and exalts pantheism.*[3] Not biblical parables but 'the parables of sunlight' are what moved him, the 'legends of green chapels' (woods) not grey ones, and twice-told *fields*, not lessons or sermons. And in the next stanza the 'truth' of his joy turns out to have been whispered not to God but 'To the trees and the stones and the fish in the tide' (unpunctuated to suggest nature in general). The 'mystery' was found not at an altar (or if at one, then at the punning one of 'the blue altered sky') but 'still in the water and singing birds' — which brings us back to the beginning of the poem, and back to the present as the weather turns around again 'And the *true* / Joy [i.e. checked by memory and found *not* to be romanticised] of the long dead child sang burning / In the sun.' Below, however, the town is 'leaved with October blood' — both beautiful and lethal, and a reminder of reality.[4]

3. If some lingering suspicion remains that we may be reading into the poem what is not really there, a little scholarship may provide psychological reassurance: 'It is my aim as an artist . . . to prove beyond doubt to myself that the flesh that covers me is the flesh that covers the sun, that the blood in my lungs is the blood that goes up and down in a tree. It is the simplicity of religion.' (Letter, Jan. 1934, quoted in *Poet in the Making* (Dent, 1967), ed. Ralph Maud, p. 24). 'I employ the scenery of the island to describe the scenery of my thoughts, the earthquakes of the body to describe the earthquakes of the heart.' (Letter, Feb. 1933, *ibid.*, p. 27).
4. Note the comparable double-edged imagery, and consequent tonal complexity, of 'To Autumn' 's last stanza (see pp. 53 and 64–5).

The poise between elation and sadness, summer and winter, past and future, is maintained to the end. An end, however, that refers to 'my heart's truth' — significantly *not* the head's, so we are reminded that it is still mainly an expressive poem, and one whose 'truth'* seems to have been sufficiently guaranteed by the fluctuations of mood, the shadows accompanying the sunlight, and the check by the resurgence of unsophisticated childhood feelings. A maturity appropriate to a thirtieth birthday, too, seems inherent in the last line: not the normal 'in a year's *time*', but 'in a year's *turning*', as if to insist that the full range of moods and seasons, wintry as well as summery, of the sadness as well as the gladness of life are to be accepted and indeed welcomed as part of nature's plenitude.

So, then, *A Poem in October* has been looked at in terms of mode, type, and kind, as a check on its assumed purport. Closer inspection, flexibly taking into account stanza-form, diction, punctuation, sound-effects, symbolism, ambiguities, and tone has found it not to be wanting, in the light of that purport — though the purport had to be slightly amended. Baffling as any other sort of poem, it has turned out to 'make sense' as a mainly expressive one, to be coherent though complex, rounded and unified though not simplified, its pantheistic 'message' thoroughly absorbed into, and expressed through the autumnal birthday experience. This sort of approach served to reduce to a minimum any possibly misleading preconceptions due to knowledge of the author and his environment. Where we did turn to that knowledge, in later stages of the critique, it tended to confirm, psychologically if not logically, what the purely literary approach seemed to bring out. What we should beware of now is any extension of this particular assessment to the whole of Dylan Thomas's poetry. Much that starts baffling stays so, some that is interpretable nevertheless may be found wanting as relatively incoherent and dis-unified, or as oversimple in attitude, or in some way inauthentic: self-dramatising or self-deceiving. This poem, however, escapes all such strictures. Put aside for a month or two, to allow this dissecting critique to sink to the bottom of the mind, and then re-read for pleasure, it should prove a richly rewarding poetic experience.

# 2. John Crowe Ransom

### 'Piazza Piece'

— I am a gentleman in a dustcoat trying
To make you hear. Your ears are soft and small
And listen to an old man not at all,
They want the young men's whispering and sighing.
But see the roses on your trellis dying
And hear the spectral singing of the moon;
For I must have my lovely lady soon.
I am a gentleman in a dustcoat trying.

— I am a lady young in beauty waiting
Until my truelove comes, and then we kiss.
But what grey man among the vines is this
Whose words are dry and faint as in a dream?
Back from my trellis, sir, before I scream!
I am a lady young in beauty waiting.

Even the most perfunctory first reading makes one thing clear about this poem: it is different in almost every way from Dylan Thomas's. Most importantly, it differs in being neither expressive in mode nor lyric in type. It is dramatic in type; and in mode fictional, formal, and artificial. The author retires behind his characters, tells — or appears to let them tell — of their life not his own, chooses a given pattern,* the sonnet, and uses an oddly 'literary' diction.

This last characteristic may seem even odder if we happen to know the author to have been famous as both a modernist critic and poet (of Eliot's generation rather than Thomas's), for early modernism abjured Victorian and Edwardian poetic diction with particular sternness.

To assume that a writer's life must always provide insights into his work is one form of the biographical fallacy,* a notorious critical pitfall.[1] After all, he might sometime kick over the traces or just lapse from his

1. For further discussion see critique 9, pp. 75–7, as well as the glossary.

normal standards (even Homer 'sometimes sleeps'). Still, the oddity
suggests that this information about Ransom could be cautiously taken, at
some stage, as a tip to question the authenticity of this diction. Certainly,
the chosen structural\* form\* and the dramatic presentation together give
grounds for being wary of taking this poem at face value as a sort of
Romantic précis of Milton's *Comus*. A regular Petrarchan sonnet,\* traditionally a typical vehicle for lovers' lyric self-expression, is here used
dramatically: octave (or octet) for the gentleman's speech, sestet for the
lady's. If Ransom has anything of his own to express, he is being provoca-
tively oblique about it. A tip, perhaps, to test for allegory or symbolism?
But not just yet, for all oblique, or potentially oblique, works present in
an acute form the standard critical dilemma of parts-and-whole.

Any work as a whole results from the combination of its parts. To
know the whole, then, we must understand the parts. But an understanding of the parts often presupposes knowledge of the kind of whole they
are parts of.[2] For instance, if we do not know that a poem purports, as a
whole, to be a parody we shall take its constituent parts seriously and mis-
construe them as clumsy and irritating instead of finding them clever and
funny. But we gather the poem's purport (what, in general, it is up to)
only from a cumulative interpretation of the parts. Happily, this vicious
circle can usually be broken by turning it into a spiral, gradually narrowing
until it reaches the point of reasonable conviction. Some parts at first
reading will seem to indicate a certain kind of whole. A second reading,
with that hypothesis in mind, and paying regard to other parts, may tend
to confirm or disconfirm it but leave some parts unclear. A somewhat
revised hypothesis may illuminate those parts. And so on.

In the present instance, a *suspicion* of symbolic or allegorical purport
seems warranted — hardly worth dignifying as a *hypothesis*, for the evidence is as yet mostly vague and external. So, before going any further in
that direction we ought to look at the parts in more detail. And where
better to begin than at the beginning?

Why 'Piazza Piece'? As a word for an Italian square, perhaps, 'piazza'
reminds us that the piece has just a hint of *Romeo and Juliet* in it, a very
faint hint indeed. It may remind us a little more strongly of those Jacobean
tragedies in which cloaked villains skulk in midnight piazzas, and speak of
their murderous Italianate intrigues as 'night pieces': elegantly plotted
little dramas of death within the main play. The archaic language in
general at any rate does not conflict with such a reading, and 'dying' and
'spectral' in particular positively encourage it. 'Vines' too, might possibly

2. This matter is further touched upon on pp. 43 and 106, and in the glossary under
   *Mode* and *Purport*. It is viewed from a different, and wider, angle in critique 14.

be considered vaguely Italianate. But what are vines doing in a piazza? Indeed where is there any mention, any hint even, of a piazza in the poem? Sensitivity to overtones is all very well but it needs some support from the plain sense.

It is at this point that background knowledge really comes into its own. Far more relevant than Ransom's modernism is the fact that he was born in the Old South of the United States — and there we find that a verandah — the counterpart here to Juliet's balcony — may be called a 'piazza'. The fact that Ransom chose the latter alternative, and added 'piece' rather than, say, 'romance', suggests that the Renaissance-drama hints we suspected were indeed meant to exist as a shadowy presence behind the more modern drama, or melodrama, in the foreground. Also important is the fact that Ransom was born in 1880, a time still steeped in nostalgia for that lost Southern chivalry to which a rather oldfashioned diction and traditionally proper young lady would not be inappropriate — especially if both were faintly inauthentic. That date, too, means that the writer was brought up in the earliest age of the motor car: the era of dusty, unmacadamed roads and open cars, when motorists wore caps, goggles, and long coats down to the ankles — dustcoats.

Here, surely, as early as the first line we get sense and symbolism in combination. The first line distances us a little. What would-be seducer ever began so? But a car owner would then be a gentleman. Why does he tell her that he is in a dustcoat? Cannot she see that for herself? She sees that he is 'a grey man'; and in what other sense than covered in dust would he be grey (grey-*haired* men always being so described)? However, there is one personage who would certainly not call himself merely a man, might be unseeable at first, and could well wear a 'dustcoat': namely, Death (compare the phrase 'wearing the earth for overcoat' for those dead and buried). Could this poem, then, be a modern rendering of the age-old allegory* of Death and the Maiden? On closer inspection it seems hardly possible that it could not. The formality of structure and diction, the title, and many ambiguities of detail (like the 'dustcoat') all point to such a reading. Interpreted so, the poem is tonally complex, brilliant, and coherent. Interpreted 'straight' it is muddled and stilted — and thus untypical of Ransom.

Let us look at the sonnet more closely, triangulating form, tone, and implied story, to minimise the possibility of going too far wrong in any one direction. One item of structural form stands out. In an otherwise orthodox sonnet, the end-words of the first and last lines of each speech are not rhymes but repetitions. In terms of textural form there is a difference: in each case the first use is transitive, the line and the sense running on from 'trying' and 'waiting', while in the second case they come to what we may call a dead end. That the gentleman has to *try* to make her hear, implies a certain ghostliness, as does his suggestion that she should listen, Renaissance-like, to the music of one of the spheres (now more sinisterly rendered as 'the spectral singing of the moon'). The latter 'trying' (line eight) being unqualified, suggests acting as judge, testing for quality, and putting under strain. The first 'waiting', taken straight, implies the brief period before an expected and welcome meeting. Taken symbolically it conveys dramatic irony: we know, though she does not, that the 'truelove' — the only one that will be faithful for ever and take her completely, body and soul — is Death. An interpretation that accords with line seven's 'I must have my lovely lady soon' — which would be wildly overconfident for a real elderly gentleman. The latter 'waiting' appropriately ends the poem. She now awaits only an unexpected, unwelcome full-stop.

All the other details now fall into place. 'Want' in line four is enriched by the ironic implication 'but that is not what they are going to get'. 'Must have' in line seven is prophetic as well as sexual. The grey man among the vines becomes a grim travesty of Bacchus, for the time of wine and roses is over — and sadly early for this maiden. 'Dust', 'grey', 'dry', 'spectral', 'dying', as against 'soft', 'roses', 'lovely', 'vines', tonally reinforce the idea of the encounter of Death with Life. The feminine rhymes too contribute a number of contrastive dying falls. And if the poem is symbolical then the roses may also be taken as the bloom of health (as in 'rosy' cheeks) and '*your* trellis' also as her body or, even more specifically, her bones. No wonder she cries 'Back from my trellis, sir, before I scream'. We may smile at the Victorian innocence and prudery implicit in this example of burlesque melodrama, on the literal level, but the author's joke is on us at the allegorical level. How could a young and beautiful woman accept a fate worse than seduction? The literary joke obliquely reflects one of life's many tasteless jests.

The *purport* and *mood* of the poem are now clear. It is an ironically presented miniature allegorical drama, obliquely suggesting to the reader that he should prepare to meet his last end, for Death is not to be denied, whenever he may call. Sad as a whole, though parodic and punning in the parts, the poem yields an overall effect of wry fatalism. But what of *performance*? To bring out this wryness, to make apparent the puns, the parody, the allegorical symbolism, will need highly skilled reading (a somewhat — but not ludicrously — ghostly voice for the octet, perhaps a tiny hint of emphasis on 'your' in line five, though it is metrically unstressed, for instance?). In particular, though, should we read the identical lines nine and fourteen differently (especially as we have agreed that 'waiting' carries different implications in each line)? The choice is between (1) 'I am a lady young/in beauty waiting' and (2) 'I am a lady/ young in beauty/waiting'. If we decide that in the other two repeated lines 'gentleman' should be slightly more emphasised in the first (not to make the allegory obvious too soon) and 'dustcoat' in the second (to bring out the element of allegorical menace), then we seem to be given a reason for choice between (1) and (2). (1) emphasises 'young' and thus seems appropriate for line nine, underlining the ironic pathos of her innocent eager expectation. (2) emphasises 'lady', which seems appropriate for line fourteen, since it accords both with the Victorian melodrama of the preceding line and with the more moralistic irony required when the allegory has become established (Death respects neither wealth nor class); furthermore, this reading isolates 'waiting', which accords with the implication proposed earlier. But arguments could be adduced for reversing the performatory readings of these four lines. We are now at the point where objective critical interpretation passes over to legitimate personal opinion. And that is the place to stop.

# 3. Andrew Marvell

### 'To His Coy Mistress'

Had we but World enough, and Time,
This coyness Lady were no crime.
We would sit down, and think which way
To walk, and pass our long Loves Day.
Thou by the Indian Ganges side
Should'st Rubies find: I by the Tide
Of Humber would complain. I would
Love you ten years before the Flood:
And you should if you please refuse
Till the Conversion of the Jews.
My vegetable Love should grow
Vaster than Empires, and more slow.
An hundred years should go to praise
Thine Eyes, and on thy Forehead Gaze.
Two hundred to adore each Breast:
But thirty thousand to the rest.
An Age at least to every part,
And the last Age should show your Heart.
For Lady you deserve this State;
Nor would I love at lower rate.
    But at my back I alwaies hear
Times wingèd Charriot hurrying near:
And yonder all before us lye
Desarts of vast Eternity.
Thy Beauty shall no more be found,
Nor, in thy marble Vault, shall sound
My ecchoing Song: then Worms shall try
That long preserv'd Virginity:
And your quaint Honour turn to dust;
And into ashes all my Lust.
The Grave's a fine and private place,

But none I think do there embrace.
    Now therefore, while the youthful hew
Sits on thy skin like morning dew,
And while thy willing Soul transpires
At every pore with instant Fires,
Now let us sport us while we may;
And now, like am'rous birds of prey,
Rather at once our Time devour,
Than languish in his slow-chapt pow'r.
Let us roll all our Strength, and all
Our sweetness, up into one Ball:
And tear our Pleasures with rough strife,
Thorough the Iron gates of Life.
Thus, though we cannot make our Sun
Stand still, yet we will make him run.

Another maiden crying 'Back from my trellis, sir!' but in a very different scene, though this poem too pits Life against Death, refers ironically to an earlier kind of poetry, and is rhymed and metrical. For one thing, if we follow the sensible practice of taking everything literally unless there is some positive indication to the contrary, this maiden is not symbolic. She may be imaginary — we need not assume her to be part of Marvell's biography; nor indeed need we assume the persona of the poem to be Marvell as himself; such assumptions would add nothing to the poem — but, imaginary or real, she is not symbolic. For another thing, it is paradoxically evident even on an uninquisitive first reading that this poem is less literary and oldfashioned than Ransom's appeared at first, though written long ago (*c.* 1650) *in* one traditional literary kind, the *carpe diem*,\* and, to begin with, directed *at* another, the Petrarchan.[1] Paradoxical but not perhaps surprising, for Ransom deliberately used an earlier idiom as part of his stage-effect, whereas Marvell is writing in the idiom of his own day, so it does not sound oldfashioned, though it is. Moreover, this is a direct presentation of the persona's case, not an oblique one; the monologue of a man who wishes his words to work. Unlike Death, he cannot 'have the lovely lady' against her will.

    A second reading, surely, confirms the element of *address*. It is not artificial speech, in the sense of seeming inauthentic, phoney, yet neither is it colloquial speech. Rather it is the heightened speech of one urging a case. Forensic rhetoric might best describe the mode; and that is why it

1. See p. 44, note 2.

seems better to type the poem as more dramatic than lyrical, though it has some lyric qualities. The mood is not musing, but forceful; we are not so much overhearing as being addressed — imaginatively identifying ourselves in part with the maiden who is, so to speak, in the dock, and in part with the persuasive presenter of the case.

The presentation is neither fictional nor, really, non-fictional (despite appeals to the facts of Time and Death), but logical. The argument of its three verse paragraphs is that of If—But—Therefore. *If* we had world enough, and time . . . *but* we have not . . . *therefore* we must sieze the day' (*carpe diem*). An argument neither particularly original nor subtle; as with most poems (why else write a poem rather than a treatise?) the paraphrasable theme is less important than the impact of its presentation — and, of course, that presentation will contribute an unparaphrasable element to the theme; the difference being akin to that between a living body and a skeleton. That contribution could be summed up by saying that the logical development is completed by several kinds of non-logical development.

For instance, the mood seems to be playful in the first paragraph, scornful in the second, and passionate in the third. Other *carpe diem* poems express one similar mood, and thus tend to seem charming exercises in a tradition rather than heartfelt statements of feeling. Compare Marvell's 'Coy Mistress', for instance, with the well-known and rightly admired 'To the Virgins, to Make Much of Time' by Herrick:

> Gather ye rosebuds while ye may,
>     Old Time is still a-flying:
> And this same flower that smiles today
>     Tomorrow will be dying.
>
> The glorious lamp of heaven, the sun,
>     The higher he's a getting;
> The sooner will his race be run,
>     And nearer he's to setting.
>
> That age is best, which is the first,
>     When youth and blood are warmer;
> But being spent, the worse, and worst
>     Times still succeed the former.
>
> Then be not coy, but use your time;
>     And while ye may go marry:
> For having lost but once your prime,
>     You may for ever tarry.

Clearly Marvell uses the kind much less conventionally. Not only is his

poem more dramatic, but it is cumulatively forceful; it changes-up as it
goes on.

The first section humorously parodies those Elizabethan poets who
followed, indeed exceeded, Petrarch in poems of improbable promises and
incredible patience for idealised lovers. Here in Marvell excess is itself
exceeded, extravagance piled on extravagance till no one could believe
this sort of courtship reasonable, or even sane. Appropriately this is the
hypothetical part of the argument; an inflation to be followed by a
recession:

> I would
> Love you ten years before the Flood:
> And you should if you please refuse
> Till the Conversion of the Jews.
> My vegetable Love should grow
> Vaster than Empires, and more slow.

The second section turns from teasing to warning — with an apt change of
gear in the metre: from the stately formality of the iambics concluding the
first paragraph, to the psychologically stressed opening of the second:

> Fŏr Lád/ў yóu/dĕseŕve/thĭs Státe;
> Nŏr wóuld/Ĭ lóve/ăt lów/ĕr ráte.
>  Bŭt ăt/mў bắck/Ĭ ál/wăies héar
> Times wińg/ĕd Chár/rĭŏt húr/rўińg néar

Three unstressed syllables hurry in the first line of this latter couplet, so
that particularly heavy stress is required somewhere (preferably on 'back'?)
to redress the balance. The next line has two feet containing extra
unstressed syllables, thus encouraging a hurrying in performance, and the
opening spondee gives us three stressed syllables in succession ('heár Times
wíng') to emphasise an important point — the whole couplet, together
with the succeeding one, underlining the change from playfulness.

Perhaps we have moved a little too soon from the general to the particular. But since other metrical and rhythmical points deserve attention,
it may suffice simply to note the urgency of the third section (introduced
by the stabbing 'Nŏw thérefőre'), and carry on with them, finally turning
to the various other textural items that also help to flesh out the bare
bones of thematic structure.

Blank verse* would have been easier to turn to three different uses, and
might have seemed more convenient for attaining an effect of heartfelt
directness. But this is a controlled, sophisticated heartfeltness. The couplet
enhances that sense of control, and, being farther from natural speech than

blank verse, it harmonises better with the literary reference of the first section, with the traditional element of the *carpe diem* kind chosen, and with the plethora of figurative language throughout. Moreover, the compact neatness of the couplet form, however illogically, seems to support the logic of the argument, and it nicely clips together those points that are made epigrammatically, such as:

> The Grave's a fine and private place,
> But none I think do there embrace.

In addition, however, it provides a stricter norm than blank verse, against which variations may show up significantly. Those at the watershed of the first and second paragraphs have already been noted. The stressed long vowels of ' . . . shóuld grów / Váster . . . and móre slów' (taken, it must be said, *along with the sense*) are equally notable, as is the chewing movement of ' . . . slów-chápt [i.e. *jawed*] pów'r' and also the tension with which ' . . . róll áll oúr Stréngth, aňd áll / Oúr swéetněss' can properly be read. But even more effective in contributing formally to the sense of living rhythms, a varying pulse of feeling, of control threatened and therefore needed, is the flexible way in which some couplets run on from the first line to the second while othere are end-stopped, in which the sense is confined to one couplet or flows through the next, or in which rhythms sometimes stop and start in mid-line rather than at the end.

These small-scale, textural, rhythms and sense-groups blend with and enrich the large-scale, structural ones. Can the same be said of other textural details, epithets, metaphors, and so on? In general, it is apparent they do, but a number of particular examples merit discussion, especially in the third paragraph. Does 'vegetable', witty though it is, too much disparage the persona's love? No, 'vegetable' at that time was not necessarily derogatory. True, it did imply slowness and a lack of passion but it also had connotations of vital power (witness the ability of vegetable growth to split rock, given time enough). More tricky is 'your quaint Honour'. Should we, as some critics do, read a pun on 'cunt'? It is tempting to reject the suggestion out of hand, on the ground that Marvell was a Puritan; but this is an instance where a reminder of the biographical fallacy is salutary, for it is impossible to reconcile the whole of the last section with any stereotype of puritanism. And if Marvell is not a typical puritan there, why should he be here? There is, however, a linguistic problem: from Chaucer to the beginning of Marvell's century the word 'quaint' was in common use in this sense. Thereafter that meaning seems to have been ousted in favour of 'quaint' as 'elegant, finicky, overrefined'. Still, the Petrarchan parody shows Marvell to have been well-read in Elizabethan literature, and it seems quite possible that the older usage could have lingered on after the word (never of course very common in print in any spelling) ceased to appear in books.[2] Certainly, it is consistent with worms trying 'That long preserv'd Virginity', and would be an apt enough ambiguity to apply to a young lady concerned only with the technical preservation of her virginity while her 'willing Soul transpires / At every pore with instant Fires'. On balance it seems right to accept the reading. It causes no incoherence, adds a relevant overtone, and prepares the reader for the highly unusual conclusion of the poem.

In a *carpe diem* poem we are entitled to expect Venus's doves or at most lecherous sparrows. What do we get? 'Amorous birds of prey'! Suddenly we are worlds away from the traditional modes of Petrarchan and *carpe diem* poetry. The playfulness and scorn have turned to passion, not merely directly sexual but sado-masochistic. Hence the appropriateness of the tension in the lines:

> Let us roll all our Strength, and all
> Our sweetness, up into one Ball:
> And tear our Pleasures with rough strife,
> Thorough the Iron gates of Life.

These take the traditional image of the chaste maiden as a besieged castle and give it a quite new power. The 'ball' is primarily a cannonball smashing through the castle gates; it is also, however, an image of the lovers — male strength and female sweetness — locked together in that lust which all too soon will turn to ashes, and an image of a hymen torn 'with rough strife' rather than gentlemanly tenderness. Here the violence needing civilised control becomes vividly evident. But what of the last two lines? Taken literally they are puzzling, though their gist is clear enough: we cannot be immortal but we can make the most of life. The puzzle comes in the word 'run'. We cannot stop time (to give us world enough and time for an infinitely prolonged courtship) but we can do the opposite by cramming the time we have with action. That rounds off the poem well enough by referring us back to the beginning and it is a neat Q.E.D. to the argument. But is there not an esthetically displeasing gap between this couplet and the 'strife' imagery? No, for 'run' *is* ambiguous: an enemy made to run is an enemy routed. So, paradoxically, though the advance of an enemy, time ('our Sun') cannot be halted it can be defeated by being speeded up. A witty, complex conclusion to a highly original 'traditional' poem.

2. According to Partridge's *Dictionary of Historical Slang* (Penguin, 1972) it continued as a dialect word into the present century 'in parts of the North Country'. Marvell came from Hull.

# 4. e.e. cummings

## 'Two X'

16 heures
l'Etoile

the communists have fine Eyes

some are young some old none
look alike the flies rush
batter the crowd sprawls collapses
singing knocked down trampled the kicked by
flics rush (the

Flics, tidiyum, are
very tidiyum reassuringly similar,
they all have very tidiyum
mustaches, and very
tidiyum chins, and just above
their very tidiyum ears their
very tidiyum necks begin)
                          let us add

that there are 50 (fifty) flics for every
one (1) communist and
all the flics are very organically
arranged
and their nucleus (composed
of captains in freshly-creased
– uniforms with only-just-
shined buttons
tidiyum
before and behind) has a nucleolus:

the Prefect of Police

(a dapper derbied
creature, swaggers daintily
twiddling
his tiny cane
and mazurkas about tweak-
ing his wing collar pecking at his im

-peccable cravat directing being
shooting his cuffs
saluted everywhere saluting
reviewing processions of minions
tappingpeopleontheback

'allezcirculez'

— my he's brave . . .
the
communists pick
up themselves friends
& their hats legs &

arms brush dirt coats
smile looking hands
spit blood teeth

the Communists have (very) fine eyes
(which stroll hither and thither through the
evening in bruised narrow questioning faces)

The previous poems, on a first reading, revealed some obvious differences
from each other, and a good many more on further reflection. 'Two X'
reveals itself as strikingly different from all of them, without any reading
at all, merely by its untidy appearance on the page, its obviously dis-
orderly form. A tip to approach it from that aspect?[1]

Reduced to essentials any work is a combination of *form* and *content*,
each of course being subdividable. A thoroughgoing modernist might even
reduce these to one, arguing that form and content are inseparable or,
more, vigorously, that form *is* content. Neither argument is really tenable,
either pragmatically or logically, at any rate if by the content we mean

---

1. No *rule* is implied. For different reasons, dependent on the context of the poem
   as a whole, an approach through form may also seem appropriate to some highly
   regular verse (witness critiques 19 and 20).

what is paraphrasable and by the 'form' a way of putting something that could in principle have been put in some other way. Authors revise, thus changing the form of an established content; synopses are made; Ben Jonson wrote his plays in prose before drastically altering their form by putting them into verse; and so on. Moreover, it is logically evident that 'X hit Y' and 'Y was hit by X' say the same thing in different forms. Form and content, then, are separable though it remains true to say that in creative literature the total experience will be the result of their marriage.

e.e. cummings's poem, looks like an attempt to demonstrate the modernist thesis on form and content. Even at first glance it is apparent that a difference of form — say, putting the poem into rhyme and metre would make an enormous difference to the total effect. Form very nearly *is* content, though not quite (the only way it could quite become so is the neo-dadaist* way of making 'shape-poems' not out of sentences or even words, but letters or bits of letters thus eliminating meaning entirely; but it is less confusing to define such pieces as (sub-) art than as literature). So, let us approach 'Two X' formally — always being prepared though, to find it necessary to speak of content, almost in the same breath.

Very generally, we can say: that the poem has a beginning, middle, and end, in so far as it deals first with the communists, then with the French police (from 'Flics, tidiyum, are' to 'allezcirculez'), and finally with the communists again; that the first and last sections are smaller than the middle one; and that the blocks of print *within* the first and last sections tend to be smaller than those in the middle. So the poem does have a certain balance, a roundedness, an emergent form, so to speak, within an apparently total informality — and a form that 'physically' suggests the middle to be bigger and more powerful than the ends. The fact that, on closer inspection, the middle is seen to be almost correct in punctuation and grammar while the ends are not, also 'physically' suggests that the middle is better organised. Do these suggestions of shape, organisation and grammar tally with the contentual ones of sense, tone, and purport, and with those of such other formal suggestions as sound-effects and typographical effects (white spaces, indentations, line-endings, word-splitting)?

A contemporary structuralist might well ignore this question, resting content with our large-scale analysis, and going straight on to point out, in the metacritical fashion characteristic of French Structuralism, that the structure we have discerned was a sign of the power-structure of society, or, in its combination of surface chaos, underlying order, and the conflict of groups, of a capitalist oligarchy, or again, in its combination of vague general ideas and particular defiances of verbal conventions, a reflection of the structure of the author's psyche (typical romantic leftist perhaps?).

Structuralists tend to be more interested in skeletons than bodies, in maps than places – in sociology, anthropology, or psychology, in fact, than in literature. A perfectly proper interest, of course, but one that may well cause such a critic to go too quickly from what the work *is* to what it may be a *sign of* for his conclusions to carry much weight in these extra-literary fields (though they may do well enough as large generalisations). Certainly someone with primarily literary interests will feel that there is more to be said about the poetic experience before going beyond it (if he wishes to); that, in fact, it might be well to look at the detail of form-and-content – and in the order in which it comes, for after all poems are temporal experiences at least as much as they are 'spatial' ones. We may perceive at first broad patterns (octet–sestet, triple sense-division, and so on) and finally, as precipitates of memory, such 'outlines' as character, theme, plot,* story,* mode, or purport. But the poem, as literature, is more importantly the temporal experience we have as we read it from line to line – with some of these generalities in mind and others growing as we read. This continuous and varying experience is not a matter of memory – which accounts for the fact that we can re-read good poems with pleasure, though we already know the theme, or twist in the tale (if any), but do not get much pleasure from a paraphrase or synopsis.

Well, then: '16 heures / l'Etoile'. Obviously it sets the scene: 4.00 p.m. in Paris. Why '16', not 'seize' or 'sixteen', and why the curtness of these lines? Surely a mock-military order, as portrayed in so many bad films? The next line by comparison is positively expansive, and it makes the communists the more human by giving them all (implausibly? propagandistly? sentimentally?) 'fine Eyes', emphasised in a sort of verbal big close-up by a capital letter. Thereafter the camera pulls back to take in the crowd, but no farther back than medium close-up: we see the charged crowd in detail – detail rendered graphically by the speed and confusion engendered by an absence of punctuation and a telescoped syntax. Suddenly we cut to a different scene, a move marked by brackets, a syntactical hiatus ('the'), and a white space. Even the background music one might hypothesise seems to change: in literal terms, there is a change of rhythm. 'Tidiyum' itself seems to call up the fleeting ghost of a brisk military march, the drums going *tidiyum–tidiyum–tidiyum–tum-tum*; and the whole section is neater and tidier – a childish tidiness also being suggested by 'tidiyum' (perhaps tedium too). This one word, as much by form as connotational content, caricatures the flics as boring children spruced up to play at being soldiers; an element of caricature enhanced by concentration on chins, moustaches, ears, and necks; parts of the physiognomy by convention more ridiculous than eyes ('the windows of the soul').

'Let us add' by its isolation at first suggests an accountant's version of 'Let us pray', a suggestion that picks up the subliminal effect of the figures and the officiality of the use of the twenty-four hour clock in '16 heures', and anticipates the bureaucratic habits implied in the repetitions of '50 (fifty)' 'one (1)' – repetitions that contentually also point up the unfairness of the conflict. The reversal (number, word/word, number) seems to be another formal way of indicating the complete contrast and opposition between the two groups. 'Arranged' again points up the difference of the flics from the sprawling crowd. Here the formal effect (giving the word a line to itself) obviously enhances the importance of the content (the semantic meaning of 'arrange'). The same applies to the one-line 'tidiyum', and a similar, though less obvious, ludicrousness accrues to the lesser emphases (as unstopped line-endings) on 'composed', 'creased', 'just', and 'buttons', to say nothing of the likening of the police to the lowest form of life, the single-celled amoeba. There can be no doubt on which side cummings's sympathies lie; and subtleties of form much more than the *overt* or paraphrasable content lure the reader's in the same direction.

Formally 'the Prefect of Police' dominates the scene and the poem. He comes right in the middle (rightly for a 'nucleolus'), has not only a line but a little block to himself, and is granted the dignity of two capital letters (by a writer spurning their use for his own name). This domination soon becomes ironic and indeed downright ridiculous in the course of the following portrait. Alliteration, line-emphasis ('twiddling'), sound-effects ('-ing . . . wing . . . [peck]ing', 'peck . . . at, -peccable'), word-splitting (unnatural, and giving silly emphases), typographical effects (the fussy rapidity of 'tappingpeopleontheback'), and the bit of fused grammar after 'being' (quite different in effect from that of the opening and closing sections – as they in turn are quite different in effect from that of Thomas's opening stanza: an indication of the importance of context, the *varying* effect of anything because of its relation to everything else) – all these things, and more, soon reduce the Prefect of Police to a pretentious mechanical toy jerkily prancing about and looking for all the world like a hen pecking seed. ' – my he's brave . . . '!

Then, back to the beginning, presumably about 16.05 heures. The big battalions have won, the communists are in a distressing, pitiful mess – but they are not mechanical dolls or the lowest form of life. They may still be as disordered as the punctuation and grammar imply, yet they remain human, they help their friends, still have fine eyes ('very' rather than capitalised ones, for they are not now in big close-up), and can still question.

In the end, the reader finds he has been given much entertainment, a good deal of esthetic pleasure from the matching of form and content, large-scale and small, some not too difficult puzzles (save for the title), and the satisfactions of partisanship. Whether these last are *justified* must be largely a matter of opinion. The poem ostensibly purports, by its striking emphasis on expressive form, to convey an experience. Close analysis shows it to be far from neutrally conveyed. There is therefore a latent purport, or implication. Not very latent; we can hardly accuse cummings of attempted deception (propaganda, in a strict sense of the word). Indeed it is sufficiently clear for us to be able to assert with confidence that, despite its modernist, highly formalistic appearance, the poem has an abstractable theme: that communists are more human and likeable than cops. But put like that it sounds pretty simplistic, even untrue — certainly impossible to prove. Is the poem then, behind its avant-garde bravura, rather sentimental? Probably, yes — and probably it does not matter, for this makes no pretence of being a Great Poem; it offers and gives a clever unpretentious verbal circus-turn, the ringmaster being much in evidence, cracking his whip with gusto.

# 5. Anon.

### 'The Twa Corbies'

As I was walking all alane,
I heard twa corbies making a mane;        (*carrion-crows*)
The tane unto the tither did say
'Whar sall we gang and dine the day?'

'In behint yon auld fail-dyke,            (*turf-wall*)
I wot there lies a new-slain knight;
And naebody kens that he lies there,
But his hawk, his hound, and his lady fair.

'His hound is to the hunting gane,
His hawk to fetch the wild-fowl hame,
His lady's ta'en anither mate,
So we may mak our dinner sweet.

'Ye'll sit on his white hause-bane,       (*neck-bone*)
And I'll pike out his bonny blue e'en;
Wi ae lock o' his gowden hair
We'll theek our nest when it grows bare.  (*thatch*)

'Mony a one for him maks mane,
But nane sall ken whar he is gane;
O'er his white banes, when they are bare,
The wind sall blaw for evermair.'

### 'The Three Ravens'

There were three ravens sat on a tree,
They were as blacke as they might be.
The one of them said to his mate,
'Where shall we our breakfast take?'
'Downe in yonder greene field,
There lies a knight slain under his shield.

'His hounds they lie down at his feete,
So well can they their master keepe.
'His haukes they flie so eagerly,
There's no fowle dare him come nie'.
Downe there comes a fallow doe,
As great with yong as she might goe.
She lift up his bloudy head,
And kist his wounds that were so red.
She got him up upon her backe,
And carried him to earthen lake.
She buried him before the prime,
She was dead herselfe ere even-song time.
God send every gentleman,
Such haukes, such hounds, and such a leman.

'The Twa Corbies' differs from all our preceding poems: it tells a tale, the tale does not even *seem* to be told by the poet in his own person, and it has two narrators, of whom the most important by far is a carrion-crow. These may well be differences of degree rather than kind, but they are sufficiently striking to warrant differences of critical emphasis.

Suppose, after a preliminary 'innocent' reading to get the feel of the poem, we ask after mode, type, and kind — not because it really matters how we categorise a work but because such preliminary enquiries may lead to more interesting perceptions. Indeed some degree of doubt about the classification may be of more practical use than an easy certainty. Moreover, we should keep in mind the desirability of an interplay between generalities (or wholes) and particulars (parts), so that we neither allow a too hasty general classification to dictate a forced interpretation of certain details nor, on the other hand, leap to general conclusions by focussing only on highly selective details.[1]

The mode is clearly fictional (crows do not talk) and, in a sense made apparent by comparison with 'The Three Ravens', realistic. Is it mimetic*? To some extent, yes, if only by reason of one or two vigorous words (especially 'pike' and 'theek') and the general curtness and consonantal clutter of the Scottish dialect. In Northrop Frye's terms it is an example of the Low Mimetic (protagonists not superior to other men, or to circumstances), which inclines to the ironic. Again, what it is ironic about is made clear by comparison with 'The Three Ravens'. Is it metaphoric? Not necessarily; the fact that these talking crows are not real crows does not

1. See pp. 26 and 106 for remarks on the dilemma of parts-and-whole. See also glossary under *Mode* and *Purport*.

automatically turn them into metaphysical or symbolic crows. Indeed, they are imaginatively *realistic*, if not literally real. Oddly enough this very fact helps to give them a certain symbolic quality – at any rate when taken in combination with the introductory 'I' and the concluding wind that 'sall blaw for evermair'. They seem to symbolise the ruthless indifference of nature.

It would be possible to interpret the whole poem simply by following up the leads given by our asking after mode, but the result would lack the surety of checks and balances. So, leaving these matters for the moment, on to type and kind, and story, style, and theme – even though this procedure will involve some repetition and overlapping.

At first sight the type appears to be dramatic and nothing but dramatic; very nearly a dramatic monologue, since the human prologue has no personality and takes no action. Certainly the poet in his own person does not even appear to play a part; so this is not a lyric poem (as defined: see glossary under *Type*). However, a second look reveals an implicit narrative – a murder mystery, to which the solution is fairly obvious, though shocking. The knight has not met with an accident, for he is 'new-*slain*'. He has not been killed in battle or ambushed by an enemy or his killer would know where his body was. Moreover, the body has clearly been hidden in a lonely place, 'In behint yon auld fail-dyke' and this suggests a murder. Since '*naebody* kens' where it is except his hawk and hound, who could not have done it, and the lady, the culprit is obviously 'his fair lady' (whose motive is implied in 'ta'en anither mate').

What, then, is the relationship between the dramatic and narrative elements in this poem? Do we read it *for* the grisly little story? In so far as it is a very different story from that implied in 'The Three Ravens', we do. We are meant to pick up the ironic contrast with the established literary behaviour of a man's pets and his lady fair.[2] But since the poem is mainly dramatic in type, the teller becomes more important than the tale – and this requires a brief digression on the complicated business of the persona or personae in poems (and novels).

'Narrator' might be a better term save that, strictly speaking, all lyrics as well as all narratives should be considered as the expression of at least one persona. 'Voice' would get round this difficulty and, like 'narrator', is often used as a synonym for the more common 'persona'. As 'persona' originally referred to the mask worn by actors in classical Greek drama that term does get to the heart of the matter. For the creative writer is probably always wearing a mask – or at any rate is best considered as

---

2. For other, contrastive, uses of literary tradition see critiques 3, 13, and 18.

doing so, since even if we knew that it was exactly like his own face the knowledge would be of no use to us — unless we were engaged in the meta-critical activity of using the text as a document for the author's biography. When the narrator is a crow, as in this case, or a member of the opposite sex, as in Defoe's *Moll Flanders*, it is obvious that the author is wearing a mask, using a persona to tell the tale. In the case of 'omniscient-narrator' novels or intimate lyric poems, it is not so obvious; and indeed the narrator may in practice be almost identical with the author. Still, in that it is the author *as* jester, *as* sage, or *as* lover, or even *as* neutral retailer of alleged facts, a persona is operating. A particular sort of voice is setting the tone of the work, suggesting an attitude, a kind of approach, to the reader. Sometimes there may be an ostensible and an implied persona (or, more plainly perhaps, a primary and a secondary narrator). One of these may be reliable, the other unreliable. Thus, both Swift's *A Modest Proposal* and Browning's 'My Last Duchess' are clearly the expressions of characters very different from the real authors (as we know from their biographies) and from the implied authors, the secondary personae. But how do we know this latter fact, and know also that the primary personae are unreliable narrators? Largely, because these dramatic monologues are not *quite* fully dramatic, the author has not disappeared behind his characters; a ghostly dramatist — in persona, we must say, rather than in person — is to be glimpsed ironically making the primary narrators give themselves away.

In 'The Twa Corbies' much of the chilling effect comes from the fact that the primary narrator is neither shocked nor surprised by what has happened, and indeed regards it as of merely incidental interest: a guarantee that nobody will meddle with this windfall of food and raw material. But what is the function of the secondary narrator? Well, one function is to create a sense of plausibility, or at least to increase the possibility of that 'willing suspension of disbelief' that Coleridge required of readers. He is a colourless character and he speaks matter-of-factly, so that we are predisposed to accept him as a reliable narrator. More importantly, though, he helps to infuse a symbolic element into the poem. For he too is neither shocked nor surprised. Why should he be? What other attitude would you expect of carrion-crows? This tends to further the idea that the crows are indissolubly associated with nature. If they did not strip the knight of his clothes, his hair, and finally his flesh, other natural forces would — the forces typified by the constant bleak wind. However, the mere fact that the introductory narrator is human and is writing in a kind that usually took nature to be at least a little less neutral and indifferent, ladies less again, and hounds a lot less, does give this second function an extra dimension: namely the idea that he must have been *struck* by the neutrality of nature and even more struck by the fact that pets and people do *not* transcend it, as we feel they should. The mere fact that he feels the crow's remarks to be worth reporting, and in an ironic variant of a traditional kind, gives rise to this idea.

The toughness of the diction, the curt idiom, the dramatic manner, and many of the details (especially the blue eyes and golden hair of the young hero who normally dies in combat) are all characteristic of the early Scottish Border ballad.[3] What is not so characteristic is the neat plot, so cleverly brought in as of incidental interest to the crow, though in human terms it ought to have been of overwhelming importance. This has led to the suggestion that it is not there at all, but is merely a bit of careless writing (the 'naebody' not to be taken strictly, but merely as 'nobody except the man who killed the knight'). Such an interpretation, however, not only distorts the plain sense, and minimises the ironic contrast with such a ballad as 'The Three Ravens', but it relinquishes another irony. The lady, already associated on equal terms with the hawk and hound, as just one more item in a list, is then said to take 'anither *mate*' as if she too were just another beast of prey like the hawk, the hound — and the carrion-crow, whose callousness now seems no more than hers.

Now this indicates the great danger of rushing one's fences. If most Border ballads do not have a certain characteristic it does not logically follow that there can be no exceptions, and the sense of a particular ballad should never be distorted to fit a Procrustean bed of kind. As it happens, there are good reasons for supposing that this is *not* a genuine Border ballad anyway. Let us refer to a ballad scholar:

> It is from Sir Walter Scott's *Minstrelsy of the Scottish Border*. Scott said that it had been 'communicated by C. Sharpe, as written down from tradition by a lady,' but it is poorly supported by folk-tradition. For that reason and from internal evidence it is likely that the version is largely of Scott's making.
>
> (M.J.C. Hodgart, *The Ballads* (Hutchinson, 1950), p. 43)

Hodgart takes 'The Twa Corbies' to be a rewriting of 'The Three Ravens', and, though he concedes that Scott is a great ballad poet, comes to the conclusion that the latter is the better. There is, however, no reason why a fake — to put the case at its worst — should not outdo an original, nor does Hodgart argue that there is. The reasons he gives for his preference, indeed, are rather vague and mystical, and hardly seem to outweigh

---

3. For other variations of the ballad see critiques 9, 17, and 21.

the muddle he admits to in 'The Three Ravens', let alone the positive
virtues of 'The Twa Corbies':

> The point of the story has been lost: a magical transformation of a
> maiden into a deer lies in the background but has become suppressed
> . . . Earthen lake is inexplicable and there are obvious gaps. There
> remains an evocation of that intuitive sympathy between man and
> nature which is characteristic of the ballads' folklore.
>
> (pp. 42–3)

As we have seen, it is precisely the main point of 'The Twa Corbies' to
shock us into recognising that if there is an 'intuitive sympathy' between
us and nature, it is not reciprocated by nature, and that there is a certain
sentimentality in unthinkingly supposing it is. Perhaps, on the other hand,
we should concede a certain cynicism in the suggested animalism of fair
ladies. But in many other ways 'The Twa Corbies' seems to score: the
rhyming is better, the idiom more colloquial (yet appropriate for a crow),
the harsh diction more in keeping with the theme, and the progression and
prevailing emotional climate more consistent. But what Hodgart has
neglected above all is the matter of the handling of personae. Scott's
handling was both simple (in giving the whole as a crow's-eye view) and
subtle (in allowing an 'I' to *imply* a normal human viewpoint). 'The Three
Ravens' — one more than is necessary, by the way — seems thoroughly
muddled. It is impossible to say with any assurance which is the primary
narrator, the crow of the first half or the moralist of the second. Nor is
any obvious interplay between them discernable. Two poems seem to be
arbitrarily yoked together, apart from the fact that the lady (as a doe that
lifts and carries!) is as true as the haukes and hounds. There is no plot, and
we do not know why 'She was dead herselfe ere even-song time', or
whether the last couplet is tinged with irony (as perhaps Scott read it) or
merely a formal piety. Quite possibly, a lost original version of 'The Three
Ravens' might turn out to be a finer ballad than 'The Twa Corbies'. This
version seems merely to highlight the superior quality of the latter.

# 6. Marianne Moore

## 'To A Steam Roller'

The illustration
is nothing to you without the application.
　　You lack half wit. You crush all the particles down
　　　　into close conformity, and then walk back and forth on
　　　　them.

Sparkling chips of rock
are crushed down to the level of the parent block.
　　Were not 'impersonal judgement in esthetic
　　　　matters, a metaphysical impossibility,' you

might fairly achieve
it. As for butterflies, I can hardly conceive
　　of one's attending upon you; but to question
　　　　the congruence of the complement is vain, if it exists.

Whatever rhythm is, this poem seems not to have it. Indeed it seems to go
out of its way to frustrate the reader's expectation that a poem, if not
metrical, will at least be rhythmical. A legitimate expectation, for rhythm
is a normal requirement of all good writing, prose included. In fact it is a
normal requirement of effective living; a fit animal's movements are rhythmical, a lame one's unrhythmical, hobbling and jerky; the first-rate sports-
man's actions are rhythmical, the rabbit's awkward and relatively ineffective.
　　Physically speaking, then, rhythm is a natural concomitant of effective
and economical action. The good tennis-player plays faster than the poor
one, hits the ball harder, and yet seems to expend less effort and have
more time. His strokes look better not because they are abstractly more
beautiful but because they are doing the job more effectively, and each
kind of stroke will have its own distinctive rhythm.
　　Does this idea of rhythm have any bearing on literature? In so far as
literary rhythms involve both the natural and the physical, it does. As
D.W. Harding says:

It is from rhythms inherent in the natural speaking of the language that all rhythmical writing begins. In strict metrical verse speech-rhythms have been selected in a way that produces successive repetitions of the same movement pattern, or the same combination of patterns.

(*Words Into Rhythm* (Cambridge University Press, 1976), p. 157)

We may add that the natural impulse to form rhythmical sub-units within sentences, thus clarifying sense, tone, or feeling, as the good speaker does, involves some physical activity. The lifeless monotone of the bad speaker, weighing his words as if they were separate pebbles, has to be replaced by an active grouping of words that involves changes of stress, pitch, and tone — and therefore activity of all the vocal apparatus. A physical activity reproduced in a very minimal way by the good reader of poetry, who reads 'aloud' to himself.

Such rhythmising activity, however, seems to be positively discouraged by this poem. It might almost have been written not merely on a type-writer but *by* a typewriter, so far does it depart from rhythmical natural speech. The second sentence, for instance, by choosing 'half wit' rather than 'half-wit' or, say, 'one half of wit' (to indicate a specialist rather than a moron) not only makes the sense ambiguous but virtually rules out any rhythmical reading. To keep open the possibilities of meaning, we have to give a ploddingly even emphasis to each word. The rhyming of the first two lines of each stanza sets up a mild expectation of metre, but immediately fobs us off with blatantly ill-matched lines. Thus line one has one stress ('the illustrátion'), line two at least three stresses ('nóthing', 'yóu', 'applicátion') — though precise stressing is difficult because the line is so unrhythmical. Nor is any obvious stanzaic rhythm set up. The first line of the next stanza, for instance, has three stresses, that of the last stanza has two. The rhyming, moreover, is inexplicably dropped for the third and fourth lines of each stanza. And whereas in most free verse line-endings are used to help to establish rhythmical units, or at any rate to emphasise matters of sense or feeling (as in 'Two X'), these lines positively do the opposite by apparently beginning and breaking off anywhere, regardless of sense or feeling (witness the random pauses of 'down / into . . . ', 'esthetic / matters', or 'achieve / it'). The diction too, is abstract and toneless.

So consistent is this effect of inorganic, unrhythmical writing that we are bound to put it down to malice aforethought rather than incompetence. Here, in short, we have a poem that insists on being 'unpoetic' — that is to say on crushing all our ideas of what poetry ought to be and

49

walking back and forth on them, steamrollering over our protests. The very title is provocative. 'To a Nightingale', 'To a Skylark', 'To Phyllis', 'To the West Wind', 'To Summer . . . Autumn . . . Winter . . . ' – to almost anything natural we allow poems to be addressed, but to a *steamroller*!

Of course, it is possible to romanticise steamrollers – almost certainly a society somewhere is doing just that for these mechanical dinosaurs – but this poem takes pains to prevent us. *Is* the poet talking of a steamroller though? Steamrollers do not walk, and illustrations are nothing to them either with or without applications, as they have no minds. On the other hand they do crush particles into 'conformity' (uniformity?). These words mean much the same thing, but uniformity is more often applied to materials, conformity to ideas or beliefs. So the answer to our question is yes and no, but more no than yes. In short, this is obviously a symbolic steamroller; a steamroller used as a metaphor for a type of person – to whom, therefore, the effects of the crunching monotony of the rhythm and the deadening jargon of the diction are transferred.

On closer inspection, we find that there *is* a sort of rhythm, or parody of rhythm, in the poem. Not an organic, but a mechanical one appropriate to an unfeeling machine. For one thing, the large-scale structure of the poem goes back and forth like the roller from rhymed to unrhymed lines. For another, in each stanza the runs get longer from line to line, and then start again. But the small-scale structure, the innards of the machine, so to speak, is more interesting, for it adds a key element to our explanation of the peculiarly unnatural anti-rhythm of the lines. Each one is based on a mechanical principle that enhances neither sense, tone, nor feeling but on the contrary just brutally ignores them, walks back and forth on them. The principle is that of counting syllables, regardless of stress: every syllable counts as equal to every other syllable. The first line of each stanza has five, the second twelve, the third twelve, and the fourth fifteen.

Diction and rhythm, then, suggest we have a poem that purports to show up the repellent characteristics of a type of person or group – a type so insensitive that comparison with a rhinoceros would be too flattering; only a steamroller will suit. If we triangulate by theme we seem again to get confirmation. For we are told that such a type crushes individuals into conformity, eliminates sparkle, is impersonal, and could not conceivably be associated with beauty. So far, so good, but something is not quite right.

What kind of poem is this? A satire? If so, it is a very unusual one. Most satires tend to individualise, to focus the faults of a class on one figure; and, what is more to the point, they adopt a personal voice – usually of scornful mockery – and clearly purport to reform. In this poem, although the word 'I' is used once, the tone, diction, and movement are so flat, that the persona comes across as quite neutral; it is a sort of computer voice. And this, surely, indicates what is not yet quite right.

Were we not premature in saying that the abstract diction and the anti-natural syllabic structure were 'appropriate' to a steamroller? They are, of course; and these repellent qualities do act in a satirical way (enforced by a deadpan humour of pedantry) but though they refer to the steamroller they actually belong to the persona. We are hardly likely to end by *favouring* the steamroller type, yet on the other hand, the feeling of the poem does not move us to reform, since it feels unindignant and unconcerned. The persona seems more perceptive, but no less inhuman than the steamroller itself. For, after all, this is not the steamroller's voice, however 'appropriate' it may be in one way. In today's terms we might say that we seem to have a computer coolly rebuking a steamroller for its lack of sensibility! However – to bring in a touch of scholarship – Marianne Moore wrote this poem before the age of computers (and, what is more apropos, before the sixties, when America belatedly ceased to be about as conformist as Victorian England). So perhaps we should go back to our original analogy and say that it seems to be a case of a clever typewriter calling the dull steamroller mechanical. In short, the satire is two-edged; and that is why it is uncharacteristically muted, 'if it exists'. The matter satirises the 'steamroller', but the manner tars with the same brush the neutral satiriser (to coin a phrase that is almost a contradiction in terms).

In various ways, then, this poem teases the reader: by frustrating his reasonable expectations of rhythm, diction, and satire. It teases, too, by not allowing *all* poetic vitality to be crushed into close conformity; some sparkling chips still show through. For example, 'Sparkling chips', in association with 'parent block', suggests the proverbial 'a chip off the old block'. But the normal implication of a lively son of a lively father is here inverted. The 'parent block' – basic, national, institutional, or familial authority – is here ensuring that liveliness and brilliance are going to be put a stop to ('block' suggesting both obstruction and stupidity). Again, the opening lines of the poem are so neutral in tone and movement that they could imply praise of practicality (a possibility, however, that in retrospect becomes ironic). 'You lack half wit' could, then, mean 'You are no half-wit' or, on the other hand, 'You are not even a *half*-wit', or 'You make your mind up', or 'You lack half of human wit (mind, intelligence)' – namely the fanciful half. Wholly impersonal judgement in esthetic matters *is* a metaphysical impossibility (see the introduction on the need for *subjective* objectivity) but the philosophic axiom as quoted here is itself of a machine-like impersonality.

By the time we get to the last stanza the 'typewriter's' extra cleverness and perception have established a mischievous dominance. Whatever our reservations, we are more against the steamroller than the persona, and are likely to pick up a faint echo of the phrase about 'breaking a butterfly on the wheel' — a likely fate that would account for the inconceivability of the butterfly of beauty (or imaginativeness, fancy, sensibility) going anywhere near such a stolid brute as the steamroller. That is to interpret the last sentence somewhat as follows: 'It is so inconceivable that there is no point is discussing the appropriateness of such an association.' However, such an interpretation renders 'if it exists' superfluous and requires 'but' to be read as if it were 'so' or 'therefore'; yet the pedantic precision of the writing forbids such liberties. The fact is that just as the tonally dispraising 'You lack half wit' allowed the logical possibility of praise for down-to-earth practicality, so 'but' and 'if it exists' (and for that matter 'hardly') allow the faint possibility that after all this Beast might get together with Beauty. We should interpret, then, rather like this: 'If such unions occur it is useless to complain of their incongruity.'

But *why* would such questioning be 'in vain'? Because a flower on a dunghill is still a thing of beauty? Because words will not alter facts? Because such a chilly Euclidean, or esthetic, approach to Beauty-and-the-Beast mismatchings is simply inappropriate? Perhaps something of all these is hinted. What seems certain, though, is that the hardly conceivable does happen to the poem itself. A butterfly, as it were, is finally seen to be attending upon the typewriter. Nor would there be any point in questioning the congruence of *this* complement, for it is precisely from the mischievous accumulation of incongruities, from breaking the rules of poetry, that this poetic butterfly perversely emerges. It is like a good photograph — in the negative.

# 7. John Keats

## 'To Autumn'

### I

Season of mists and mellow fruitfulness,
    Close bosom-friend of the maturing sun,
Conspiring with him how to load and bless
    With fruit the vines that round the thatch-eves run;
To bend with apples the mossed cottage-trees,
    And fill all fruit with ripeness to the core;
        To swell the gourd, and plump the hazel shells
    With a sweet kernel; to set budding more,
And still more, later flowers for the bees,
Until they think warm days will never cease,          10
        For Summer has o'er-brimmed their clammy cells.

### II

Who hath not seen thee oft amid thy store?
    Sometimes whoever seeks abroad may find
Thee sitting careless on a granary floor,
    Thy hair soft-lifted by the winnowing wind;
Or on a half-reaped furrow sound asleep,
    Drowsed with the fume of poppies, while thy hook
        Spares the next swath and all its twinèd flowers;
And sometimes like a gleaner thou dost keep
    Steady thy laden head across a brook;          20
    Or by a cider-press, with patient look,
        Thou watchest the last oozings hours by hours.

### III

Where are the songs of Spring? Ay, where are they?
    Think not of them, thou hast thy music too —
While barred clouds bloom the soft-dying day,
    And touch the stubble-plains with rosy hue;
Then in a wailful choir the small gnats mourn

> Among the river sallows, borne aloft
> > Or sinking as the light wind lives or dies;
> And full-grown lambs loud bleat from hilly bourn;      30
> > Hedge-crickets sing; and now with treble soft
> > The red-breast whistles from a garden-croft;
> > > And gathering swallows twitter in the skies.

### 'Ode on a Grecian Urn'

I

Thou still unravished bride of quietness,
> Thou foster-child of silence and slow time,
Sylvan historian, who canst thus express
> A flowery tale more sweetly than our rhyme:
What leaf-fringed legend haunts about thy shape
> Of deities or mortals, or of both,
> > In Tempe or the dales of Arcady?
> What men or gods are these? What maidens loth?
What mad pursuit? What struggle to escape?
> > What pipes and timbrels? What wild ecstasy?      10

II

Heard melodies are sweet, but those unheard
> Are sweeter; therefore, ye soft pipes, play on;
Not to the sensual ear, but, more endeared,
> Pipe to the spirit ditties of no tone:
Fair youth, beneath the trees, thou canst not leave
> Thy song, nor ever can those trees be bare;
> > Bold Lover, never, never canst thou kiss,
Though winning near the goal — yet, do not grieve:
> She cannot fade, though thou hast not thy bliss,
> > For ever wilt thou love, and she be fair!      20

III

Ah, happy, happy boughs! that cannot shed
> Your leaves, nor ever bid the Spring adieu;
And, happy melodist, unwearied,
> For ever piping songs for ever new;
More happy love! more happy, happy love!
> For ever warm and still to be enjoyed,
> > For ever panting, and for ever young —

All breathing human passion far above,
   That leaves a heart high-sorrowful and cloyed,
      A burning forehead, and a parching tongue.        30

IV

Who are these coming to the sacrifice?
   To what green altar, O mysterious priest,
Lead'st thou that heifer lowing at the skies,
   And all her silken flanks with garlands dressed?
What little town by river or sea shore,
   Or mountain-built with peaceful citadel,
      Is emptied of its folk, this pious morn?
And, little town, thy streets for evermore
   Will silent be; and not a soul to tell
      Why thou art desolate, can e'er return.        40

V

O Attic shape! Fair attitude! with brede
   Of marble men and maidens overwrought,
With forest branches and the trodden weed;
   Thou, silent form, dost tease us out of thought
As doth eternity: Cold Pastoral!
   When old age shall this generation waste,
      Thou shalt remain, in midst of other woe
Than ours, a friend to man, to whom thou say'st,
   'Beauty is truth, truth beauty, — that is all
      Ye know on earth, and all ye need to know.'      50

### 'Ode to a Nightingale'

I

My heart aches, and a drowsy numbness pains
   My sense, as though of hemlock I had drunk,
Or emptied some dull opiate to the drains
   One minute past, and Lethe-wards had sunk:
'Tis not through envy of thy happy lot,
   But being too happy in thine happiness —
      That thou, light-wingèd Dryad of the trees,
         In some melodious plot
   Of beechen green, and shadows numberless,
      Singest of summer in full-throated ease.       10

II

O, for a draught of vintage! that hath been
   Cooled a long age in the deep-delvèd earth,
Tasting of Flora and the country green,
   Dance, and Provençal song, and sunburnt mirth!
O for a beaker full of the warm South,
   Full of the true, the blushful Hippocrene,
     With beaded bubbles winking at the brim,
      And purple-stainèd mouth,
   That I might drink, and leave the world unseen,
    And with thee fade away into the forest dim —       20

III

Fade far away, dissolve, and quite forget
   What thou among the leaves hast never known,
The weariness, the fever, and the fret
   Here, where men sit and hear each other groan;
Where palsy shakes a few, sad, last grey hairs,
   Where youth grows pale, and spectre-thin, and dies;
     Where but to think is to be full of sorrow
      And leaden-eyed despairs;
   Where Beauty cannot keep her lustrous eyes,
    Or new Love pine at them beyond to-morrow.       30

IV

Away! away! for I will fly to thee,
   Not charioted by Bacchus and his pards,
But on the viewless wings of Poesy,
   Though the dull brain perplexes and retards.
Already with thee! tender is the night,
   And haply the Queen-Moon is on her throne.
     Clustered around by all her starry Fays;
      But here there is no light,
   Save what from heaven is with the breezes blown
    Through verdurous glooms and winding mossy ways.    40

V

I cannot see what flowers are at my feet,
   Nor what soft incense hangs upon the boughs,
But, in embalmèd darkness, guess each sweet
   Wherewith the seasonable month endows
The grass, the thicket, and the fruit-tree wild —

White hawthorn, and the pastoral eglantine;
   Fast fading violets covered up in leaves;
     And mid-May's eldest child,
The coming musk-rose, full of dewy wine,
   The murmurous haunt of flies on summer eves.     50

### VI

Darkling I listen; and, for many a time
   I have been half in love with easeful Death,
Called him soft names in many a musèd rhyme,
   To take into the air my quiet breath;
Now more than ever seems it rich to die,
   To cease upon the midnight with no pain,
     While thou art pouring forth thy soul abroad
      In such an ecstasy!
   Still wouldst thou sing, and I have ears in vain —
     To thy high requiem become a sod.     60

### VII

Thou wast not born for death, immortal Bird!
   No hungry generations tread thee down;
The voice I hear this passing night was heard
   In ancient days by emperor and clown:
Perhaps the self-same song that found a path
   Through the sad heart of Ruth, when, sick for home,
     She stood in tears amid the alien corn;
      The same that oft-times hath
   Charmed magic casements, opening on the foam
     Of perilous seas, in faery lands forlorn.     70

### VIII

Forlorn! the very word is like a bell
   To toll me back from thee to my sole self!
Adieu! the fancy cannot cheat so well
   As she is famed to do, deceiving elf.
Adieu! adieu! thy plaintive anthem fades
   Past the near meadows, over the still stream,
     Up the hill-side; and now 'tis buried deep
      In the next valley-glades:
   Was it a vision, or a waking dream?
     Fled is that music — Do I wake or sleep?     80

### 'Ode on Melancholy'

**I**

No, no, go not to Lethe, neither twist
    Wolf's-bane, tight-rooted, for its poisonous wine:
Nor suffer thy pale forehead to be kissed
    By nightshade, ruby grape of Proserpine;
Make not your rosary of yew-berries,
      Nor let the beetle, nor the death-moth be
        Your mournful Psyche, nor the downy owl
A partner in your sorrow's mysteries;
    For shade to shade will come too drowsily,
      And drown the wakeful anguish of the soul.      10

**II**

But when the melancholy fit shall fall
    Sudden from heaven like a weeping cloud,
That fosters the droop-headed flowers all,
    And hides the green hill in an April shroud;
Then glut thy sorrows on a morning rose,
    Or on the rainbow of the salt sand-wave,
      Or on the wealth of globèd peonies;
Or if thy mistress some rich anger shows,
    Emprison her soft hand, and let her rave,
      And feed deep, deep upon her peerless eyes.      20

**III**

She dwells with Beauty — Beauty that must die;
    And Joy, whose hand is ever at his lips
Bidding adieu; and aching Pleasure nigh,
    Turning to poison while the bee-mouth sips:
Ay, in the very temple of Delight
    Veiled Melancholy has her sovran shrine,
      Though seen of none save him whose strenuous tongue
    Can burst Joy's grape against his palate fine;
His soul shall taste the sadness of her might,
      And be among her cloudy trophies hung.      30

Just before his death, at the early age of twenty-four, Keats finally transcended the doubts and conflicts characteristic of the rest of his better
poetry — conflicts still lingering in the other great odes — and celebrated
the richness of life on earth. Like the Shakespeare of *King Lear* he had

come to accept that 'Ripeness is all.' So runs a well-established critical view of the ode 'To Autumn', a poem generally agreed to be one of the finest lyrics in the language.

Is this view correct? It is certainly plausible. On the other hand, the minimal scholarship of knowing the companion odes of the same period suggests that such a view might do less than full justice to the greatness of this poem. For one thing this account implies that an optimistic view of life is preferable to a realistic one; for another, it tacitly approves an acceptance based on exclusion, on turning a blind eye to the difficulties of that acceptance. Of course, Keats might have done just that, the general agreement as to the poem's greatness being a case of mass-sentimentality. But it is more likely to be critical intuition outrunning comprehension.

The essence of Romanticism seems to lie in a conflict between spiritual desires and material realities, strong wishes and hard facts – and there is a tendency for Romantic poems to be better in proportion as they grapple with this human dilemma, as against plumping for one side or the other and, usually, hoping that rhetoric will create conviction. Certainly the other three of the four odes acknowledged to be the crown of Keats's brief career do grapple with it. Perhaps, then, the ode 'To Autumn' does also, but subtly enough for the fact to have been obscured, and appreciation of the poem therefore less precise than it deserves?

That is why it seems worthwhile to set this poem in the context – especially the thematic context – of its companion-pieces, the odes 'on Melancholy', 'on a Grecian Urn', and 'to a Nightingale' – though it would have been quite possible to approach it through Keats's revisions, of which we have a good record (why was 'The vines with fruit(s)' altered to 'With fruit the vines', 'Dazed' to 'Dos'd' to 'Drows'd', and so on?). After all, the four do form a contemporary group.

The 'Ode on Melancholy' is the least acclaimed, perhaps because both tone and theme seem vaguely puzzling. Much of the puzzle disappears if we recognise something never noticed, which this poem shares with the other odes, a considerable element of *wit*. True, it is not what is usually called wit (wisecrack, epigram, or aphorism), and no doubt that is why it has gone unnoted. But it is difficult to give this quality, a quality of perceptive paradox, any better name. In the first stanza it is most obvious, or seems most obvious, for Keats adopts the mantle, as it were, of the Peacock of *Nightmare Abbey* or the Jane Austen of *Northanger Abbey*, and mocks the posturing melancholy of second-rate Romanticism (including perhaps his own 'Isabella'), with its well-worn stock of scary properties. But it is the twist in the tail of this stanza that makes it an example of a peculiarly Romantic wit. Why should one not indulge in such melancholic antics? Not because it is better to pull your socks up and be sensible, but because they will actually anaesthetise a real melancholy ('drown the wakeful anguish of the soul') and prevent its being savoured! The second stanza suggests that melancholy is as necessary a component of life as rain. So we should *glut* our sorrow on the rose, rainbow, or globèd peony. Why sorrow in connection with these things of beauty? Surely, as stanza three confirms, because their beauty is brief. But why is it good to glut sorrow, rather than pushing the brevity out of mind, repressing it into the sub-conscious, and simply concentrating on the beauty?

Stanza three, surprisingly, may be approached through a famous enigmatic phrase in Wallace Stevens's 'Sunday Morning': 'Death is the mother of beauty.' The point seems to be this: the spirit yearns to enjoy for ever the beauties of life, so we invent immortality and a changeless heaven to go with it, not realising that beauty is largely a mental or spiritual matter; at any rate it needs a perceiver as well as an object. Any object is beautiful only in the act of perception – and perception is not purely physical. Stevens then goes on to indicate that eternal summer, eternal ripeness, and so on would be boring, not beautiful. We appreciate beauty fully and keenly only because we know that we and it have one brief life, just as we savour the flowers of summer and fruits in their season, knowing they will soon be gone. In that sense, death is the mother of beauty, and we are wrong to long for a changeless eternity. Keats had come to a similar conclusion, in even more subtle form, well over a century before.

The last stanza of the 'Ode on Melancholy' seems confused. The tone is apparently one of triumph (' . . . none save him . . . / His soul shall taste . . . ') while the sense is apparently that of disaster (' . . . Turning to poison / . . . be among her cloudy trophies hung'). Actually the stanza is witty in the Romantic sense mentioned above. The contradiction of tone and sense is *paradoxical* – conveying a complex sense through seeming nonsense – rather than *confused*. Melancholy dwells with beauty because even as we appreciate the beauty we know it will pass – and that is why joy is ever 'bidding adieu', and pleasure is 'aching'. But the beauty, joy, and pleasure would be humdrum, zombie-feelings, were the 'wakeful anguish of the soul' drugged either by self-indulgent pessimism (as the first stanza suggests) or false optimism ('A thing of beauty is a joy for ever' as Keats had once put it, lying to himself). Hence the suggestion of achieve-ment in penetrating to the very shrine of melancholy, and the paradox of achieving this through a strenuous joy. And that explains the paradoxical contrast between the tone of triumph in tasting melancholy's might and the sense of defeat in being hung among her trophies. Triumph and defeat are wittily taken to be interdependent. The typical Romantic conflict of spiritual or emotional desires and material realities has been resolved by a subtle psychological integration.

We are now in a position to approach the 'Ode on a Grecian Urn' at its most thematic point, the didactic and much-discussed conclusion:

> 'Beauty is truth, truth beauty, — that is all
> Ye know on earth, and all ye need to know.'

If the whole statement, as here, is attributed to the urn it can be made to seem plausible, as a biassed utterance by a work of art. If only the first epigram is attributed to the urn, as in many editions, and the rest to Keats (or, strictly, the persona who speaks in these odes for Keats at peak points of apprehension), it seems absurdly limited. In fact, of course, the whole thing, either way, has been written by Keats and placed as a ringing conclusion. Too ringing, it must be said. However interpreted, these lines, in their didactic definiteness, are somewhat out of keeping with the subtle sadness, sense and humour of the rest of the poem. But they can be brought a good deal nearer to common sense. That a mental or spiritual feeling is a truth in its own right, that what is not material is not necessarily *false*, is a point Keats has made before. In that sense 'Beauty is truth'. Another idea of truth, however, is material fact — including the harsh facts of change, of ageing, of one generation being superseded by the next, and of death. But this very harshness, as we have seen, can be regarded as a necessary component of a keen perception of beauty, and therefore as something that rightly viewed can itself be considered a thing of beauty. In that sense, a different sort of truth is a different sort of beauty. This may still not be *all* we need to know, but it is a great deal more than appeared at first. The 'disguised' provocative form of the epigram is presumably deliberate. It is, again, paradoxical, as is the poem as a whole — and as, indeed, are works of art. They seem to be useless but are in fact 'a friend to man' for they do transcend those destructive effects of time that must mingle melancholy with deep joy and beauty. A great work of art represents a pinnacle of human perceptive achievement, a compound creativity that cannot long be sustained in life. But once materialised in art it is constantly available to recreate that human pinnacle time after time, age after age. In art, time seems to have been defeated, intense beauty purged of melancholy. There is, though, a snag, as Keats perceives and that is why he needs to insist, perhaps over-insist, that *truth* is beauty as well as beauty truth.

That snag is summed up in the phrase '*Cold* Pastoral'. There is a price to be paid for eternal beauty. The idyllic world of the first stanza is seen in the second to be a less than wholly satisfactory model for the real world; a place of paradoxical *un*heard melodies piping only to an inner spiritual ear. Love and beauty will never fade, but neither will they have their bliss. And surely the exaggerated assertions of this happiness, as contrasted with that of life, in stanza three, are *ironically* exaggerated — for after all this love is *not* warm and panting, as 'Cold Pastoral' acknowledges. True, this 'silent form' does 'tease us out of thought / As doth eternity', but eternity, as Stevens also saw, has its drawbacks. Without time there is no intensity, without the prospect of loss no real gain. All that can be claimed is that for those who are human and therefore mortal such an idyllic work of art will be 'a friend' — but only in part because it offers a resting-place to contemplate visions of beauty that are truths of a kind; the other part is that its limited mode of being as *art* (not life) also points towards the beauty to be found in life's truth of ceaseless change, with its different limits.

The same quality of realism within Romanticism informs the 'Ode to a Nightingale'. The desire is explicitly stated, to:

> Fade far away, dissolve, and quite forget
>   What thou amongst the leaves hast never known,
> The weariness, the fever, and the fret
>   Here, where men sit and hear each other groan;
> Where palsy shakes a few, sad, last grey hairs,
>   Where youth grows pale, and spectre-thin, and dies;
> Where but to think is to be full of sorrow
>   And leaden-eyed despairs;
> Where Beauty cannot keep her lustrous eyes,
>   Or new Love pine at them beyond to-morrow.

It seems *almost* worth dying ('*half* in love with easeful Death') at a moment of felt transcendence; but common sense immediately corrects this notion ('still wouldst thou sing and I have ears in vain'), and 'the fancy' is finally seen as a cheat — or possibly something better. *Was* it 'a vision' or merely 'a waking dream' (i.e. a form of inner truth or mere escapism)? The question is unanswered, and the poem seems to hover on the verge of reconciling Beauty and Truth, Joy and Melancholy, in theme, as the 'Ode on Melancholy' does, and of reconciling ideal fictions with hard facts, in tone, as the 'Ode on a Grecian Urn' does. In the light of these three marvellously sane, subtle and sensitive attempts to come to terms with a major human problem, it seems at least possible that the ode 'To Autumn' owes its greatness to the fact that it succeeds in combining all these elements into one complex unity of form, feeling, and implication. At least, there is a prima-facie case for bearing such a possibility in mind as we examine it, for being alert to recognise the expression of something more than a simple celebration of nature's bounty.

If 'To Autumn' is as fine a poem as it is usually intuited to be, it should be densely coherent; texture, structure, theme, tone, rhythm, imagery should all contribute to a variegated but unconfused unity. At first sight the clarity and ease of the poem seem to belie this. Surely a work so comprehensible on first reading must be simple? Certainly, the thematic and tonal complexity we noted in the other odes has not commonly been noted in this one. Perhaps, then, it does not exist? There is indeed a danger of assuming that because it exists in contemporary poems it must (rather than may) do so here. As a safeguard, then, against going too far too fast in a thematic direction, let us triangulate with major features of content, and the most evident aspects of structural form, the rhyme-scheme and the progression of the stanzas (if any).

The rhyme-scheme is highly elaborate but shows no sign of having created difficulties with sense or syntax. It does seem to go wrong slightly in the first stanza. At any rate there appears to be no point in its ending with the rhymes *edcce* whereas the other two end with *ecdde*. On the other hand, this does not appear to matter; it is not a *felt* difference. What is felt is a sense of intricate involvement – which would be formally appropriate to an unsimple theme. Contentually, the stanzas change. The first certainly loads us with ripeness; it does unarguably celebrate the richness of nature. So, it might be said, does the second. But there is a change of emphasis, from ripening to harvesting. The riches of nature are being reaped, almost plundered. And in the last stanza they have gone; we are left with stubble plains. The poem is always autumnal but always altering – like life, and unlike a Grecian urn. Structurally speaking, we find that the three stanzas act as the beginning, middle, and end of a natural drama that concludes with death. More particularly, the first stanza suggests early autumn and mid-morning, the second, mid-autumn and afternoon, and the third, late autumn and twilight. Time, change, and the brevity of perfection are already implicit in this structure – and are perfectly in keeping with the contentual movement from ripeness to reaping to regret.

But in saying 'regret' we have insensibly moved from content to tone. The fact that it seems impossible to separate them for long, or to keep either out of any real investigation of form tends to confirm that the poem is more complexly coherent than the surface clarity suggests. Already it seems to be turning out to be an example of the highest kind of art, the art that conceals art. A more detailed examination, stanza by stanza, taking all aspects as they occur, should conform or disconfirm this provisional judgement, of complexity within apparent simplicity.

The first stanza slightly personifies autumn ('bosom-friend', 'conspiring') thus preparing for the stronger personification of the second, which enables a great deal to be said very economically. This element of personification (and that of the third stanza: 'thy') also enables a hint to be infiltrated, that the progress of autumn is like the progress of life itself as well as the progress of a day. The statement of plenitude is backed up by images of muscular tension ('bend', 'fill', 'swell', 'run', 'plump'), of touch, ('mossed', 'clammy') and of an alliteration that impedes the rhythm to reinforce the sense of surfeit (*'fill all f*ruit'): 'wa*r*m days . . . *c*ase . . . su*mm*er . . . bri*mm*ed . . . *c*la*mm*y . . . *c*ells'. Into this evocation of perfect plenitude, however, 'conspiring' and 'think' (the bees are wrong) come as two chilly drops of anticipation.

In stanza two 'careless' must mean not only 'without a care' but also 'uncaring' (the 'next swath' is not spared out of mercy, and there is a tiny suggestion of the torture of pressing to death in the last line, a shadow to the onomatopoeic richness of 'oozings hours by hours'). In this context the 'twinèd flowers' become emblems of the beauty that must die.

In the first stanza, it is worth noting, there are no interrogatives; in the second there is one; in the third two. Within the sustained praise of autumn a questioning grows. In the first stanza imagery of touch and tension predominates, in the second of sight, and in the third of sound. Since music is the least substantial and the most directly emotional of the arts, this too seems to add another pointilliste* touch to the changing atmosphere of the poem. We have run a sensory gamut. It is worth remarking, too, that each stanza, within its own scope, seems to have a movement similar to that of the poem as a whole: from lighter to darker.

The third stanza starts bravely enough: 'thou hast thy music too'. But what is it? A *wailful* choir of *mourners*; and the bleating of 'full-grown lambs' — an image of genius. Suppose Keats had simply said 'sheep'. We should have lost the link with spring, the reminder of the loss of youth and beauty, and the pathos of the fact that they, like the fruit and the grain, have achieved maturity only to be ready for the knife. Death has already been insinuated in connection with the 'day' and the 'light wind', so we are conditioned to pick up this reminder. Yet, the day is *'soft*-dying' and the barren spikes of stubble are *'rosy'*, and the *bars* of the looming prison house give a *'bloom'* (like that on ripe fruit) and the hedge-crickets *'sing'*. So the sunny richness, ripeness, and beauty of autumn's heyday is still fragilely present in the twilight of the late season. But the hedge-crickets' song is paired with the whistling of the red-breast 'from a garden-croft'. It is moving near to the house in readiness for winter. And finally, there is the beauty seen in what must have been a terrible symbol for the youthful, dying Keats: 'gathering swallows twitter in the skies', ready to depart. Thus the poem, like a broadening waterfall, changes within same-ness, grows more complexly unified[1] to the last stanza in which all four seasons make their presence felt, where warmth, life and beauty are woven with chill, dying, and barrenness in one seamless web, thus enacting the subtle inseparability, indeed the complementarity, of contraries that is asserted in the other odes. This poem is a greater work of art than the Grecian urn Keats wrote of, for its beauty is based on the full acceptance of necessity — 'full' in the sense that it has passed beyond the merely conceptual, without, however, leaving it behind.

1. Compare Dylan Thomas's modern-Romantic use of complexly expressive nature-imagery (see p. 23, note 4).

# 8. William Cowper

### 'The Poplar Field'

(A)  The poplars are fell'd and adieu to the shade
     And the whispering sound of the cool colonnade,
     Their winds play no longer and sing in the leaves,
     Nor Ouse in its bosom their image receives.

     Twelve years had elaps'd since I last took a view
     Of my favourite field and the bank where they grew,
     When behold on their sides in the grass they were laid,
     And I sat on the trees under which I had stray'd.

     The blackbird has sought out another retreat
     Where the hazels afford him a screen from the heat,
     And the scene where his notes have oft charm'd me before
     Shall resound with his sweet-flowing ditty no more.

     My fugitive years are all hast'ning away,
     And I must alas! lie as lowly as they,
     With a turf on my breast, and a stone at my head,
     Ere another such grove rises up in its stead.

     The change both my heart and my fancy employs,
     I reflect on the frailty of man, and his joys;
     Short-lived as we are, yet our pleasures, we see,
     Have a still shorter date, and die sooner than we.

(B)  The poplars are fell'd farewell to the shade
     And the whispering sound of the cool colonnade,
     The winds play no longer, and sing in the leaves,
     Nor Ouse on his bosom their image receives.

     Twelve years have elaps'd since I first took a view
     Of my favourite field and the bank where they grew,
     And now in the grass behold they are laid,
     And the tree is my seat that once lent me a shade.

The blackbird has fled to another retreat
Where the hazels afford him a screen from the heat,
And the scene where his melody charm'd me before,
Resounds with his sweet-flowing ditty no more.

My fugitive years are all hasting away,
and I must ere long lie as lowly as they,
With a turf on my breast, and a stone at my head,
Ere another such grove shall arise in its stead.

'Tis a sight to engage me, if any thing can,
To muse on the perishing pleasures of man;
Though his life be a dream, his enjoyments, I see,
Have a being less durable even than he.

In so far as Cowper is read at all — apart from 'John Gilpin' and 'The Cast-away' — it is with mixed feelings; and perhaps rightly so. He stands some-what uncomfortably on a borderline, one foot in the Augustan world, one in the Romantic; a descendant of Pope, a precursor of Wordsworth. Cer-tainly 'The Poplar Field' is not in a mode likely to arouse instant admir-ation today. That in itself might be one reason for attending to it — supposing it to be a *good* example of a kind not now in vogue. For much verse of the past is valuable not for what is 'for all time' in it but for what is of its age only. Not that Cowper is any different from us, of course, in regretting the despoliation of nature. The difference lies in the precise manner of his recognition and rendering of that regret, the way emotion is filtered through morality and reflection, and — even more different — the way it is stylised, distanced by formalities of diction. There is also, however, a second reason for paying attention to this poem: comparison of the two versions shows up not only the peculiar pleasures and rewards of a polite kind of experience now difficult of access but also the limitations of the organic* theory of literature which has been a critical dogma since Coleridge's day. Like olives, this sort of poetry is an acquired taste; and it would be a pity if a false dogma prevented any attempt to acquire it.

(A) is Cowper's first version, clearly a finished version, since he pub-lished it in *The Gentleman's Magazine* in January 1785, and even felt it to be worth translating into Latin at the same time. (B) was published in 1800, the revision having been made sometime after 1786. No question, then, of revision in the first flush of inspiration — nor indeed are the revisions of that Romantic kind. According to the organic theory, any literary work of worth is a complete whole, like a plant or animal, such that the alteration of any part will mutilate the whole. Such a theory fits in well with the Romantic doctrine of creative inspiration, in which the imagination acts like God or nature or the World Spirit by creating out of chaos a unified world. It does not fit in so well with the Augustan doctrines of art as imitation and craftsmanship, of inspiration as largely perspiration. Both theories provide useful rules of thumb for judging different kinds of literature; neither is logically watertight. On organic principles, for instance, it is difficult to see how readers would ever get through a novel, since they could be aware only of mutilated fragments till they had reached the end. Similarly, it is rather difficult to account for successful revision once the whole is completed, since the alteration of any part ought to involve the alteration of every other part so as to produce an entirely new organic whole. And this is clearly not consistent with common authorial practice. True, Romantics do tend to distrust revision, even to disclaim it, but in fact commonly indulge in it.[1]

Cowper is obviously Augustan in that he has no such inhibitions about careful and considered revision, long after the first creative mood has passed. He is Augustan too in so far as he is not only craftsmanly but also shows a care for clarity, logic, and good sense. Some Romantics would be more likely surreptitiously to revise such qualities *out* of a poem, on the ground that they were inconsistent with depth of feeling. What is different about Cowper is that he dispenses his feelings to his guest, the reader, slightly chilled and with a twist of lemon. Like most Augustans he would normally have felt abandonment to feeling to be vulgar and unworthy of a civilised man. Today we find the poems of abnormality, in which he does not try for the sort of balance of sense and sensibility aimed at in 'The Poplar Field', far more accessible: poems such as 'The Castaway' and 'Yardley Oak' that are emotive, personal, and Romantic. Probably they actually are better poems, even when all allowance has been made for our post-Romantic prejudices. The present poem, however, offers some quieter, more esthetic pleasures that the revisions may bring to the notice of our current, somewhat coarsened sensibilities, apt to overlook such niceties. One final caveat: if we ask *why* Cowper made such and such an alteration, the question is not to be taken literally (that would be to commit the intentional fallacy,* for we can only guess at what went on in Cowper's head). It is merely a short cut to getting at the actual *effect* of the alteration.

1. Further comments on organic (and imposed*) form and/or on Romanticism (and Augustanism) are to be found in the different contexts of critiques 10, 11, 12, and 22. See also p. 102 for an amplification of the matter of organic and imposed form in the context of a poem that is neither Romantic nor Augustan.

So 'why' did Cowper change 'and adieu' in the first line to 'farewell'? Surely on grounds of rhythm for one thing. The run of anapaests* in the first version is all too light and tripping for a sad poem ('The póp/lărs ăre féll'd/ănd ădiéu/tŏ thĕ sháde'). The revised version, however, is not only less metrical; it is more dramatic. The pause (caesura) that takes the place of the missing syllable hints at the stunned moment before the significance hits the viewer: 'fárewéll . . . ' 'Farewell', moreover, is native English and less attuned to the drawing-room than 'adieu' and thus carries more conviction of feeling. As a minor point — the alliteration bridges the gap of the caesura and subtly links cause (the *f*elling) and effect (the *f*arewell). The alteration of 'Their winds' to 'The winds' seems to be purely logical. Cowper has seen that the winds do not belong to the trees, and certainly are not produced by them, and therefore — with a care for correctness not common in Romantic, Victorian, or modern poetry — has emended the word. The comma after 'longer' is presumably to minimise sing-song in the metre. But why should 'in its bosom' be revised to 'on his'? The answer seems to lie in an entirely different direction, that of euphony. 'Ouse on his bos-' flows smoothly, as is appropriate for the scene. 'In its' would be more appropriate to choppy waters. In the first stanza, then, Cowper subtly improves the verse in four ways: rhythmical, dramatic, logical, and melodic.

The second stanza is more radically revised, largely in the interest of good sense (though good grammar and good logic are also involved). '*Had* elaps'd' is not really grammatically consonant with the present tense of the first stanza, but more importantly it is not consonant with his shocked sense of loss. If it is twelve years since he last walked under the poplars, the reader is inclined to think, why fuss about their destruction; he did not take much advantage of them when they were available. '*Have* elaps'd since I *first* took a view', on the other hand, suggests frequent visits over a twelve-year period. The past tense of 'were laid', too, is tonally inept (though grammatically required by the previous 'had'); it implies someone telling about the scene after some interval, and is thus less immediate than 'are laid' in the revised version, as well as being inconsistent with the first stanza's present-tense immediacy in both versions. Good sense, then, accounts for the alterations of 'were' to 'are' and 'sat' to 'is my seat' and probably of 'When' to 'And now'. All these cause the second stanza to accord better with the time-scheme and tone of the first, and are clearly improvements by the principle of coherence. But what was wrong with 'on their sides'? Surely this is a matter of logic. How else *could* trees be laid? The Augustan care for sense and logic is something that Romantic and modern poets have neglected; it is one of the things that show Cowper

69

to be at most *pre*-Romantic. 'Shade' too contrasts more tactfully with 'seat' than does 'stray'd' with 'sat', which could easily seem comic.

The next stanza's changes are less complex. 'Sought out' is deliberate, where 'fled' implies alarm and even, distantly, the idea of a destructive invasion — an idea subconsciously reinforced by the other meaning of 'retreat'. '*No*tes *have oft ch*arm'd' sounds like someone speaking with his mouth full; 'melody charm'd' is rather hackneyed but more melodious. And 'resounds', again, accords with the greater immediacy of this version — an extra immediacy much needed, since the poem is more reflective than expressive, and therefore needs to convey as well as possible what the feeling is that is being reflected upon.

In the fourth stanza, 'ere long' seems better than 'alas' in several ways. For one thing 'alas' is rather melodramatic, for another it is illogical (we must all die some day, and for all the line tells us Cowper may be expecting to live to a hundred). 'Ere long' implies *alas*, since it foretells an early death, and it tallies better with the general unmelodramatic mood of the poem; and 'shall arise' seems right because the poet is looking into a future he will not be sharing.

So far, all the revisions seem to be indisputable improvements. Is this true of the completely rewritten final stanza? There is certainly *more* in the revised version. The question is: should it be there? 'If anything can' suggests a deep-seated depression. This was in fact characteristic of the suicidally-inclined Cowper, but is not really in keeping with the controlled and relatively mild sorrow at the loss of the poplars. The previous line was superfluous, as the poem clearly indicates that both heart and fancy have been engaged by the loss; but the revision simply seems to substitute one kind of flaw by another. And the revision of the last two lines is even more questionable. In particular, 'Though his life be a dream' brings in a huge new area of speculation — or rather it seems to take for granted what is in fact highly speculative. Even more to the point is that the idea is not very relevant. Admittedly, the poem has progressed on the whole from feeling to reflection, heart to fancy, from establishing the facts, emotional and natural, to musing on their significance; but with this statement we leap to a quite different level of abstraction. If Cowper is introducing the philosophical idea that the whole of what we take to be a series of sleepings and wakings may be a dream in some other, unknown, life, then the topic needs a poem to itself — and in any case gives no reason why his 'enjoyments' should not be less durable, since dreams are not instantaneous. If he just means, in a religiose way, that in some sense life on earth is illusory, the statement is far too vague to be an improvement on the common sense of the first version; nor does the revision tally with the concern for good logic shown elsewhere.

Possibly Cowper felt that the whole thing was too slight as it stood, but in attempting to make it grander (if in fact that was the purpose of that last stanza) he has brought it perilously close to the self-centredness and vague portentousness that often mar Romantic poetry. The very slightness and modesty of the subject and treatment is where the poem's agreeably minor virtues lie, and the revisions of the preceding stanzas appropriately display a pleasing concern for getting things right on a small scale within an accepted convention of form and style — pleasing anyway if we can put aside the idea that originality and depth are prerequisites of poetry.

# 9. William Wordsworth

## 'She Dwelt Among Th' Untrodden Ways'

She dwelt among th' untrodden ways
    Beside the springs of Dove,
A Maid whom there were none to praise
    And very few to love.

A violet by a mossy stone
    Half hidden from the eye!
— Fair as a star, when only one
    Is shining in the sky.

She lived unknown, and few could know
    When Lucy ceased to be;
But she is in her grave, and, oh,
    The difference to me!

At first sight this little poem presents no problems, either of theory or of practice; on further reflection it bristles with them. The most obvious problem, involving major questions of both theory and practice, is one that has never been noticed. Why? Presumably because it is a problem of extreme rarity. Possibly, too, because we are so used to ignoring the intentional and biographical fallacies that we always tend to read texts in the light of what we know about the author.

The theoretical aspect of the problem is this: what kind of whole is this, an elegy or a lampoon? The practical aspect: what, if anything, in the text indicates that all its parts are to be taken seriously?

No one has ever doubted that the poem is in fact a serious lyric elegy, expressing Wordsworth's grief at the death (or imagined death) of Lucy (whoever she was, if anybody). And certainly what we know of Wordsworth, a man with as little sense of humour as anyone who ever lived, tends to confirm this. The nature of the other Lucy poems, too, tends in the same direction. But suppose we knew nothing of Wordsworth or his poems? Suppose this one page turned up, to be read by some beetle-eating survivor of a nuclear holocaust? How would he know *not* to read the last two lines of each stanza sardonically, concluding with a tone of delighted release for 'and, oh, / The difference to me!'? Normally, little inconsistencies or incoherences would indicate which reading we should plump for. Here nothing internal to the work seems to help. Each reading is perfectly self-consistent, the sad elegy or the humorous lampoon. This is probably part of the price Wordsworth has to pay for rejecting the devices of traditional poetic rhetoric. Naive vocabulary and simple syntax may give a gain in naturalness but run the risk of bathos – and of course the humorous reading does depend on emphasising the bathetic possibilities at the end of each stanza. Since Wordsworth's principles at the time of the *Lyrical Ballads* prevented him from guarding himself against this possibility, and since his lack of a sense of humour probably prevented him from even seeing it, we have to say that in terms of strict logic we have here two quite different poems expressed in precisely the same words, the difference depending on the way we look at them and the tone we read them in. It is all rather like those trick drawings: looking one way you see two facing black profiles, changing focus you see a white vase against a black background. Nothing has altered and both views are perfectly consonant with what is given in the drawing. Moreover, there is no possibility in seeing both at once, nor would there be any gain if one could, since the two are incompatible.

So we have to choose. And since there is no record of Wordsworth's falling into temporary madness, or going on to drugs, while writing the Lucy poems at Goslar, elementary scholarship clearly indicates that we should choose the serious reading, thus assimilating this poem to his life and the rest of his work. It simply remains an interesting literary aberration, that anyone wearying of Wordsworth's solemnity could parody him without altering a word or comma of one of his own poems.

Possibly the potentially ironic meaning does not quite disappear in a serious reading. At any rate, other potential discrepancies (which *have* been noted) seem to contribute to its precarious success: that of a man amazingly walking a tightrope over disaster. For instance, is not an untrodden way a contradiction in terms? Is it not absurd to liken Lucy to a violet and also a star – especially if the one is 'half-hidden' and the other dominating the whole sky (presumably Venus, the most likely candidate for this lone splendour, but hardly a good candidate for a shy maid!)? And is it not contradictory to say that she lived unknown, since obviously the writer knew her and so did those 'few' who loved her (but why did they not praise her?)? All this surely gives hostages to the hostile reader, and nudges him towards the lampoon reading. Really, rather a lot depends on the reader's goodwill. How does Wordsworth manage to obtain it?

What might at first seem to be yet another difficulty about the poem may well give most of the answer: its restraint, which is of course closely linked with its dangerous simplicity. Donne goes to the other extreme in his elegy 'A Nocturnal upon St Lucy's Day, being the Shortest Day'. (Did Wordsworth have this fact in mind when he chose the name Lucy, or did he choose it simply because it was a common name in popular ballads?)[1] Donne becomes extravagantly ingenious and hyperbolic about his grief, saying little or nothing about the dead girl. The poem is so ingenious that the grief seems contrived, and one enjoys the wit rather than shares the alleged feeling. If the feeling *were* to be taken seriously it would seem self-centred; witness, say, stanza four:

> But I am by her death (which word wrongs her)
> Of the first nothing the elixir grown;
> > Were I a man, that I were one,
> > I needs must know; I should prefer,
> > > If I were any beast,
> Some ends, some means, yea plants, yea stones detest,
> And love; all, all some properties invest;
> If I an ordinary nothing were,
> As shadow, a light, and body must be here.
>
> But I am none . . .

Wordsworth, on the other hand, tells us practically nothing of himself, simply that Lucy's death has made a 'difference' — and that comes in the last line; so any sadness we may have felt in the poem up to that point cannot be the result of its implications. Anyway, why do we take it to imply a *sad* difference? Where indeed does the impression of sadness come from in the rest of the poem? The metre is common ballad metre, equally suitable for comedy or tragedy; its function here surely just the 'framing' one of all formal verse: an indication that the piece is to be set apart and considered as a verbal artefact, not simply a report on reality, certainly not as reality itself. The properties, too, are not notably associated with sorrow: springs, violets, stars.

The answer must lie in a combination of reasons. Firstly, the poet tends to gain our goodwill by speaking far more of Lucy than of himself and his

---

1. Though 'She Dwelt' comes from the *Lyrical Ballads* it seems nearer to folk-song, since the element of story is minimal. For more central, though differing, uses of ballad form see critiques 5, 17, and 21.

own loss, and by speaking of her in appropriately simple terms – so simple that he risks bathos; but his readiness to take that risk may itself engender goodwill, provided we already have a little to start from. Secondly, there *seems* to be no exaggeration of her good qualities; so that, again, what could be taken as sardonic, looked at one way, becomes praiseworthy honesty, looked at another ('none to praise', 'very few to love', 'unknown' and therefore not great or famous). Thirdly, the first of the contradictions tends to arouse sympathy. The (relatively) 'untrodden ways' suggests a lonely life, and that suggestion conditions us to accept 'none to praise' and 'very few to love' as further indications of loneliness rather than horrible-ness. Fourthly, the violet and the star – again, taken with goodwill, which the poem certainly makes quite *possible* – have in common ideas of beauty and loneliness that override the element of contradiction. The violet, too, perhaps accords with Lucy's living 'unknown' (to the public), while the star hints at the way she appears to the poet, the only person, it would seem who knew her really well. Gray made a very similar point, but in a typically Augustan way: not bringing in any personal relationship at all, speaking generally about the *class* of the meritorious unknown rather than one instance of it, and using the rhetorical resources of poetic diction – thus avoiding the risk of bathos and contradiction but losing something in intensity of feeling:

> Full many a gem of purest ray serene,
> > The dark unfathom'd caves of ocean bear;
> Full many a flower is born to blush unseen,
> > And waste its sweetness on the desert air.     (*uninhabited area*)
>
> Some village Hampden . . .
>
> ('Elegy Written in a Country Churchyard')

The fact that this poem of Wordsworth's, despite its restraint, despite its folk-song form, does come over in the last analysis as an expressive lyric, a very personal utterance, has led to a great deal of speculation about the 'real' Lucy. Although the Lucy of the poems differs somewhat from poem to poem – as one might expect, if only as a way of fictionalising her to extend the merely personal into the significant – the most likely origin seems to be his sister Dorothy (though she outlived William). She is cer-tainly the 'Lucy' of 'The Glow-worm', and Coleridge suggested her as the original of 'A Slumber'. Furthermore, Wordsworth's feelings for his sister were uncommonly intense. Few men going on honeymoon take their sisters along too. Such material is clearly relevant to a biographical study of Wordsworth, but what relevance has it to a literary-critical study of this poem?

To value a poem for what it happens to reveal of the author and to imagine this to be a *literary* evaluation is to fall into the biographical fallacy. None the less, biographical data, like any other, can be used in the pursuit of intrinsic\* criticism; that is, as an aid in moving into the poem (rather than out from it to some other area). Suppose the poem is, psychologically speaking, a more or less subconscious attempt by Wordsworth to exorcise incestuous feelings by symbolically killing off his sister. How is this reflected in the poem? How does it affect its nature or quality, if at all?

There is a sense in which we could say that the poem purports to be biographical,[2] in that it seems to aim at truth, plain truth in plain language. Not 'truth about' (such as the *idea* that beauty and virtue flourish best in the remote countryside − though this Wordsworthian notion may be sensed in the background); but 'truth to', truth of *experience* − not of the external world, in this case, but rather of the inner realm of feeling. On the other hand, the mere fact of putting something into rhyme and metre removes it from documentary, suggests that any truth purveyed is being purveyed through art: in other words the *truth* in question, even if it is a truth *to*, need not be related to literal and *particular* facts. A certain degree of fictionalising is implicitly claimed, perhaps to allow the truth to be purified and clarified, given in its essence or as a typical, rather than an actual case. The change from Dorothy to Lucy would be an instance of this licence − 'Lucy' being both a saint and a typical figure of folk-ballad. In short, whatever the psychological origin of a work, the poet can legitimately claim that the finished artefact represents a truth achieved rather than a truth simply reported.

In the present case, it is clear that Lucy is so generally characterised that she could not be related to the particular characteristics of anyone. They are not in question; she is more like a spirit of the wilderness. If Wordsworth did start from incestuous feelings he has certainly exorcised them very thoroughly. The most one could say might be that the vagueness of 'the difference', the lack of information as to what sort of difference, could be a result of such a source. By extension, then, we might account for some of the other peculiarities of this lyric: in particular, for the general reticence, and the sense of hidden qualities in Lucy, known only to the persona. Perhaps, too, it could be held to account for the possibility of two contradictory readings, the 'lampoon' one being connected with a subconscious guilt at allowing through even the reticent feelings that are here expressed. However, to say how something may have

2. For discussion of the biographical fallacy see p. 25 and the glossary.

come about is not to say what it now is, let alone to evaluate it. And as we have seen: granted goodwill, the possible sardonic reading need not infect the serious reading; the same qualities that invite another reading also make it easy to grant that goodwill; and the minor contradictions all turn out to be more apparent than real — or, perhaps, all but one: if there were a few to love, why were there none to praise? This seems to be the one place in the poem where we might legitimately suspect that a latent implication beneath the ostensible purport is being glimpsed in a small flaw, the one little *unresolvable* incoherence in the poem. Were Lucy, say, a mongol, the sentence would make perfectly good sense. But 'Fair as a star' rules that out. Could it then represent the repressed idea that *if anyone knew* . . . there would be none to praise? It does not seem impossible; but all we can say as critics is that this unusual lyric elegy does contain one flaw that is difficult to explain away.

# 10. D.H.Lawrence

## 'Hibiscus and Salvia Flowers'

Hark! Hark!
The dogs do bark!
It's the socialists come to town,
None in rags and none in tags,
Swaggering up and down.

Sunday morning,
And from the Sicilian townlets skirting Etna
The socialists have gathered upon us, to look at us.

How shall we know them when we see them?
How shall we know them now they've come?

Not by their rags and not by their tags,
Nor by any distinctive gown;
The same unremarkable Sunday suit
And hats cocked up and down.

Yet there they are, youths, loutishly
Strolling in gangs and staring along the Corso
With the gang-stare
And a half-threatening envy
At every forestière,
Every lordly tuppenny foreigner from the hotels,
    fattening on the exchange.

Hark! Hark!
The dogs do bark!
It's the socialists in the town.

Sans rags, sans tags,
Sans beards, sans bags,
Sans any distinction at all except loutish commonness.

How do we know then, that they are they?
Bolshevists.
Leninists.
Communists.
Socialists.
-Ists! -Ists!

Alas, salvia and hibiscus flowers
Salvia and hibiscus flowers.

Listen again.
Salvia and hibiscus flowers.
Is it not so?
Salvia and hibiscus flowers.

Hark! Hark!
The dogs do bark!
Salvia and hibiscus flowers.

Who smeared their doors with blood?
Who on their breasts
Put salvias and hibiscus?

Rosy, rosy scarlet,
And flame-rage, golden-throated
Bloom along the Corso on the living, perambulating bush.

Who said they might assume these blossoms?
What god did they consult?

Rose-red, princess hibiscus, rolling her pointed Chinese petals!
Azalea and camellia, single peony
And pomegranate bloom and scarlet mallow-flower
And all the eastern, exquisite royal plants
That noble blood has brought us down the ages!
Gently nurtured, frail and splendid
Hibiscus flower —
Alas, the Sunday coats of Sicilian bolshevists!

Pure blood and noble blood, in the fine and rose-red veins;
Small, interspersed with jewels of white gold
Frail-filigreed among the rest;
Rose of the oldest race of princesses, Polynesian
Hibiscus.

Eve, in her happy moments,
Put hibiscus in her hair,
Before she humbled herself, and knocked her knees with repentance.

Sicilian bolshevists,
With hibiscus flowers in the buttonholes of your Sunday suits,
Come now, speaking of rights, what right have you to this flower?

The exquisite and ageless aristocracy
Of a peerless soul,
Blessed are the pure in heart and the fathomless in bright pride;
The loveliness that knows noblesse oblige;
The native royalty of red hibiscus flowers;

The exquisite assertion of new delicate life
Risen from the roots:
Is this how you'll have it, red-decked socialists,
Hibiscus-breasted?

If it be so, I fly to join you,
And if it be not so, brutes to pull down hibiscus flowers!

Or salvia!
Or dragon-mouthed salvia with gold throat of wrath
Flame-flushed, enraged, splendid salvia,
Cock-crested, crowing your orange scarlet like a tocsin
Along the Corso all this Sunday morning.
Is your wrath red as salvias,
You socialists?
You with your grudging, envious, furtive rage,
In Sunday suits and yellow boots along the Corso.
You look well with your salvia flowers, I must say.
Warrior-like, down-cock's-comb flaring flower
Shouting forth flame to set the world on fire,
The dust-heap of man's filthy world on fire,
And burn it down, the glutted, stuffy world,
And feed the young new fields of life with ash,
With ash I say,
Bolshevists,
Your ashes even, my friends,
Among much other ash.

If there were salvia-savage bolshevists
To burn the world back to manure-good ash,

Wouldn't I stick the salvia in my coat!
But these themselves must burn, these louts!

The dragon-faced,
The anger-reddened, golden-throated salvia
With its long antennae of rage put out
Upon the frightened air.
Ugh, how I love its fangs of perfect rage
That gnash the air;
The molten gold of its intolerable rage
Hot in the throat.

I long to be a bolshevist
And set the stinking rubbish-heap of the foul world
Afire at a myriad scarlet points,
A bolshevist, a salvia-face
To lick the world with flame that licks it clean.

I long to see its chock-full crowdedness
And glutted squirming populousness on fire
Like a field of filthy weeds
Burnt back to ash,
And then to see the new, real souls sprout up.

Not this vast rotting cabbage patch we call the world;
But from the ash-scattered fallow
New wild souls.

Nettles, and a rose sprout,
Hibiscus, and mere grass,
Salvia still in a rage
And almond honey-still,
And fig-wort stinking for the carrion wasp;
All the lot of them, and let them fight it out.

But not a trace of foul equality,
Nor sound of still more foul human perfection.
You need not clear the world like a cabbage patch for me;
Leave me my nettles,
Let me fight the wicked, obstreperous weeds myself, and put them
    in their place,
Severely in their place.
I don't at all want to annihilate them,
I like a row with them,

But I won't be put on a cabbage-idealistic level of equality with
    them.

What rot, to see the cabbage and hibiscus-tree
As equals!
What rot, to say the louts along the Corso
In Sunday suits and yellow shoes
Are my equals!
I am their superior, saluting the hibiscus flower, not them.
The same I say to the profiteers from the hotels, the money-fat-ones,
Profiteers here being called dog-fish, stinking dog-fish, sharks.
The same I say to the pale and elegant persons
Pale-faced authorities loitering tepidly:
That I salute the red hibiscus flowers
And send mankind to its inferior blazes.
Mankind's inferior blazes,
And these along with it, all the inferior lot —
These bolshevists,
These dog-fish,
These precious and ideal ones,
All rubbish ready for fire.

And I salute hibiscus and salvia flower
Upon the breasts of loutish bolshevists,
Damned loutish bolshevists,
Who perhaps will do the business after all,
In the long run, in spite of themselves.

Meanwhile, alas
For me no fellow-men,
No salvia-frenzied comrades, antennae
Of yellow-red, outreaching, living wrath
Upon the smouldering air,
And throat of brimstone-molten angry gold.
Red, angry men are a race extinct, alas!

Never
To be a bolshevist
With a hibiscus flower behind my ear
In sign of life, of lovely, dangerous life
And passionate disquality of men;
In sign of dauntless, silent violets,
And impudent nettles grabbing the under-earth,

And cabbages born to be cut and eat,
And salvia fierce to crow and shout for fight,
And rosy-red hibiscus wincingly
Unfolding all her coiled and lovely self
In a doubtful world.

Never, bolshevistically
To be able to stand for all these!
Alas, alas, I have got to leave it all
To the youths in Sunday suits and yellow shoes
Who have pulled down the salvia flowers
And rosy delicate hibiscus flowers
And everything else to their disgusting level,
Never, of course, to put anything up again.

But yet
If they pull all the world down,
The process will amount to the same in the end.
Instead of flame and flame-clean ash,
Slow watery rotting back to level muck
And final humus,
Whence the re-start.

And still I cannot bear it
That they take hibiscus and the salvia flower.


## 'Kangaroo'

In the northern hemisphere
Life seems to leap at the air, or skim under the wind
Like stags on rocky ground, or pawing horses, or springy scut-tailed
    rabbits.

Or else rush horizontal to charge at the sky's horizon,
Like bulls or bisons or wild pigs.

Or slip like water slippery towards its ends,
As foxes, stoats, and wolves, and prairie dogs.

Only mice, and moles, and rats, and badgers, and beavers, and
    perhaps bears
Seem belly-plumbed to the earth's mid-navel.
Or frogs that when they leap come flop, and flop to the centre of
    the earth.

But the yellow antipodal Kangaroo, when she sits up,
Who can unseat her, like a liquid drop that is heavy, and just touches
    earth.

The downward drip
The down-urge.
So much denser than cold-blooded frogs.

Delicate mother Kangaroo
Sitting up there rabbit-wise, but huge, plump-weighted,
And lifting her beautiful slender face, oh! so much more gently and
    finely lined than a rabbit's, or than a hare's,
Lifting her face to nibble at a round white peppermint drop which
    she loves, sensitive mother Kangaroo.

Her sensitive, long, pure-bred face.
Her full antipodal eyes, so dark,
So big and quiet and remote, having watched so many empty dawns
    in silent Australia.

Her little loose hands, and drooping Victorian shoulders.
And then her great weight below the waist, her vast pale belly
With a thin young yellow little paw hanging out, and straggle of a
    long thin ear, like ribbon,
Like a funny trimming to the middle of her belly, thin little dangle
    of an immature paw, and one thin ear.

Her belly, her big haunches
And, in addition, the great muscular python-stretch of her tail.

There, she shan't have any more peppermint drops.
So she wistfully, sensitively sniffs the air, and then turns, goes off in
    slow sad leaps
On the long flat skis of her legs,
Steered and propelled by that steel-strong snake of a tail.
Stops again, half turns, inquisitive to look back.
While something stirs quickly in her belly, and a lean little face
    comes out, as from a window,
Peaked and a bit dismayed,
Only to disappear again quickly away from the sight of the world,
    to snuggle down in the warmth,
Leaving the trail of a different paw hanging out.

Still she watches with eternal, cocked wistfulness!

How full her eyes are, like the full, fathomless, shining eyes of an
    Australian black-boy
Who has been lost so many centuries on the margins of existence!
She watches with insatiable wistfulness.
Untold centuries of watching for something to come,
For a new signal from life, in that silent lost land of the South.

Where nothing bites but insects and snakes and the sun, small life.
Where no bull roared, no cow ever lowed, no stag cried, no leopard
    screeched, no lion coughed, no dog barked,
But all was silent save for parrots occasionally, in the haunted blue
    bush.

Wistfully watching, with wonderful liquid eyes.
And all her weight, all her blood, dripping sack-wise down towards
    the earth's centre,
And the live little-one taking in its paw at the door of her belly.

Leap then, and come down on the line that draws to the earth's
    deep, heavy centre.

Romanticism is as much a matter of temperament as of period. Conditions
towards the end of the eighteenth century provided a favourable environment[1] for the expression of that temperament and provoked a fairly
coherent, if amorphous, set of ideas for it. When those conditions changed
the period petered out, but some of the ideas, or derivatives of them, lived
on to give support to those still of a Romantic temperament, like
Lawrence, though no longer living in so favourable an environment as the
great Romantics, like Wordsworth, Blake, and Keats.

Theory and temperament combine to push Romantic poetry away from
traditional verse-form, away from moderation in tone, and away from public or impersonal subject-matter. One consequence of this movement
towards the unorthodox, the emotional, and the personal is that such
poetry suffers greater variation in quality than that of preceding ages — or
perhaps, more accurately, there is less poetry of reasonably middling
quality. Romantic poetry is like the little girl with the curl: when it is
good it is very very good and when it is bad it is horrid. Of no recent
Romantic poet is this more true than of Lawrence.

The major Romantics reacted against Augustan ideas of good sense
and decorum in verse. Though they took over more than they intended

---

1. A hostile environment — but that is what Romanticism thrives on. See p. 68, note
   1 for comments on Romanticism in other critiques.

from the Augustans, they nevertheless agreed in abandoning the 'tyranny' of the heroic couplet, agreed that a natural diction for all kinds of verse was to be preferred to special registers of poetic diction for different kinds of verse (e.g. for satire, epic, or narrative), and agreed in preferring emotional self-expression to the expression of opinion on matters of public concern — for the self was seen as related to something bigger than society: nature, the Life Force, or a Universal Spirit. In Lawrence, two centuries away from the moderating influence of Augustanism, these preferences find an extreme expression.

Wordsworth took popular songs and ballads as his model and tried to use the real language of men. Keats argued that poetry should grow as naturally as the leaves on a tree. And Coleridge codified the attitude behind these reactions against the older view of art-poetry in his doctrine of organic form: the form should grow out of the content, rather than the content's being poured into a pre-set form like wine into a bottle, and the whole and the parts should be mutually interdependent; the result, not of consideration and adjustment, but of a vital inner necessity. Clearly, the logical end of such a doctrine, technically speaking, is free verse and an idiosyncratic and colloquial diction. Clearly, too, such an end may encourage, on the one hand, irresponsible self-indulgence, and on the other, subtle individual expressiveness — the extremes, in fact, that seem to be exemplified by the two poems we have here.

Setting Lawrence against this background, of course, neither excuses the vices of his poems nor detracts from their virtues; it simply helps to illuminate their nature. But since individualism — even to the point of self-centredness — is a prime characteristic of Romantics, we can expect that nature to be a uniquely Lawrentian variant of the type. Thus, while he is like most Romantics in being better when dealing with the non-human world than he is when dealing with men and ideas, we find that 'Hibiscus and Salvia Flowers' is unusually unsympathetic to humanity and exceptionally virulent in its 'ideas', and 'Kangaroo' departs from the usual Romantic concern with nature as landscape — by now an exhausted topic — to deal with animal nature. In terms of form, too, these poems are peculiarly Lawrentian in the particular ways in which they dissolve prose syntax, vary line-length, and manipulate rhythm to imply a personal and very recognisable tone of voice.

That these poems represent almost opposite ends of the Lawrentian spectrum is made evident by the sketchiest analysis. The mode of 'Hibiscus and Salvia Flowers' is rhetorical and vaguely symbolic, that of 'Kangaroo' mimetic and wittily metaphoric. Despite its highly personal tone, the former seems not so much lyric as dramatic — or melodramatic — in type:

we do not overhear the persona's musings, we are ranted at; whereas the type of the latter is clearly narrative – with a touch of lyric, for though the writer's personality is subdued to his subject it seeps back through the very perceptiveness of the rendering, through the shock of originality that is a necessary element in rendering the subject *vividly*. In the one case, the mood is sneering, petulant and arrogant, in the other, intrigued and amused. The content of the one expresses irrational antipathy, that of the other, sensitive empathy.* Both poems have a loose freewheeling texture and structure, but in the case of the former the free verse has little unity (and is mixed with rhyming tags) and the structure seems random, whereas the texture of the latter preserves a sense of form, though fluent rather than rigid, and the structure is purposive and not unshapely. What might pass for an attempt at shaping in 'Hibiscus and Salvia Flowers', namely, its repetitiveness, comes over in fact (taken in conjunction with tone and diction, as it must be) as neurotic obsessiveness. These differences are pretty evident on the most casual first reading, but a closer look at each poem is warranted, if only because such differences occur throughout Lawrence's work, in prose as well as verse, and often in juxtaposition (where they are harder to distinguish).

'Hibiscus and Salvia Flowers' is certainly a highly emotional poem, but it also purports to be conveying some ideas, or at any rate to be expressing a case. And though it is true that *how* poems say is probably more important than *what* they say, nevertheless the paraphrasable ideas expressed (if any) are certainly part of the poem and warrant discussion. That they are confused and irrational in this case is more likely to be a cause of the fact that both structure and texture seem to vary randomly rather than to be a result of it. As parts of the total experience of the poem, of course, the deficiencies of content and form are mutually reinforcing and can well be taken together in a rapid survey.

> Hark, hark
> The dogs do bark
> Beggars are coming to town.
> Some in rags
> Some in tags
> And some in velvet gown.

So goes the nursery rhyme. Lawrence substitutes 'socialists', thereby suggesting that they wish to live off society, like beggars, without earning their keep – which is not part of the doctrine of any kind of socialism. And yet he seems aggrieved that they are not in rags – which would be rational only if socialists *were* beggars. Later on, though, he seems aggrieved that the Sunday suits of these Sicilian peasants are 'unremarkable'. Does he expect them to be individually styled? They are described as 'swaggering', 'loutish', envious, and common, before the introductory descriptive section ends, with an abrupt change of rhythm and line-length that suggests hardly controlled hysteria, on:

> Bolshevists.
> Leninists.
> Communists.
> -Ists! -Ists!

Reasonable enough, perhaps — especially as a Romantic — to be opposed to people who are not individualistic. But since the poem is saying we cannot know these people, and is obviously violently biassed, we tend to react by asking how he knows they *are* any of these '-ists'. The only hint of evidence is the allegation that they look with 'half-threatening envy' at 'Every lordly tuppenny foreigner . . . fattening on the exchange'. They might well do so without being bolshevists — and anyway how does Lawrence know the foreigners *are* fattening on the exchange? Is he himself? The only thing that comes over clearly is that the poet hates both the natives and the visitors of Sicily. The frequent repetition of the parodied nursery rhyme, too, tends to be counter-productive. Perhaps it was meant as a structural nut-and-bolt but it comes over as sneering in lieu of argument, which implies a bad case.

We then have a long section largely addressed to the flowers, but intermingled with unanswerable rhetorical questions, such as:

> Who said they might assume these blossoms?
> What god did they consult?

or:

> Come now, speaking of rights, what right have you to this flower?

What right, one feels, has Lawrence to ask these absurd questions? Why should peasants not wear Sunday suits and wear a buttonhole in them? The 'answer' seems to be that they are not aristocrats, but the exaggerated repetition of such words as 'princess', 'noble', 'royal', and the like, in long lines loaded with epithets, seems to indicate a distinct lack of confidence in this case — as does the virulence and overwriting of the passage that ends this section:

> You with your grudging, envious, furtive rage . . .

It all seems rather like the pot calling the kettle black, since the only rage we have witnessed has been that of the author, irrationally outraged at what seems a harmless, even charming, local custom.

Next comes a long, hectoring reflection, centred on the idea of burning 'these louts' and indeed the rest of humanity:

> I long to see its chock-full crowdedness
> And glutted squirming populousness on fire
> Like a field of filthy weeds

(But note a few lines later: 'Leave me my nettles'. Who are they? Similarly fascistic characters?) The verse-structure seems simply to mirror surging irritation. Though it makes gestures towards a case ('new real souls', 'not a trace of foul equality') the content matches this formless form. In that sense the poem is organic to its detriment. Again, the case gets support only by way of repetition, as if something will become true if said often enough: witness the recurrence of words like 'anger', 'rage', 'fire', 'flame', and 'hot' – so inappropriate for flowers that one is not surprised the author feels it necessary to beat the drum so loudly. Again, the symbolism is extremely vague. It is even harder to associate nettles, roses, hibiscus, grass, and fig-wort with specific types of person than it is to see salvia flowers as representing a natural aristocracy and therefore being 'above' mere peasants who tastelessly wear yellow boots. (Are we to assume the suits were *blue*? We are not told so.)

It is difficult to make any kind of sane case out of this polemic. The poet is apparently hostile to peasants and traditional aristocrats, to socialists, communists, and capitalists alike. Only natural aristocrats are approved of. But how are these human salvia flowers and hibiscus to arise as 'new real souls' when all the world – except nettles – has been destroyed? Does it make sense to envisage a world in which everyone is an 'aristocrat'? And if it does is indiscriminate destruction the way to achieve it? Moreover, would not such a world be one in which people *were* equal, in so far as each was an aristocrat? Can Lawrence really mean, by 'not a trace of foul equality', that there is not to be equality of opportunity? If so, how will these natural aristocrats emerge? Could there not be some amongst the despised peasants (who do anyway seem to appreciate salvia flowers and hibiscus)? If he just means that he does not want everything the *same* – well, whoever would say that the cabbage and the hibiscus were the *same*? In fact it rather appears that only one person is just right:

> What rot, to say the louts among the Corso . . .
> Are my equals!
> I am their superior . . .
> The same I say to the profiteers . . .

> to the pale and elegant persons        (*esthetes? the intelligentsia?*)
> . . . all the inferior lot —

The last two lines surely give the game away. All the apparent reasons in the poem are in fact rationalisations — excuses for unjustifiable feelings — the real root of the polemic lying in an insecure sense of personal superiority that seems threatened by peasants suspected of having ideas and some esthetic sense instead of fulfilling the earthy, inarticulate role Lawrence admired (but never adopted). In short, what happens in this poem represents the danger of free verse: namely that it offers no safeguard against self-indulgence (whereas an imposed form may act in literature rather as the restraints of society act in life). The writer feels under no obligation to order his thoughts; he is able to pour them forth without pause, to take thought and feeling as much the same thing, and to accept subconsciously the notion that whatever is strongly felt is right. And here, of course, we come up against the matter of sincerity in literature.

In life we can decide whether someone is sincere by checking what he says against what he does. In literature we have only what is said — and if it is said perfectly (i.e. there are no betraying implications) it is for all practical purposes sincere, though the author might not believe a word of it. On the other hand, if as in this case, sincerity in the writer seems proven by the very badness of the work, it is clear that sincerity *per se* is of very little value. Probably Hitler was sincere in his view of the Jews, but this in no way justifies his statements about them or his treatment of them. In 'Hibiscus and Salvia Flowers' the twitchy way the form reflects bursts of irrational abuse or argument, jumps from description, to address, to reflection, to prophecy, from rhyme to unrhyme, long lines to short, seems to guarantee that the writer was genuinely putting down what came into his crotchety head at the moment it arrived there. And the oddities of the content tend to confirm this. No one who wished to make friends and influence people would have written in this way, however strongly he felt. It offers, then, the attraction of sincerity — and the temptation to lapse into the delights of the tantrum, but this is all it offers.

'Kangaroo', on the other hand, represents the *opportunities* offered by free verse and the idea of organic unity. The rhythms of this verse are just as obviously Lawrentian in kind, but how different they are in effect! One can only assume that this is mainly because this is rather a descriptive poem than an expressive one. Lawrence is here getting into the essence of something other than himself rather than getting out what is bottled up in his own psyche. So he has to pause and ponder, and work imaginatively for organic unity. It is a kind of truth, 'truth to', that is in question, not sincerity.

Now, this pondering has led to a much more shapely general structure. We start with a general presentation, placing the kangaroo in relation to the southern hemisphere, go on to a particularised presentation (starting at the face and working down to the tail), then we see it in action, and finally move back to its affinity with the southern hemisphere, and indeed with the most primitive life-forces of the earth. Each section is subtly interwoven with the others, so that what has gone before and what is still to come are kept in mind. The divisions are not schematic and mechanical. Such a form fuses very naturally with the theme — of alien earth-centred otherness — and with the content, the comic but co-ordinately shaped kangaroo.

Lawrence clearly likes animals and flowers better than people. When there is no compulsion to compete, his brilliant gifts of sympathy and empathy (feeling *with* and feeling *in*), and his preference for the unconventional, come into their own. Instead of automatic hostility at difference there is a delight and wonder at it, which are conveyed in the very act of trying to identify with it. Real identification, of course, would be impossible. As Wittgenstein has profoundly said: 'If a lion could speak we should not understand it.' So we cannot get right inside the kangaroo's world; inevitably we end with a human idea of it. What the poem does, however, is to make us aware that there *are* other modes of being, in some ways inferior, in others superior to ours, but in any case *different*. It puts our ruthless human-centredness in its place by vividly evoking the otherness of the kangaroo and the closer relationship it has with its alien physical world. We come from it with a sense of having enlarged our human limitations, if we have not transcended them.

There is a great deal of repetition in this poem too. Lawrence was never an economical writer. But here it is functional, not merely rhetorical. Thus the repetitions of *slip* and *slippery*, *come flop* and *flop to*, or *The downward drip / The down-urge*, all reinforce the empathy the opening section is striving for. On the larger scale of structure, repetitions knit sections together so that the poem as a whole does seem as organic a unity as the kangaroo itself, different though one part might be from another, considered in isolation. So 'her great weight below the waist' in the second section picks up and amplifies 'Who can unseat her, like a liquid drop that is heavy' in the first, both recurring, still further amplified, in the conclusion: 'And all her weight, all her blood, dripping sack-wise down towards the earth's centre'. In a similar way — but not the same way — the creature's eyes are referred to in each of the last three sections (of description, action, and return). In this case, they refer us to a difference of scene and outlook, to an aspect of theme (of an *inner* alienness related to the outer one), and finally — in 'wonderful liquid eyes' — prepare us for another aspect of theme (that initiated by the opening 'liquid drop'), namely, the kangaroo's primordially powerful relationship to the most basic and powerful of all natural forces, the force of gravity.

What is most likely to strike the reader, however, after the cantankerousness of the previous poem, is the poet's subordination to his subject, the paragraphic rhythms, smooth and downward-falling as the kangaroo they are concerned with, the easy, goodnatured, conversational tone and idiom, and above all, the beautiful wit and humour — beautiful because it is apt, not smart. At its most subtle, perhaps, it is to be found in the opening lines' exhilarating idea — an exaggeration of a real difference, one feels — that life in the northern hemisphere tries to defy the force of gravity:

> Life seems to leap at the air, or skim under the wind
> Like stags on rocky ground, or pawing horses, or springy scut-tailed
> rabbits.

How delightfully rhythm, diction, sound effects, and examples combine — with slightly humorous exaggeration — to highlight this vitality which is to contrast with the 'slów sád leáps' of the kangaroo (and the flop of the comic frogs). At its most brilliant, this quality is seen in those incongruous metaphors, bridging a huge gap, that turn out to be just right, perfectly evocative of kangarooity: 'Her . . . drooping Victorian shoulders', 'the long flat skis of her legs'. But throughout, serious implications of alienness — conveyed with marvellous simplicity: 'empty dawns', 'that silent lost land' — are kept from solemnity by gentle comic touches such as the addiction to peppermints (very *un*primitive), the paw hanging out, or ' . . . a lean little face comes out, as from a window, / Peaked and a bit dismayed' — as it might well be at the sight of the world it must enter. (It is worth noting, too, how the short line here is perfectly justified, for this is a humorous aside, contrasting with the larger action of the grown kangaroo.)

Two poems, then, equally Lawrentian, similarly organic and free in form — and utterly different in effect and quality.

# 11. Ted Hughes

## 'Thistles'

Against the rubber tongues of cows and the hoeing hands of men
Thistles spike the summer air
Or crackle open under a blue-black pressure.

Every one a revengeful burst
Of resurrection, a grasped fistful
Of splintered weapons and Icelandic frost thrust up

From the underground stain of a decayed Viking.
They are like pale hair and the gutturals of dialects.
Every one manages a plume of blood.

Then they grow grey, like men.
Mown down, it is a feud. Their sons appear,
Stiff with weapons, fighting back over the same ground.

Both Augustans and Romantics claim to have 'nature' on their side,[1] and
both are right, though in the one case nature usually leads towards con-
servative conclusions, in the other case to radical ones. It all depends on
which aspect of 'nature' is chosen as the essential one; and that choice
presumably depends largely on temperament (though in certain periods
fashion may play a part). Look at the regular movement of the planets, the
permanent positions of the fixed stars, the repetitive cycle of the seasons,
or the general pattern of man's life from the 'infant / Mewling and puking'
to 'second childishness, and mere oblivion', and it seems evident that
nature is order, stability, regularity. Look at falling stars, comets, the
weather, the incessant and murderous struggle for existence among species,
or the chancy variety of men's lives, and it seems equally evident that
nature is change, spontaneity, struggle, vitality. For Augustans (or
Apollonians*) the contrary view seems to lead straight to chaos; for

1. For other aspects of Romanticism and Augustanism, touched upon in the context
of different critiques, see pp. 68, 85, 98, and 163.

Romantics (or Dionysians*) the contrary view seems to lead to a deadening mechanical rigidity. Again, both are right; and it seems lucky that in most periods most people take a balanced, or muddled, view of the nature of nature.

The two extremes are vividly portrayed in *King Lear*, in which Edmund is the main spokesman for the Dionysian view of nature and Gloucester for the Apollonian. The chaos that ensues from the attempt by Edmund and his allies to overthrow Order fits in well enough with both Renaissance political theory and literary theory. The poet's creation was seen as analogous to God's: so it should display order, proportion and harmony, all being appropriate to the subject, according to the rule of *decorum*. Hence, imposed form was regarded as a good *per se*. So too, as we have seen, for eighteenth-century Augustans, though perhaps by that time the underlying image was more architectural than theological. A poem was to be constructed like a fine building, not to be organic like a plant or an animal.

Like that of Blake and Lawrence, Hughes's poetry is in direct opposition to this outlook, both in its celebration of power, passion, and the primitive, and in the freedom of its form. He may be taken as the most striking contemporary example of post-Romanticism, as Larkin (who comes next) is of post-Augustanism — in an age that has been on the whole no more hospitable to one kind than the other (though at the moment it appears to be in a Romantic phase).

'Thistles' admirably encapsulates his virtues — and perhaps hints at a corresponding danger in such an extremist temperament. Nothing could more brilliantly evoke the specific and essential quality of this plant. But, as we noted with 'Kangaroo', in the last analysis we find that we are inevitably seeing something of our own reflected in the alien form of life. For a plant, uncompromising revengefulness, indomitability, and the inheritance of bloodlust may well seem admirable qualities, ensuring survival of the species. If one applies these qualities to men (say, the Irish, to stay near home) their admirableness seems far less self-evident. And, of course, the poem does encourage such a transfer by its imagery (the only kind of imagery, of course, that could enable human beings to identify with non-human beings); witness, especially, the last stanza:

> Then they grow grey, like men.
> Mown down, it is a feud. Their sons appear,
> Stiff with weapons, fighting back over the same ground.

This, however, is implication rather than purport; primarily the poem is

94

about its title — or more accurately, about feelings evoked by an empathetic consideration of thistles.

What sort of feelings? Surely those typified by its first word: 'Against'. Against all that is implied by the easy rhythm of the opening line, rising and falling like a pastoral landscape, against the civilising of nature, indicated by 'cows' and 'hoeing'. Note how 'rubber', besides being physically right and poetically unexpected, also gives a tiny suggestion that cows are somehow artificial animals.

After that first line the poem itself enacts its theme, crackling with the same energy that is attributed to its subject. 'Spike', as a verb, inevitably suggests spears and battle, and prepares for 'weapons', 'Viking', and the 'plume of blood'. That cows' tongues and hoeing hands are vulnerable and blameless indicates that the celebration of indomitable uncompromising energy is not altogether uncritical. Certainly it is in the foreground, but in the background we have the overtones of 'revengeful' (made the more reprehensible by association with 'resurrection' — normally connected with the idea of forgiving one's enemies). The 'underground stain of a decayed Viking', too, has connotations very different from those of, let us say, 'the buried remains of a long-dead Viking'. 'Underground', 'stain', and 'decayed' are all tainted with some unfavourable connotations, as is 'feud'. 'Stiff' is not so clear a case, but it does seem to hint that the sons have sacrificed natural grace and freedom for the encumbrance of arms.

Against this secondary theme, however, we must surely set the overriding impression of fierce energy enjoyed and shared by the persona. 'Crackle' is a marvellous use of synesthesia (transfer from one sense to another; in this case from the visual to the aural) and so, more subtly, is 'pressure'. The onomatopoeia of 'Thistles spike' is repeated and reinforced by the spiteful hiss and throaty growl of 'grasped fistful' or 'frost thrust'. And stress plays its part, as in 'Blúe-bláck préss-', 'grásped físt-', and 'fróst thrúst' — not to mention 'grów gréy', 'Mówn dówn', and other examples. With similar effect, lines often end on forceful words: ' . . . *burst* / Of', ' . . . *fistful* / Of', ' . . . *up* / From', '*pressure*', '*blood*'. And alliteration clearly lends effective aid. Together with the sense, all these things combine to convey a sense of clenched anger, jagged aggressiveness; all that is the contrary of mildness and harmony in fact.

Yet what is even more striking — in this poem where identification far outweighs meditation — are the almost surrealistic imaginative complexes. 'A plume of blood' is the simplest of them, but nevertheless unites a picture of the red top to the thistle's head, the idea of swanky knighthood, and the grisly acknowledgement of arterial blood spurting from a bad

95

wound: i.e. it unites realistic, esthetic, and brutal elements. 'They are like pale hair and the gutturals of dialects' is the most improbable of them — yet it does come off. Thistles *are* pale at the top and Vikings are thought of as fierce, cold, Nordic blondes. They invaded and pillaged more civilised peoples as thistles invade cultivated land and are a curse to it. 'Gutturals of dialects' implies barbarians, uncouth and incomprehensible, coming into a more cultured world (and the sound of the phrase picks up the effects previously noted in 'grasped fistful', and so on). Thistles too seem as uncouth among plants as the rhinoceros among animals, and as formidable. So, against all expectation, one agrees they are 'like pale hair and the gutturals of dialects', and finishes the poem with a feeling of having been forcibly introduced to powers that civilisation has always struggled, often unsuccessfully, to contain, whether in the farms or the minds of men.

# 12. Philip Larkin

## 'Deceptions'

*'Of course I was drugged, and so heavily I did not regain my con-
sciousness till the next morning. I was horrified to discover that I
had been ruined, and for some days I was inconsolable, and cried
like a child to be killed or sent back to my aunt.'* – Mayhew,
*London Labour and the London Poor.*

Even so distant, I can taste the grief,
Bitter and sharp with stalks, he made you gulp.
The sun's occasional print, the brisk brief
Worry of wheels along the street outside
Where bridal London bows the other way,
And light, unanswerable and tall and wide,
Forbids the scar to heal, and drives
Shame out of hiding. All the unhurried day
Your mind lay open like a drawer of knives.

Slums, years, have buried you. I would not dare
Console you if I could. What can be said,
Except that suffering is exact, but where
Desire takes charge, readings will grow erratic?
For you would hardly care
That you were less deceived, out on that bed,
Than he was, stumbling up the breathless stair
To burst into fulfilment's desolate attic.

The value of much poetry (and fiction) lies in the way it revives the over-
familiar, gives new life to what has become dead and habitual; it 'cleanses
the doors of perception'. Much, however, is of value for the opposite
reason, for its demonstration of unfamiliar areas of scene, action, or
experience. The one kind enlivens, the other enlarges our sensibility or
knowledge. On the whole – though not entirely – Lawrence and Hughes

were seen to fall into the latter class. And being Romantics, they chose to take the reader into areas of unfamiliar feeling. The sort of truth they were dealing with was truth *to* (to personal perception and emotion). For that reason it seemed most profitable to start exploring their work through its expressive and empathetic qualities, to prove it on our pulses. A first open-minded reading of 'Deceptions' at once reveals Larkin to be at the other end of the poetic spectrum: an Augustan or Apollonian writer. His poem is more related to truth *about* (to 'placing', to what depends less on personal impression than on appeal to good sense and *common* sensibility). On the whole he is refreshing the familiar (by rewriting more vividly a personal but hackneyed account of a rape) and then pondering on its implications. It is in the pondering, the attempt to extend understanding, that he is most obviously Augustan.[1] Through subtle reason he appeals to a potentially *public* intelligence. So theme and paraphrasable meaning may properly loom larger in the analysis of 'Deceptions' than they did in that of 'Thistles'.

Quite evidently these distinctions are not absolute. It is a matter rather of different emphasis. Some critical intelligence was to be discerned in 'Thistles' and very clearly the first paragraph of 'Deceptions' is largely concerned with sharing experience rather than reflecting on it (with truth *to* rather than truth *about*). It is very different from the second. Nevertheless, the distinction holds good, taken with a pinch of salt. Larkin is more meditative than emotive. Even while, in the first paragraph, we are made to feel anew the girl's plight we are also considering it, placing it in a social context. Moreover, he is not meditating on a personal experience, nor even on someone else's current experience, but on a *report* of a long-past experience by someone different in every way — save the way of common humanity — from himself. On the other hand, the last paragraph, though detached and appealing to subtle good sense, is not *coldly* detached; nor is it wholly abstract in style.

The twin themes of the poem, we may say in crude summary, are that pity is useless and — coming as a twist in the tale, a sort of intellectual plot-denouement — that the act was self-punishing, the deceiver being the more deceived of the two. To say this reveals how little even the most meditative of poems depends on its conclusions, true and clever though they may be. The real merits of this poem are implied in the reader's recognition that he has come not only to understand the event better than the girl herself but also that the poet's words, a century later, have brought home her feelings far better than her own verbatim account to Mayhew.

1. See pp. 68, note 1 and 93, note 1 for references to further commentary in other critiques.

Technically, the poem is masterly. Every word is a normal everyday word, every phrase and sentence in perfectly ordinary syntax, the rhythms those of natural self-communing speech. There is no trace of ostentation or preaching, so the reader is prepared to trust the poet, to go along with him in what seems an unpretentious honest exploration: what was it like? and how is it to be placed? The rhyming is strict, but the many run-on lines render it unobtrusive, and the iambic pentameter is subordinated to speech-rhythms (though it is never at odds with them). Together, rhyme and metre are just evident enough to 'frame' the piece as an artefact, an object of disinterested interest. It combines form with informality; and in that the verse seems a perfectly natural embodiment of the content, it is an example of organic form without free verse.

In its quieter way, this poem co-ordinates imaginative complexes at least as widely spread as those of Hughes. 'Bitter and sharp with stalks' transfers mental suffering into vivid physical terms. ' . . . he made you gulp' suggests the enforced swallowing of a nasty draught, and is analogous to the rape. Since the throat has thus become analogous to the vagina, 'sharp with stalks' recalls her pain, the physical counterpart to her grief. And 'Bitter', of course, implies feeling as well as taste. 'I can taste the grief' is so unemphatically phrased that one is apt to overlook the daring synesthesia that makes the complex image of the next line possible. 'The sun's occasional print' indicates that the day was more cloudy than sunny, and that the girl lay miserably looking at the wall on which the sun from time to time printed its window-pictures – the light that 'forbids the scar to heal' (a sensitive suggestion of shame's longing for the cover of darkness). ' . . . the brisk brief / Worry of wheels' supports its reference by alliteration and rhythm, but through 'Worry' indicates their constant reminder that she must go out eventually to the hypocrisy of Victorian 'bridal' London, which will henceforth accept her only as a teenage prostitute. The final line of the paragraph, with its brilliant domestic image – appropriate to the girl – takes us back to the opening mixture of the mental and physical, though again only the mind is explicitly referred to. How much more telling an account of her feelings than the conventional idiom of her own account: 'horrified to discover that I had been ruined . . . cried like a child', which rings true but not true *to*.

Having brought the fact to life in its physical, psychological and social reality, Larkin then goes on to ponder its wider implications. 'I would not dare / Console you if I could' is clear enough. Consolation would be no compensation, and therefore an impertinence, and anyway it is all over and done with. But what does it mean to say, instead of consolation, 'that suffering is exact, but where / Desire takes charge, readings will grow erratic'? Since hers is the suffering, the desire the deceiver's, the point must be this: that what she has suffered she has suffered; no words will diminish it, no reflection make it more acceptable; yet there is this to be said, that when possessed by desire the readings on our moral dial, so to speak, become abnormal and cease to be a guide.

That she, personally involved and deeply injured, 'would hardly care' in no way reduces the perceptiveness of the paradoxical truth of the conclusion. Unlike her, we *are* able to take a god's-eye view, aided by the marvellous symbolism of the last two lines. They are at once straightforwardly realistic and perfectly expressive of the sexual act. She *was* carried up to an attic, by a man no doubt panting with desire and the physical effort involved. At the same time, stumbling up a breathless stair perfectly suggests the clumsy rape of an inert unco-operative body, and 'burst into fulfilment's desolate attic', the simultaneous orgasm and disillusion that must have followed the act — an anticipated paradise that turns into a desolate attic as desire disappears and moral readings return to normal.

That the 'Augustan' outlook and practice necessarily leads to a deadening conventionality is thus seen to be at least as untrue as the notion that the 'Romantic' one necessarily leads to wild chaos: though these are possible extremes. 'Deceptions' turns out to be no less feeling than 'Thistles', despite its thoughtfulness. The difference lies in the kind of feelings: those associated with man as a civilised and communal being as against those of man as a primitive and private one.

# 13. William Shakespeare

## Sonnet 138

When my love swears that she is made of truth
I do believe her, though I know she lies,
That she might think me some untutor'd youth
Unlearnèd in the world's false subtleties.
Thus vainly thinking that she thinks me young,
Although she knows my days are past the best,
Simply I credit her false-speaking tongue:
On both sides thus is simple truth suppress'd.
But wherefore says she not she is unjust?
And wherefore say not I that I am old?
Oh, love's best habit is in seeming trust,
And age in love loves not to have years told.
  Therefore I lie with her, and she with me,
  And in our faults by lies we flatter'd be.

Since the sonnet is a given pattern, any sonnet is likely to be perceived as a poem in which paraphrasable content interacts with imposed form. The wise sonneteer will not try to make form and content indistinguishable, but on the contrary will use the perceived pattern' and its interplay with paraphrasable content as the components of an esthetic experience (disinterested delight from the relationship of parts to the whole and other parts, and the complementarity of form and content). Shakespeare does in fact use the sonnet form in this way. We are always aware of its structuring effect; but as the content it is structuring is subtle, difficult, and realistic, that effect is not artificial but rather comparable to the way we have to structure experience, in life, in order to cope with it. In this it is significantly different from most Elizabethan sonnets, which tend to be artfully artificial. They exploit the formality of the given pattern, even flaunt it, rendering it acceptable by matching it with highly conventional diction and subject-matter. This Renaissance *decorum* of the sonnet means that appreciation is almost *purely* esthetic: an appreciation of clever play within the twin confines of conventional form and content. Shakespeare offers a more mixed pleasure — made up in part of the plain esthetic pleasure of perceiving the artificial form so effortlessly accommodated to an unusually naturalistic content, in part of the more subtle esthetic pleasure in noting the contentual play *against* decorum (rather like that of deliberate discords in music),[1] and in part of the non-esthetic pleasure of exploring an unfamiliar area of emotional experience (so super-civilised as to make Larkin look almost primitive). This is a far more deeply indecorous poem than the anti-conventional sonnet 130, 'My mistress' eyes are nothing like the sun . . . '

Sonnet 138 shares with poems of organic form the feeling that neither sense nor syntax has had to be strained or contorted to accommodate itself to the verse-form. However, the reader is always fully aware that he is reading a sonnet: firstly, because it is obviously a given pattern and the sense goes along with it, each quatrain dealing with a different aspect of the matter and the couplet summing up epigrammatically; secondly, because the structural form is in no way blurred by run-on lines or half-rhymes.

In fact, a fully perceptible form is necessary to the poem for it lacks almost all the other devices used in poetry (or literary fiction) for enriching or intensifying the paraphrasable meaning and for giving esthetic pleasure — the two main reasons for writing in a literary rather than a merely informative way. There are no metaphors or similes, for instance, indeed, no images at all; there are no *obvious* sound-effects, and no poetic diction.

The formal pattern, then, gives esthetic pleasure by its easy interplay with such informal diction, and it intensifies meaning by helping the reader to 'hear' sound patterns that, in speech, would indicate an inner emotion (as, for example, rapid speech might indicate excitement). Thus the metrical (iambic) stressing of the second line insists on 'do' and 'know', which natural speech-rhythm would somewhat emphasise, and thus brings out more evidently the implication of an effort of will to deceive oneself. Something similar goes on, though more subtly, in the line 'Oh, love's best habit is in seeming trust'. The last two feet are obviously iambic; the rest is more difficult to stress, but the underlying iambic current of the preceding lines encourages one to try to adapt the stress required by sense. But what *is* the stress required? If we are aware of sonnet decorum we would expect the line to read, say, 'Oh, love's best habit is in *perfect* trust'. This poem is saying it is in *pretended* trust — which makes 'best' surprising

1. Compare the different use of literary convention in the poems discussed in critiques 3, 5, and 18.

for, given 'seeming', conventional decorum would have produced 'worst'. The urge towards a compromise between speech and metrical rhythm does in fact promote extra emphasis on these two words that need it. 'Oh' requires a pause after it, so we start with a reversed foot 'Oĥ ⌣̆'. The next foot then runs iambically — provided we stress 'best' ('love's best') but 'habit is' carries an extra unstressed syllable, which tends to make us give a little more emphasis than we otherwise would have to 'seeming': 'Oĥ,⌣̆/ lŏve's bést/hábĭt is/ĭn sĕem/ĭng trŭst'. Other examples could be adduced, but we have been brought to the verge of a more important function of the given pattern, the sonnet form: namely, that it imposes unity on a potentially unmanageable state of mind and feeling; and it sets it apart from the stream of experience — where action seems to be demanded — as an art-object, for contemplation. And this allows a more sophisticated sublimation to operate. The complexity of this response to a situation that would normally have resulted in indignation and the conventional elevation of '*perfect* trust' is displayed by the theme of doublethink — more favourably viewed by Shakespeare than Orwell — and by the use of puns and other ambiguities.

Structurally, the poem is straightforward. The first quatrain discloses the persona's reaction to a trying situation, the second comments on that reaction, admitting its apparent futility, the third nevertheless finds some justification for it, and the couplet sums up the complicated position. Texturally, the matter is less simple, since almost every key word carries some kind of double meaning, thus enacting the theme of doublethink.

'Made of truth', in the first line, means wholly truthful *and* wholly faithful (maid of truth, a true lover). The second line, through the pun on 'lies' reveals her to be an unfaithful liar. And '*do* believe' though *knowing* the contrary, introduces the theme of doublethink, the willed effort to convince oneself of something known at heart not to be so. However, the very next word, 'That' (in order that) takes us to the level of treblethink, for the writer is clearly well aware that the doublethink is for the lover's own benefit — so that she will think him naive and therefore young. Since 'vainly' suggests not only the vanity of wishing to be thought as young as his mistress but also the futility of it, we seem to get into the realm of quadruplethink. For he knows that she does *not* think him young, and therefore does not think him naive, and therefore does not believe he believes her but, as later lines indicate, matches his pretence with hers by pretending to believe he believes her (and thus in a sense is not lying when she swears she is faithful, since she knows she is not deceiving him by so swearing). In short, we see that he knows she knows he knows she knows. 'False-speaking', of course, implicitly undermines '*do* believe'; the writer is too perceptive to be taken in, whether by himself or by her. 'Simply', in the sense of 'like a simpleton', then, is ironic; but as 'plainly' or 'in short' it leads into the summing up of what we may call the expository section of the poem, given in the next line, 'On both sides thus is simple truth suppress'd', in which the apparently unnecessary addition of 'simple' to 'truth' implies that there may be a truth that is *not* simple — e.g. of mutual pretences that are known not to deceive.

It is this that explains the sardonic indecorous answer to an obvious question: why do they not both confess to what each knows the other knows? The answer, that love's best habit (dress, disguise, as well as custom) is in *seeming* trust, gets its point from the perception that there can be a subtle kind of truth — even a loving kindness — in mutual pretence. It shows that neither wishes to pain the other, while both want to avoid a showdown that could end the affair. So the sonnet recognises a sort of faith in faithlessness, a sort of truth in lies — a recognition finely conveyed in the wry, resigned bitterness of the concluding couplet's summing up. It brings us back to the beginning, in that 'lie with her' means lie while she lies and lie sexually with her. 'She with me' reminds us of the sharing (and even caring) element in mutuality. And the last line acknowledges, in 'faults', that this is a second-best, while 'by lies we flatter'd be' brilliantly ties the whole thing up. 'To flatter' originally meant to smooth over, to caress. This meaning gives body to the secondary (sexual) meaning of 'lies' in so far as caresses tend to smooth over faults, sooth away consciousness of them. 'Flatter'd' is also apposite to all that has been said of the other (mendacious) meaning of 'lies', since one who is flattered, even while being pleased with the flattery, knows in his heart of hearts that it is not true.

It is, however, no flattery to say that this is probably the most original use of the genre in the whole sonnet tradition, which it both uses and abuses.

# 14. William Shakespeare

'Tomorrow, and tomorrow . . . ' (from *Macbeth*)

SEYTON: The Queen, my lord, is dead.
MACBETH: She should have died hereafter.
There would have been a time for such a word.
Tomorrow, and tomorrow, and tomorrow
Creeps in this petty pace from day to day,
To the last syllable of recorded time,
And all our yesterdays have lighted fools
The way to dusty death. Out, out, brief candle!
Life's but a walking shadow, a poor player
That struts and frets his hour upon the stage
And then is heard no more. It is a tale
Told by an idiot, full of sound and fury,
Signifying nothing.

This passage brings up a new aspect of the critical problem of parts-and-whole,[1] as it is part of a much larger whole, the entire play, while being at the same time a self-contained lyric poem — at any rate if taken from 'Tomorrow . . . ', which is where it always does begin when anthologised. In the century after Shakespeare's death, it also brought up an aspect of the problem of meaning, since it was obviously impressive while not being amenable to reasonable analysis, and it was felt that even a lyric statement, to be highly regarded should not seem mere raving. But what was the connection between time, candles, actors, and idiots? How else would time proceed, except day by day? Should not 'syllable' be 'minute'? Do not wise men also tread the way to death?

Neither problem seems unresolvable, nor even very difficult. With Seyton's remark and Macbeth's two-line reply to remind us of its place in the play, we can perfectly well consider the soliloquy as a self-contained lyric — but a *dramatic* lyric. One representing, not the self-communing of

---

1. Other aspects are to be found on pp. 26 and 43, and in the glossary under *Mode* and *Purport*.

the author or a stand-in persona, but that of a particular character at a
particular point: a man at the end of his tether, in all respects, but
especially in mind and spirit. It represents the viewpoint of a hollow man,
corrupted from within, a 'mind dis-eased'. It is an end anticipated by such
earlier insights as this:

> . . . Better be with the dead,
> Whom we, to gain our place have sent to peace,
> Than on the torture of the mind to lie
> In restless ecstasy. Duncan is in his grave;
> After life's fitful fever, he sleeps well . . .

(III.ii)

And this, of course, points towards the solution of the second problem.
One would not *expect* the lyric expression of such a mind, in a drama, to
be superficially well-ordered — though one must agree that some pro-
founder coherence should be present if it is to be seen as significant (of a
human possibility) by the uncorrupted reader, or hearer. In fact, the passage is most complexly coherent in psychological, if not logical terms.

So knowledge of the larger whole guides us to a proper interpretation
of the smaller whole and its parts. The reverse, however, is also true: the
interpretation of this brief soliloquy may lead in turn to improved knowledge of the larger whole. For it is no accident that this passage has often
been excerpted for anthologies. Shakespeare has made it stand out for
special attention (and very likely the actor came forward on the apron
stage to deliver it as a verbal aria). It has both structural 'insistence' and
textural 'coercion'; that is to say, that both by placing (at a crucial point
in the action) and by style and content it obliges us to pay it particular
attention. If, then, we treat this soliloquy as a 'key' passage, a condensation of much that is diffused throughout the play, we get the best of
both worlds, since to do so we must thoroughly grasp the piece in its own
identity. Here indeed, the principle of complementarity becomes particularly evident and necessary, as the large-scale and small-scale wholes and
parts interact within themselves and with each other to produce a local
intensification within a global body of meaning.

The curtness of Macbeth's reply to Seyton's dire news, the indifference
as to how or why his wife died, indicates how far Macbeth has come from
the time of their first meeting in the play, on his return as a war hero.
Now, it seems, things are so bad that nothing matters. The concluding
phrase of the soliloquy is already implicit in this preceding dialogue, and
we are subconsciously prepared to read the opening line of the soliloquy
proper with infinite dreariness — helped by the total abandonment of the

normal blank-verse base of iambic pentameter. Before each comma the rhythm falls to a halt, and then has to pick itself up with another un- accented syllable 'and' and yet another 'to-', rising then only to fall back again. The metre of this line does not march, it staggers; and 'Creeps in this petty pace from day to day' — in which the reversed foot at the beginning emphasises 'Creeps', and the secondary meaning of 'petty' as 'small' (not striding, therefore), preserve a physical image — confirms the implication of endless meaninglessness. But what is likely to strike the reader or hearer most forcibly on first acquaintance is the recurrent con- trast of light and dark; the whole passage indeed is reminiscent of a chiaro- scuro painting — as indeed is the play as a whole.

*Macbeth* might be regarded as *Richard III* turned inside out. In the latter, a history, attention is mainly directed to the mechanics of a tyrant's climb to power and to what it is like to live under a tyrant. In the former, a tragedy, it is mainly directed to the inner process of becoming a tyrant and to what it is like to *be* a tyrant. In terms of theme as 'message' *Macbeth* is rather like *Richard III* — and indeed it does contain a historical element to stiffen those elements, like witches, delusions, and prophecies, that suit the exploration of a less tangible reality. *That* theme could be summed up, in the play's own words, in the idea of 'Vaulting ambition which o'erleaps itself / And falls . . . ' (I.vii). But in this play, theme as 'leitmotif' is much more important. It *could* be summed up in the biblical aphorism: 'For what shall it profit a man, if he shall gain the whole world, and lose his own soul?' The point is that it is not so summarised; as a leit- motif, it is proved on the pulses by varied recurrence in different contexts — and therefore becomes known more widely and deeply though less consciously. Indeed it becomes fully conscious only in this last great speech of Macbeth's (V.v). And in the main it is conveyed through scenes and images of light and darkness.

Scenes and images of darkness are always connected, by action or dic- tion, with evil and its corrupting effect; in this they tally with the soliloquy in which they culminate. Minor motifs also culminate here, all of them relevant to each other and to the leitmotif. One has only to think of the great scene of Lady Macbeth's sleepwalking and the many references to dreams and illusions, to take the point of shadows, players, and a candle lighting the way to bed, in this passage. Shadows and players are relevant also to the motif of the nature of reality, which is introduced by the witches:

> BANQUO: The earth hath bubbles, as the water has,
> And these are of them. Whither are they vanish'd?

MACBETH: Into the air; and what seem'd corporal melted
    As breath into wind.

(I.iii)

This motif receives its most striking manifestation, perhaps, in the 'dagger of the mind' scene. Clearly, such a dagger is not real in the same way as a material one; it cannot give a stab wound. It does, however, clearly have a reality of a different kind. Mental hospitals are full of people suffering far more from such illusory realities than from the material wounds of the outside world – and often, like Macbeth in this too, causing suffering to others. Such realities impinge on those of the material world, and can indeed make life seem like 'a tale told by an idiot'.

    That the play is not to be taken literally throughout, but rather as a giant metaphor of light and darkness in humanity, is indicated early on in the alienating\* stage-metaphor

MACBETH:               Two truths are told,
    As happy prologues to the swelling act
    Of the imperial theme.

(I.iii)

This must remind the audience that they are watching a play, not seeing a slice of life and must show that the author *wants* them to be so reminded. In addition, of course, it relates ironically to the stage-metaphor of the late soliloquy. In Act I Macbeth is optimistic and illusioned, not having lost his own soul in the endeavour to gain a little world of power; in Act V he has gained his world and cannot enjoy it.

    Usually the leitmotif images of light and darkness also bring in or imply the subsidiary themes as well as the main one. Witness the following, given without further comment:

MACBETH:     ... Stars, hide your fires!
    Let not light see my black and deep desires:
    The eye wink at the hand! you let that be
    Which the eye fears, when it is done, to see.

(I.v)

LADY MACBETH:     ... Come thick night
    And pall thee in the dunnest smoke of hell
    That my keen knife see not the wound it makes,
    Nor heaven peep through the blanket of the dark,
    To cry, *Hold, Hold*!

(I.v)

MACBETH:          . . . I see thee still;
And on thy blade and dudgeon gouts of blood,
Which was not so before — there's no such thing . . .
                    . . . Now o'er the one half world
Nature seems dead, and wicked dreams abuse
The curtain'd sleep; now witchcraft celebrates
Pale Hecate's offerings; and wither'd murder,
Alarum'd by his sentinel, the wolf,
Whose howl's his watch, thus with his stealthy pace
With Tarquin's ravishing strides, towards his design
Moves like a ghost . . .

                                                  (II.i)

MACBETH:          . . . Come, seeling night,
Scarf up the tender eye of pitiful day,
And with thy bloody and invisible hand
Cancel and tear to pieces that great bond
Which keeps me pale! — Light thickens, and the crow
Makes wing to the rooky wood:
Good things of day begin to droop and drowse,
While night's black agents to their prey do rouse . . .

                                                  (III.ii)

Taken in conjunction with the action and with many other references to sleep, illusion and reality, good and evil, the nature of humanity, and self-deception, there are many touches in the above speeches to prepare us for the intricate web of implications in our soliloquy of which the dark-and-light imagery is simply the centre. There is enough, too, to prepare us for its turning out to be a psychological web, not a logical one. Conversely, the soliloquy knits up these scattered suggestions into one knotted experience at the right time, the climax of the play as a whole.

The passage now becomes fully, and complexly, coherent as an expression of nihilistic emptiness, of a man once ebulliently alive, now hard and hollow. The sense of a dreary present passing for ever into a drearily similar future, which is conveyed by the diction, of 'day' and 'morrow', and the halting rhythm of the opening lines, surely create a subliminal sense of sickness and therefore death. By association, then, we pick up the picture of life as a weary progress to death. For each day is a little area of light in an enveloping darkness (like the candle an ever-more sick man might carry down a dark passage each day on his way to what one day will be his deathbed). This, or some similar association brings in the idea of a lighted candle as a symbol of life — 'brief' in the perspective of everlasting time, and when blown out — as Macbeth wishes, in his sickness of soul — leaving nothing. This is a 'dusty' death (surely evoking the idea of 'dust to dust') leading to no glorious afterlife. In this light — if the pun may be permitted — 'Life's but a walking shadow' falls into place. A candle casts shadows, shadows are distorted images of the true self — in a way they here represent perhaps the dark side of human nature, like actors they are merely a fake reality (or a true representation if life *is* empty and illusory and morality and merit a mere dream) — indeed, they are like 'poor' actors, a travesty of reality. These seem to be some of the relevant associations, and they lead to the notion of people playing roles, trying to be popular, or powerful in Macbeth's case, exaggerating their own importance, and all to no avail: strutting and fretting only to be 'heard no more' — behaving in short like idiots, which is probably the psychological link that leads to the concluding statement that life 'is a tale / Told by an idiot, full of sound and fury / Signifying nothing'. In the context of infinitely repetitive time all human action and ambition seems meaningless.

All this by no means exhausts the associative richness of the poetry. We have not even mentioned the 'last syllable of recorded time', for example. (Is there not a hint, in the context of good-and-evil, of the Recording Angel as well as the historian, for whom Macbeth will not be famous but infamous?) And why 'fools'? Surely this refers us to such motifs as the unreliability of appearances, the illusion that peace is to be obtained by killing, the prevalence of self-deception, and the naive preference for material power and glory over peace of mind. Nor have we mentioned the quite illogical, but psychologically plausible, leap from one meaning of 'time' ('an appropriate moment') to the much wider one implicit in what immediately follows: 'Tomorrow, and tomorrow . . . ' Little has been made of 'sound and fury', though William Faulkner saw a whole book in it. But enough has been said to indicate that this passage, like many lyric poems, works as a structure of reverberations which, by their nature, have no definitive boundary. And the problems stated at the beginning have been solved by proof on the pulses (in Keats's phrase) and by setting the local and the global in reciprocal relationship.

# 15. Louis MacNeice

## 'Snow'

The room was suddenly rich and the great bay-window was
Spawning snow and pink roses against it
Soundlessly collateral and incompatible:
World is suddener than we fancy it.

World is crazier and more of it than we think,
Incorrigibly plural. I peel and portion
A tangerine and spit the pips and feel
The drunkenness of things being various.

And the fire flames with a bubbling sound for world
Is more spiteful and gay than one supposes —
On the tongue on the eyes on the ears in the palms of one's hands —
There is more than glass between the snow and the huge roses.

For a number of the poems previously criticised a certain amount of
scholarship, however elementary, proved to be a useful preliminary: setting the poem in the framework of a particular literary kind, ballad or
sonnet, for instance, or in the more nebulous, but not unreal, framework
of the Romantic or Augustan, or that of the period setting. In the case of
'Snow' nothing of this sort seems appropriate. Apart from the relative
freedom of the verse (no free-er anyway than some of Shakespeare's) there
is nothing specifically modern about it; it seems to have nothing to do
with MacNeice's politics, it is not in any traditional kind, nor is it easily
assimilable to either a Romantic or an Augustan tradition or temperament
— though in so far as it does ponder over and generalise a private and
sensuous experience it inclines towards the latter.

What may strike the reader first is a sense of oddity: the poem gives the
impression of being at once precise and ambiguous, sensuous, and abstract.
'Soundlessly collateral and incompatible' and 'Incorrigibly plural' have the
air of being precise philosophical statements (which cry out for, but
obviously do not receive, a highly formal verse). On the other hand, the

first 'it' is as loose in meaning as the verse is in stressing (roughly four stresses to the line, irregularly distributed). Was the great bay-window spawning snow-and-pink roses against the room or was it spawning snow and pink roses against the snow? (A comma would allow us to read 'Spawning snow, and [there were] pink roses against it'; something of this reading seems to come through subliminally even without the comma.) Similarly 'more than glass' seems pretty open-ended in meaning. More what?

Such a tentative approach, latching on to difficulties apparent on first reading, may well turn out to be more useful than a more systematic one – asking after mode, type, and kind, say (though we may have done this intuitively, before saying it was not of any traditional kind), or comparing form and content point by point (though we have touched on that), or working at the relationship of theme and mood. For what is likely to strike us next is that our first, slightly puzzled, impression is just the one the poem intends to convey. Oddity is what it is about; and the phrases that stand out like a sore thumb, as 'unpoetic' or 'philosophical', are precisely those that draw attention to the theme. So the mixtures of ambiguity and precision, warm and cold, regularities and irregularities of form, sensuousness and abstraction are all appropriate. The poem is coherent and unified – and if you say that is a paradoxical kind of unity, well, that too is appropriate, since the poem is dealing with the experienced world *as paradox*.

With this in mind, the detail of the piece falls into place. The first line introduces the experience of coming into a room and suddenly experiencing it anew, *un*habitually. Christmas morning might well be the occasion – in view of the snow, roses, and tangerines – though this is not a necessary assumption. The lack of commas after 'rich' and 'snow' tends to give primacy to the idea of both snow and roses being spawned against the room. 'Against' promotes *two* sets of collateral incompatibles: the room (man-made) lies alongside, but is incompatible with, the snow-and-roses (natural), and the snow (cold, white, wintry) lies alongside, but is incompatible with, the roses (organic, pink, summery). Thus the ambiguity of 'it' turns out to be right. Is there also a slight suggestion – despite the bad grammar – of 'itself'? Certainly the idea of the window combining on its two man-made surfaces these natural contraries would give another layer of implication to 'Soundlessly collateral and incompatible'. 'Spawning' is right, in visual terms, for 'snow' and wrong for roses, but is right for 'roses' in that roses, like spawn, relate to life, while snow does not. So the suddenly perceived mixed-upness, that leads to the temporary conclusion 'World is suddener . . .' penetrates into the detail of expression.

112

The next stanza explores the theme, rather than the experience, further — though it does so by filling out an abstract statement, 'World is crazier and more of it than we think / Incorrigibly plural', with the example of a small-scale sensuous experience. The tangerine is a model of the world: the same shape, and similarly a unitary variety (of peel, pips, and portions — alliteration hinting at the unity, sense at the variety). The persona's experience, too, is a model of the theme, since he is doing different things during one act (eating a tangerine) and is simultaneously aware of the incompatibilities. Hence, the 'drunkenness' — the sense of perceiving in a fresh, unhabitual way.

The final stanza amplifies the theme, mainly through sensuous references, saving its abstract statement (there is one to every stanza — but not in the same place) for an appropriately open-ended conclusion (for, after all, if there is more of it than we think, we cannot be quite definite about how much more there is). Coal fires do make a bubbling sound — but 'bubbling' combines the idea of water with that of fire. 'Spiteful' (hissing, crackling) and 'gay' also show incompatibles to be naturally combined. The absence of commas in the long list of the penultimate line encourages a rapid reading, suggesting a *gestalt* of sense-impressions, an undifferentiable variety-in-unity. What more than glass is there between the snow and the roses? Well, the difference (and relationship) of winter and summer, death and life, cold and warmth — and all the other soundlessly collateral incompatibles that we normally cut out of our conscious experience.

# 16. Craig Raine

## 'A Martian Sends a Postcard Home'

Caxtons are mechanical birds with many wings
and some are treasured for their markings —

they cause the eyes to melt
or the body to shriek without pain.

I have never seen one fly, but
sometimes they perch on the hand.

Mist is when the sky is tired of flight
and rests its soft machine on ground:

then the world is dim and bookish
like engravings under tissue paper.

Rain is when the earth is television.
It has the property of making colours darker.

Model T is a room with the lock inside —
a key is turned to free the world

for movement, so quick there is a film
to watch for anything missed.

But time is tied to the wrist
or kept in a box, ticking with impatience.

In homes, a haunted apparatus sleeps,
that snores when you pick it up.

If the ghost cries, they carry it
to their lips and soothe it to sleep

with sounds. And yet, they wake it up
deliberately, by tickling with a finger.

Only the young are allowed to suffer
openly. Adults go to a punishment room

114

with water but nothing to eat.
They lock the door and suffer the noises

alone. No one is exempt
and everyone's pain has a different smell.

At night, when all the colours die,
they hide in pairs

and read about themselves —
in colour, with their eyelids shut.

This is a most unusual poem in two ways. Firstly, it purports not to be written by a human being; the persona is a visiting Martian. Secondly, it seems to have been written only to delight. And if in fact it does delight it is largely owing to the extraordinary Martian view of our everyday world.

One could properly call this 'pure' poetry, though not in the sense in which the French *symbolistes** used the term, for poetry that attempted mystically to transcend the mundane. Rather it is pure in the double sense of not being about anything important — being indeed immersed in the mundane trivia of daily life — and of depending for its quality almost entirely on how, rather than what it means. It is a thoroughly unearnest poem, the very best sort of that kind of poetry that is styled 'light verse'.

It could be said that it 'enlarges and awakens the mind itself', though not conveying any new knowledge, in so far as it restores a childhood freshness of perception, turning the everyday into the marvellous (as Swift does, differently, by seeing it first through one end of a telescope then through the other, in *Gulliver's Travels*). This, however, would account for only part of its appeal. Some parts do work as a small child with a limited vocabulary has to work: by analogy, thus getting rid of clichés both of expression and perception. The first and the last couplets could stand as examples of this mode of operation. It would be possible for a child who knew about reading, though not reading himself, and had watched some book-story on colour television to get round his ignorance of the word 'dream' by what is to an adult the brilliant and amusing and paradoxical circumlocution 'read about themselves — / in colour, with their eyelids shut'. The same might be said of the first couplet, if we suppose a child who had heard the word 'Caxton' in connection with books but did not know the word 'books' itself — a possible rather than a probable hypothesis, which is undermined anyway by the enchanting and enchanted fifth couplet:

then the world is dim and bookish
like engravings under tissue paper.

The most we can really claim is that sometimes the poem works in a way something like that of a very young child, but not always and not altogether. More often perhaps it works like fairy-tales — of gingerbread houses, seven-league boots, and so on — in which the humdrum world of normality is transformed — and in *de luxe* editions is ensplendoured with tissue-protected illustrations.

It need not be a cause of complaint if this Martian is not entirely consistent (in knowing and not knowing books); if he sometimes seems more like a bright child, sometimes more like a not-too-bright anthropologist (the latter perhaps being in a position similar to that of the child, when he is introduced into a tribal world that is new to him). After all, the mode of this poem is obviously not realistic, as the narrator is a Martian; nor is it mimetic, attempting to prove the world on, or through, *Martian* pulses (an impossible task, for obvious reasons). Nor is any reader likely to take the persona as anything other than a convenient fictional mechanism. In short, the mode is that of fantasy, the type narrative, the mood contemplative and puzzled, and the method descriptive (in a very unusual way) rather than mimetic. So consistency can legitimately be sacrificed to novelty if the price is right.

On the whole, however, the poem is consistent enough; enough to maintain its enchanted existence in the no man's land where joke, puzzle, and wonder come together. For one thing, this extra-terrestrial narrator is all of a piece in character — a character in which human and non-human elements are nicely mixed so that the reader can at once relate to him and be amusedly amazed by him. He is comically self-confident, in fact bumptious, in this new world. *We* may be puzzled by some of his descriptions, but he is not; and he is too insensitive even to know he ought to be. Like some scientists and many inartistic people, he has no hesitation in making dogmatic pronouncements about matters that are beyond his reach. He just *knows* that the lavatory is a prison cell. What else could it be? One of his handicaps is that he has intelligence without feelings; like a scientist examining an ant colony, he can see how people behave but not share their motives or emotions. For him they are just machines. When he says their eyes melt or their bodies shriek without pain, it is not because he does not know the words 'cry' and 'laugh', as an infant might not, but that he has no conception of weeping and laughter as something more than physical mechanisms, set in motion by a merely mechanical 'bird'. Indeed, he seems to be a machine himself, a sort of self-programming computer, since he interprets the whole world in such terms:

Mist is when the sky is tired of flight
and rests its soft machine on ground . . .

Rain is when the earth is television.

Oddly, he is also consistent in the opposite way. Just as he constantly interprets human matters in mechanical terms, so he constantly interprets the inorganic in terms of the living: the sky is *tired*, time ticks with *impatience*, an apparatus is *haunted* and *snores*. He is an alien all right; perhaps not more mixed-up than we are but mixed-up differently. No wonder we are puzzled, amused, and sometimes elated by his outlandish observations.

Sometimes one element predominates, sometimes another, and sometimes the three seem to be evenly mingled, though no doubt the reactions of individual readers will differ. Not all, for instance, may agree that the eighth couplet's delight lies mainly in puzzle-solving, in the element of sudden recognition, of light dawning in obscurity (if it happens). For others it may be immediately apparent that 'there is a film / to watch for anything missed' refers to the rear-view mirror; and their pleasure will come mainly from the unexpected perception of the likeness between screen-shape and mirror-shape, the scene and a projected film. Again, no doubt not all would agree that it is in couplets ten, eleven, and twelve that amusement, elation, and puzzle-pleasure are most equally present – once one has worked through the possibilities of *baby* and *cat* to hit on a *telephone* as the only object which accounts for everything in the verse. For all the necessary limitations of its kind, the poem is elastic enough to allow not only for varied pleasures in seeing 'ourselves as others see us' but also for varied responses.

But does the verse-form add anything to the matter? At first, it seems not to. There is no rhyme, no metre, and though a three-stress beat is perceptible it is not regular, nor is it emphasised. Furthermore the lines are more often run-on than end-stopped. In brief, it is as near as could be to prose. Nevertheless, the mere fact of coupleting does add something. The mere fact that we expect couplets to be rhymed and metrical makes these appropriately alien. Furthermore they fit in with the idea of an alien tourist making random notes of what might interest those back home; these rather dead couplets seem a model of the mechanically switching gaze of a pair of dispassionate eyes – that might well be on stalks.

Texturally, too, the form adds something, for it is characterised by what seems to be a new verbal device. Traditionally, metaphor\* has served many purposes: to enliven, clarify, enrich, emotionalise, or embody the

117

literal meaning; never, wilfully, to obscure it. If the reader was puzzled it was by accident not authorial intention. When Shakespeare says that 'summer's lease hath all too short a date' it is not to cause confusion by muddling the legal idea of property-holding with that of the course of nature, but rather to add the idea that we come into 'possession' of summer but cannot hold it for ever, or even for long. Craig Raine's, how-ever, are mischievous metaphors, meant to puzzle before they enliven. *Caxtons*? Eyes do *what*? are, and are meant to be, the first reaction, how-ever brief. Only part of the reader's pleasure comes from the new light in which he eventually sees familiar things, the other part coming from problem-solving: putting the Martian right. Obfuscation precedes illumi-nation. So to the terms dead metaphor and mixed metaphor we should perhaps now add problem metaphor.

A playful poem, then, purporting only to entertain (but in the process awakening, or re-awakening, 'the mind itself'), and not afraid to be cleverly inventive. An up-to-date example of what Renaissance critics admiringly spoke of as *sprezzatura*: dazzling ease.

# 17. Robert Frost

### 'The Draft Horse'

With a lantern that wouldn't burn
In too frail a buggy we drove
Behind too heavy a horse
Through a pitch-black limitless grove.

And a man came out of the trees
And took our horse by the head
And reaching back to his ribs
Deliberately stabbed him dead.

The ponderous beast went down
With a crack of a broken shaft.
And the night drew through the trees
In one long invidious draft.

The most unquestioning pair
That ever accepted fate
And the least disposed to ascribe
Any more than we had to hate,

We assumed that the man himself
Or someone he had to obey
Wanted us to get down
And walk the rest of the way.

Craig Raine's puzzles were of the surface, visual and aural riddles in a poem not pretending to depth anyway. Frost's 'Draft Horse' on the contrary is as plain on the surface as Wordsworth at his simplest;[1] the diction is positively homespun — so much so that one is intuitively convinced that these people are not, say, artists, travelling players, escaping political rebels, or idealistic intellectuals seeking the good life in the wilderness; no,

1. Compare critique 9. Other uses of ballad form are exemplified and discussed in critiques 5 and 21.

they are clearly American small-time small-town's folk, or pioneer farmers. The tone, too, is very matter-of-fact and unexcited, as if this were an account of an everyday occurrence. This is where the puzzles begin, for it is not an everyday occurrence – or, on reflection, not *literally* an everyday occurrence. Could it, then, be symbolic of something common? That would account for the common style and for the discrepancy between tone and action? On further reflection, perhaps, the style may seem not merely simple, but simplistic; not exactly censuring the couple but showing them as almost unnaturally 'unquestioning' – or maybe all too naturally accepting whatever happens as ordained? Could Dylan Thomas's poem (prompted by his father's last illness) be relevant: 'Do not go gentle into that good night'? Questions then begin to proliferate. 'Too frail' and 'too heavy' for what? How can a grove be 'limitless'? By definition a grove is a *small* wood, or, as here, 'a cluster of trees shading an avenue'. Who is this man? Why did he kill the *horse* – and not rob the owners? What is the 'invidious draft', a draught of medicine? a chill wind? the draught of a fishing net? Why on earth should anyone want them to walk? An apparently perfectly straightforward story turns out to be almost incomprehensible as soon as one disturbs the surface. And if it is to be taken symbolically then the puzzles must go deeper than those of narrative incompetence.

Narrative incompetence, of course, would provide a simple explanation. Slightly less simple would be the explanation that Frost was taking the easy way of gripping the reader by mystification. Or, this might be a case of implication at odds with purport – uncontrolled elements of the author's psyche unwittingly intruding into the poem, thus flawing its coherence. Both scholarship and critical perception, however, seem to make these explanations less likely than that of deliberate symbolism. Frost does not normally display narrative incompetence, and the facts of the story are given clearly and economically, in verse whose control supports Frost's ironic comment on free verse: 'Well, I like to play my tennis *with* a net.' Many of his other poems are clearly symbolic. Finally, the questions prompted by a literal reading run through the poem so consistently, being apparent in every stanza, that it seems inconceivable that they could be accidental intrusions (especially in view of the evident control shown in other areas). Clearly, then, we should start with the assumption that this is a case involving both an ostensible purport and a latent purport. And since this is not an example of irony, or parody, or allegory (the most obvious cases of this kind) we can properly assume it to be an example of symbolism.

Allegory, one might say, is a mouth; symbolism, an eye. Allegory repeats, symbolism reveals. To put it less aphoristically, allegory gives a one-to-one correspondence in concrete terms to something already known more abstractly; symbolism tends to reveal through the concrete something not known, or not clearly and consciously known — often something that is not in fact clear-cut. So one may expect symbolic works to be somewhat problematical; liable to become on the one hand ineffable and inexplicable or, on the other hand, so unrealistic in concrete detail that the concrete presentation cannot guarantee the symbolic meaning. To some degree 'The Draft Horse' is open to this latter criticism. Not to any great extent though; after all, the symbolist cannot be entirely realistic or the reader would not know the work was to be read symbolically; and this story is *possible*. Moreover, the style and the properties — lantern, buggy, horse, and so on — constantly refer us to the world of recognisable material fact. But is he more open to the charge of inexplicability? Certainly, the deeper we probe the more problematical the poem becomes.

For instance, we might take the lantern to symbolise the fires of life, and the buggy the aged body — an interpretation that would square well enough with a good deal of traditional symbolism. But then what is the horse? A heart suffering from fatty degeneration, which then suffers a killing attack? But that gives us a heart which is rather separate from the body. Besides, the buggy and horse are *shared* by the couple. Moreover, they can walk still — nor is it likely that the walking is supposed to be after death, as 'the rest of the way' implies the same way they were on when travelling by buggy. Then, who is the 'man'? He makes no demands, does not rob them, or even harm them. He might be Death, but there is still that walking away to account for. If the night were drawing a *net* of darkness through the trees, sweeping them up in it, that too would suggest death. So might 'draft' in the sense of a swallowing down of light (and life). Perhaps we should admit the idea of death, but ask: death of *what*? Need it be a death of the body? The grove, taken as an avenue through a wood, certainly reminds us of 'all our yesterdays' lighting fools the way to dusty death. The light of each life, thus, is surrounded by a limitless darkness (hence *pitch-black*) and the grove is also 'limitless' because there is no destination. Our lighted lantern is not going anywhere; it is just going *out*.

The horse remains something of a puzzle. An important one, as it gives the poem its title. Why 'The *Draft* Horse' and not just 'The Horse'? Surely this suggests all it is not — not a race-, war-, or showjumping horse. Rather, a horse all right for everyday purposes, but one that in a crisis could not run, fight, or jump for its life. In short, one that is 'too heavy' *for an emergency*; and that is presumably what the buggy is 'too frail' for too. The emergency, however, does not seem to be that of a literally fatal attack.

121

We now seem on the verge of an interpretation that will leave fewer loose ends than any other, if only because it does not so insistently push the poem towards the specificness of allegory as the other did. This 'unquestioning' pair, who accept whatever happens to them as somehow right and proper, 'ordained' as we say, seem to be presented as a very average couple – the sort who would naturally have an ordinary workaday horse. They would also naturally have a dully burning lantern, especially in their later years – if we take the lantern, quite traditionally, to symbolise spirit, vitality, or the illumination of the mind, or something of that order (a fan of related meanings would be perfectly in order for a symbolic poem dealing with *areas* of human nature). The buggy we may now see as what they have built round themselves as a comfort and shield against the darkness of the illimitable unknown; partly by way of house and belongings but mainly by way of the common beliefs and conventions of society. The horse now seems to represent what has hitherto drawn them onwards through life at a steady plod – the humdrum ideals or modest ambitions that now prove 'too heavy', as the buggy proves 'too frail'.

What, though, is the 'man'. Not Death, for the reasons given, but presumably whatever gives a deathblow to one's accustomed way of life. Anything that would come under 'fate'. He is any dire crisis that puts an end to ambitions, that overturns one's scheme of things: any economic, medical, legal, political catastrophe. Such crises are undeserved, whether they result from the attack of a virus, a terrorist, the government's economic policy, or a drunken motorist. So they are unjust or 'invidious'; they come like a chill wind, a nasty draught of medicine maliciously administered, like a darkness that threatens to swallow us down or sweep us into its net; all the possibilities of 'invidious draft' seem relevant, though not *equally* relevant. Finally, though this couple do not acknowledge it (for their statement 'We assumed . . . ' is neutral), the possibility seems to be raised of a governing malevolence that wants us to make our final journey the hard way, walking, not riding, and shorn of the frail protection of our customary comforts.

Perhaps even this interpretation is a little too precise, since this is a poem that works by reverberations of meaning. If this interpretation is to be taken as the primary symbolic meaning, it is not the only one; the hints of death, sudden illness, irrational violence, the general vulnerability of man trying to maintain a brave light in the darkness of a ruthless universe – these are all relevant at some level or other. The tone, too, is not simple. If there is a sardonic note in the last two stanzas, it is not present earlier. After all, by definition most of us are near to the average. Moreover, in most of the terrible crises that can happen a less ponderous horse would make only a minor difference. The poem leaves us with a question-mark even after we have 'solved' it.

# 18. William Blake

## 'London'

I wander through each charter'd street
Near where the charter'd Thames does flow,
And mark in every face I meet
Marks of weakness, marks of woe.

In every cry of every Man,
In every Infant's cry of fear
In every voice, in every ban,
The mind-forg'd manacles I hear.

How the Chimney-sweeper's cry
Every black'ning Church appalls,
And the hapless Soldier's sigh
Runs in blood down Palace walls.

But most through midnight streets I hear
How the youthful Harlot's curse
Blasts the new born Infant's tear,
And blights with plagues the Marriage hearse.

Blake's 'London' bears some similarity to Frost's 'Draft Horse'. Both exhibit a simple diction and firm verse-form that associate them with such popular forms as the ballad and hymn. Both also appear to be making a didactic point — and in each case, despite the clarity of form, it is not immediately clear what it is. The differences, however, are probably more striking than the similarities; so a rather different approach seems called for.

The puzzles of 'The Draft Horse' arose largely from the lack of any explanatory commentary. The puzzles of 'London' arise from the fact that it is all commentary and no story; it lacks the surface realism of Frost's poem. There is no sense in which a sigh could *literally* run in blood, or a curse blast a tear (especially that of a new-born infant who could not understand it). And how should anything already dead ('hearse') be 'blighted' by plague? In what sense is the Thames 'charter'd'? What pre-cisely *are* 'The mind-forg'd manacles'? Such are the questions prompted by Blake's very different, but equally illusory clarity.

One thing is clear: Blake is not — certainly not directly — invoking large, imprecise metaphysical concepts like Catastrophe, Life, Universal Darkness. Rather, he seems to have in mind specific social ills, connected with business, propaganda, religion, war, prostitution, and marriage. So in one sense he is more precise than Frost. But though the references are specific their implications are not. Thus he refers quite definitely to the Church and comments on it — but what does the comment amount to? Presum-ably it is an unfavourable comment, since the references to all the other social matters are unfavourable; they all seem to be seen as social ills. 'Black'ning' tends to confirm this. On the other hand, if the Church is appalled at the plight of the chimney-sweeper, surely the implication is favourable? The 'Harlot's curse' proves equally baffling on investigation. At first sight it is perfectly clear. Since it is 'heard' it must simply refer to swearing. But how on earth could such a peccadillo bring about the dire effects of the next two lines? If the swearing is to be taken merely as symptomatic of some more fundamental curse, the tip of an iceberg, so to speak, what is it? Venereal disease? Rivalry for wives? Something more generally causing social disruption? It is far from clear.

It is, of course, possible that a clear surface and a crisp form simply conceal underlying confusion; but these factors do suggest that we ought to give the writer the benefit of the doubt and see first of all whether they are conveying, not confusion, but complexity in an artistic rather than an analytic way. That is, showing the knot itself rather than disentangling its separate strands — trading a clearer truth for a fuller one.

Interpretative criticism itself is necessarily somewhat analytic. If it were self-evident just what items were being knotted together — or being shown *as in fact* knotted together in life — interpretation would be unnecessary. Cases like 'London', however, cry out for some separation of strands. One simply has to remember that afterwards the knot should be pulled tight again.

Critical analysis, though it can and should be objective (in the sense defined in the introduction), is a form of reasoning that is different in kind both from the deductive (appropriate to mathematics and logic) and the inductive kind (appropriate to science). Interpretative reasoning is largely a matter of seeing things in such a way that they make more sense in relation to other things than different ways of seeing do. There is no sharp dividing line, that is to say, between seeing something as a mere fact and *interpreting* it as a meaningful fact. The interpretation is rather a matter of the fact's coming into focus and being recognised — as one might blankly see some building from an unfamiliar angle and only interpret the perceived fact as, say, Wells Cathedral on having particular features pointed out for concentrated attention. The process is objective if the features are really there and one is not being conned, or conning oneself, into taking a distant warehouse for Wells Cathedral. Since words in combination do not necessarily, or even usually, make up so well-defined a structure as building blocks do, literary interpretation will be more complicated in practice, though similar in principle. In particular, it must allow for the possibility of what was spoken of in 'The Draft Horse' analysis as a valid fan of related meanings. The range of literary meaning may be indefinite but it is not unlimited. There is nothing in nature to prevent a perverse interpreter from invoking any meanings he likes regardless of the rules of language, the agreed meanings of words, the facts of reality, or the conventions of literary forms. In that case it would not be interpretation as a mode of *reasoning*, nor would it be an objective interpretation. While if the poet wrote so loosely that there seemed to be no connection at all between *reasonably* possible meanings — i.e. not a fan but just a heap of feathers — then the work would not count as a *valid* statement.

Since 'London' does in fact seem to offer more than one possibility of meaning, our task must be to assess, first, what the reasonable possibilities are, next whether they are relatable rather than random, and finally whether such ambiguity of meaning is fruitful in terms, say, of richness, force, and memorability. Starting, as we do, with some doubts about the interpretation, we can legitimately assume this to be a case where a little scholarly reference beyond the bounds of the poem itself might not come amiss — provided we bear in mind that any such external evidence cannot conclusively prove or disprove our tentative interpretations, but only indicate some degree of probability.

Well, were we right to say that the poem seemed to be a poem of social protest? Critics have generally taken it to be so; and there seems little reason to question this assumption. Internally, words with unfavourable connotations abound and, in context, create a tone of bitterness and denunciation: *weakness, woe, cry, fear, ban, manacles, black'ning, blood, hapless, curse, blasts, tear, plagues, hearse*. External evidence, both biographical and literary tends to confirm this. Blake was a political radical, held radical views on sex and marriage, and in his work was consistently hostile to the Church, to commercial and industrial interests, and to the monarchy; harlotry he tended to relate to the Church's anti-sex ethic: 'Brothels are built with bricks of religion.'

Any interpretation, then, which is at odds with that of 'social protest'

poem may reasonably be ruled out as of lesser probability. Such evidence,
though, does not rule out differing interpretations within that category;
and in fact there are three main types of interpretation within it: historical,
moral, and psychological.

Historical critics concentrate on the facts of the contemporary background. The poem was written at the time of the French Revolution
(which Blake supported) and an English repression designed to prevent a
revolution over here. Such critics point to the government's bans on discussion, its infiltration of opposition groups by informers and *agents
provocateurs*, and its hiring of foreign mercenaries, to account for 'fear',
'ban', and 'mind-forg'd manacles', in particular. More generally, this kind
of interpretation accounts for stanza three, too, since Church and State
were opposed to the French Revolution. The opening lines also fit well
enough, as the granting of charters to businesses or institutions involved
the granting of privileges, which a radical would naturally be against. The
last stanza, however, seems to be more recalcitrant. One might also object
that though contemporary readers might be expected to pick up most of
the references, the poem does seem to express its protest in so general and
ambiguous a way that it seems unlikely to have been concerned *only* with
such specific topicalities.

Moral interpretations concentrate on Blake the metaphysician, a man
concerned with investigating States of Soul in their relation to universal
forces (and 'London' is in fact from the latter section of *Songs of Innocence and Experience*, precisely such an investigation). These critics, with
some reason, read the poem in more general terms, as a protest against the
cramping and distorting of the human soul by social institutions —
exemplified especially by commerce, marriage, the Church, and the
monarchy. Much support for this view can be found elsewhere in Blake —
particularly in the dense jungles of his long, didactic works. On the other
hand, just as the poem does not actually mention specific topical events,
so it does not actually refer to metaphysical generalities.

Psychological interpreters tend to focus more closely on the poem
itself, as obviously expressive of the writer's state of mind and his attempt
to understand it. This too is a reasonable approach, for much of Blake's
elaborate metaphysic looks much more like a rationalisation of psychological conflict than the true reasoning of metaphysical philosophy. Such
critics tend to see the mind-forged manacles as self-imposed, and the institutions as creations of the human mind built up to protect us from our
own spontaneous impulses — a view consistent with Freudian ideas of the
mechanism of repression and with clearer remarks to this effect elsewhere
in Blake's work. But again though some parts of the poem read rewardingly

as protest against what we are doing to ourselves, thus implying a need for *self*-reform before society will be reformed, others still seem much more like what we normally think of as *social* protest.

What does not seem to have been stressed is that these types of interpretation are not incompatible — at any rate not incompatible in psychological and personal terms (precisely the terms that basically charac- terise Romantics). It is not exceptional, but common to find in one and the same person the beliefs that social institutions are tyrannous, that current government policies are wicked, and that nevertheless the inner world of the psyche is a more fundamental reality than the outer world of political and social events. Moreover, there is a good deal of evidence to show that there is at any rate *some* truth in all these views — in most periods — and some degree of connection between them. Certainly it is possible to feel that the psyche and society exist in a dialectical relation- ship, each affecting the other, sometimes producing a harmonious syn- thesis but more often a vicious spiral. In short, it seems reasonable to suppose that 'London' is expressing a complex attitude compounded of various beliefs, feelings, and ideas, interlinked because all promote a similar feeling of dismay. But how, and how well, does the poem operate in detail?

It starts with the persona wandering through London, not in pursuit of any definite end, but rather like an Old Testament prophet noting differ- ent signs of a general evil and denouncing them. The hymnal form of the poem is therefore not inappropriate.[1] 'Charter'd street' and 'charter'd Thames' refer, presumably, to the privileged businesses and institutions of the capital and to the shipping on the river trading under hire (chartered). A great city given over to commerce, it would seem, is not a happy city: witness the last two lines of the first stanza. Chartering, we may tenta- tively assume, represents what is now called 'the unacceptable face of capitalism'. But surely there is something else? It is really the businesses and ships that are chartered, not the streets and the river. Does not this figurative usage carry with it a Romantic implication: that rivers as part of nature and streets as ancient ways made by the public are distorted from their essential being if given over to commerce, and especially privileged commerce?

The second stanza does not develop from the first, but rather switches — using the psychological association of 'woe' and 'cry' as a link — to a more inward sign of the general malaise. Since there are no explicit refer-

---

1. But one could equally well speak of it as an anti-hymnal form (witness 'black'ning Church'). For reference to differently contrastive ways of using literary tradition to add meaningful overtones to a poem see critiques 3, 5, and 13.

ences to current political bans and oppression, it is tempting to read this stanza as purely inward and take 'mind-forg'd manacles' as those that are self-imposed. But it is hard not to see deliberate paradox in the relationship of charters (granted to give freedom for some) and manacles (forg'd for others, one is apt to think). Perhaps the same authority responsible for the one is responsible for the other? This suspicion is strengthened by the following stanza which contrasts two major opinion-formers, the Church and the monarchy, very unfavourably, with victimised representatives of the common people, the sweep and the soldier. In short, it would seem perverse not to take 'mind-forg'd manacles' ambiguously as limitations imposed from outside through the ideals of commerce, religion, and patriotism and also limitations imposed from within by the willing acceptance of such conventional ideals. Bearing in mind the time of writing (in the early 1790s), it is reasonable to suppose that contemporary readers would have also brought to mind some of the specific current examples of such general ills. In so far as the modern reader has made himself historically aware of them, they make up a proper part of the full meaning — but a small part: in this case, we come to the particular only through the general. A point confirmed by the repetition of 'every' in this stanza.

Although stanza three, too, makes a switch rather than a development, its more concrete references clearly pick up the differing implications noted in the previous stanzas. After all, the Church, the monarchy, and the well-to-do were united against a disenfranchised and discontented populace at this time. This picking up and recombining of what has gone before probably accounts for the greater difficulty (and impressiveness) of this stanza. Before analysis, however, quotation might be useful, just to give psychological reassurance that our general idea of its viewpoint is likely to be right. Here is 'The Chimney Sweeper' (also from *Songs of Experience*) which is more plainly and bitterly ironic about employers, religion, and the monarchy. (The chimney-sweep would be a small boy, hardly able to pronounce '(s)weep', and unlikely to grow up to be a big boy, as his task of climbing up the chimneys involved burns, abrasions, and near-suffocation.)

> A little black thing among the snow,
> Crying 'weep, weep' in notes of woe!
> 'Where are thy father and mother, say?'
> 'They are gone up to the church to pray.
>
> 'Because I was happy upon the heath,
> And smil'd among the winter's snow,
> They cloth'd me in the clothes of death,
> And taught me to sing the notes of woe.

'And because I am happy, and dance and sing,
They think they have done me no injury,
And are gone to praise God and his Priest and King,
Who make up a heaven of our misery.'

The trinity at the end are clearly accused of cynical propaganda and the
parents seen as willingly brainwashed — which tends to confirm the double
meaning of 'mind-forg'd manacles'. But 'black' and 'clothes of death' may
alert us to more subtle implications of stanza three of 'London'.

Since 'appal' strictly means to grow pale, the second line appears not so
much paradoxical as plain contradictory: the Church is going black and
pale at the same time. On closer inspection, however, a genuine paradox —
of a complex kind — does manifest itself. 'Clothes of death' gives a clue.
'Appalls' could also be to cover with a (black) pall ('hearse' also suggesting
an underlying preoccupation with death, i.e. two major social institutions
are dead at heart). Moreover, 'appal' suggests fear quite as much as pity
(and this was indeed a time when the Church was under attack).
'Black'ning' too carries more than one meaning. The nearness of 'Chimney-
sweeper' suggests that the Church is going black with soot, the general
tone of the poem, however, adds the idea of increasing corruption and
deathliness. Is the Church, too, responsible, by preserving the status quo,
for making the chimney-sweeper a poor little black thing? Is it appalled
because it realises it has blackened him — and is itself blackened by that
fact? If this sense seems allowable then so must the senses of generally
spreading corruption and deathliness, and of denigration (as in the idea of
blackening someone's character). These later senses fit in with the propa-
gandist meaning of 'mind-forg'd manacles' and tally with Blake's view that
the Church in fact represented Satan (while calling him 'God'). The grammar also allows the Church to be both an active and a passive agent, like
the mind-forging: it is blackened, covered by a pall, clad in the clothes of
deathliness, by the society it supports, and in turn it further corrupts and
deadens that society. In one sense, it is as much a victim as the chimney-
sweep whose cry is at once frightening, and horrifying to its remaining
conscience.

'The hapless Soldier's sigh' that runs 'in blood down Palace walls' seems
an equally rich and powerful image, but a less complicated one. Indeed it
is problematic only if we look for some specific reference (but here, as
elsewhere — Infant, Chimney-sweeper, Harlot — the capital letters suggest
a general reference: each being the symbol of a class). If we ask, say, does
it refer to the Jacobin attack on Versailles, or to some particular battle
involving British troops sent out to die abroad, we get no answer. But it

very brilliantly condenses into memorable form the general idea that in sending soldiers to fight anywhere, for any reason, the State (typified here by the monarchy) is responsible for the blood shed and the dying sighs of those killed. Also, perhaps, one should pick up the idea, in 'sigh', of the misery of having the job of shedding blood. Like the light from a table-lamp the edge of illumination is not sharply defined, but shades off. However, a recent interpretation of the last stanza may serve to confirm that if interpretative reason can and should accommodate multiple or amorphous meaning it cannot and should not accommodate just any meaning. Valid literary meanings may be indefinite but are not infinite.

Much critical discussion has focussed on 'the youthful Harlot's curse'. If it is *just* swearing, how *does* it blast the infant and blight the 'Marriage hearse'? If we assume that the picture evoked of a drunken, swearing harlot will remind us of the 'curse' of venereal disease, this will give a definite concrete meaning to blasting the new-born infant's tear (since a baby's eyes can be infected during the course of birth) and to blighting marriage with plagues (in the plural perhaps because infection would produce mental as well as physical distress). Assigning such a meaning is rather comparable to seeing 'fear' and 'ban' as referring to concrete facts of contemporary history. However, it seemed reasonable in that case to see also a wider, less concrete level of meaning. Should we do likewise in the case of the 'youthful Harlot's curse'?

Since we have already departed from the naturalistic meaning (of swearing) to one psychologically associated but not logically so (witness 'hear'), in calling to mind the curse of venereal disease, there seems no reason in principle why we should not go further along the same path. Only common sense and literary sensibility can dictate where we stop. Certainly the interactions elsewhere in the poem of specific with general, physical with metaphysical or psychological meanings encourage us to do so. Moreover, 'hearse', which is part of the same sentence, cannot possibly be taken in a concrete sense. One has to assume that it refers to marriage as the metaphorical death of, say, free life, free choice, free love, or natural impulse. As the 'charter'd' Thames represents a perversion of the natural by the commercial, so can marriage be seen: love by contract — and in that way is also to be associated with harlotry. Does 'youthful' suggest some sympathy with the harlot, thus associating her with the other victims of society's standards, the sweep and the soldier? If so, it gives another meaning to 'curse'; like the blackening Church and the soldier she is seen then with double vision as one afflicted *by* society with the curse of her trade while in turn being a curse *to* society.

Some such complex of meaning seems reasonably called for, since the blasting and blighting cannot reasonably be seen as a consequence of mere swearing, while on the other hand the picture of a foulmouthed young harlot on the midnight streets could well call up such associations (especially as 'curse' tends to get removed from the act of hearing as the sentence goes on).

Further ramifications of meaning may be legitimate. For instance, is the new-born infant's 'tear' to be contrasted with the 'cry of fear' and the sweep's 'cry', as a sign of innocence? The spontaneous sign of natural need as against the cry induced by the imposition of mind-forged manacles? One cannot be sure, though the interpretation is not beyond the bounds of reason; it would just about fit in with the fan of relatable meanings discussed. When, however, Professor Harold Bloom[2] interprets the harlot's 'curse' as her menstruation we must surely say that this is an example of an invalid interpretation, clear evidence that an indefinite range of possible literary meaning does not imply an infinite one. It is to be ruled out of bounds on both scholarly and critical grounds: the word 'curse' did not have the slang meaning of menstruation in Blake's time, and that idea is not relatable to any of the meanings discussed or to the poem as a whole.

To come up against such a notion, though, may give us pause. Could it possibly be that *all* the other, relatable meanings are wrong (as they would have to be if this were right)? Is there any way of rechecking? As it happens, there is, for an earlier version of 'London' exists in manuscript — and the alterations might prove useful.

In the first stanza we find 'dirty' street and 'dirty' Thames. The alteration to 'charter'd' certainly tends to confirm our view that Blake regarded the takeover by privileged institutions and businesses as a form of pollution. Next, we may notice that the capital letters for Infant, Chimneysweeper, Church, Soldier, Palace, Harlot and Marriage are absent. This indicates that they are not accidental in the final version. Blake deliberately changed small letters to capitals — a fact, again, that strongly tends to confirm our idea of symbolic generality; an idea further strengthened when we notice that 'Church' was formerly 'the churches'. A merely social reference to specific buildings has been given an added abstract dimension. In fact the line read 'Blackens o'er the churches' walls' rather than 'Every black'ning Church appalls'. The first version only slightly suggests that the 'Church' is getting corrupt while the 'churches' are getting sooty. (We have to deduce this from the fact that the chimney-sweeper's *cry* rather than his brush is adduced as the cause.) Altering 'blackens' to 'black'ning' strengthens this double implication, by reason of the grammatical ambi-

2. *Poetry and Repression* (Yale University Press, 1976), p. 40.

guity of the participle which allows the Church to be actively denigratory and corrupting as well as passively suffering corruption. And the ambiguous 'appalls' — now clearly seen to be a deliberate importation of complexity — by its personification underlines the idea of the Church as an *agent* (which could, for example, forge manacles for the mind). In the last stanza 'the harlot's curse . . . Weaves around the marriage hearse / And blasts the new born infant's tear.' This, interestingly, gives us the harlot as a sort of Wicked Fairy weaving an evil spell over parents and child. Such a meaning for 'curse' fits in perfectly well with the idea of hearing — a difficulty our former interpretation never quite satisfactorily resolved. If we go on to ask 'In practical terms, what *sort* of spell?' we can still suggest the destruction of innocence, and venereal disease (perhaps why Blake inserted 'plagues' and omitted 'Weaves' — gaining in body but losing in clarity). But this earlier version rules out menstruation even more firmly, if that were possible.

The evidence of this early manuscript version, then, tends to confirm our interpretation, and gives us a new and better primary meaning for 'curse' (spell rather than mere swearing). It also indicates that the historical interpretation can be only part of the truth — that more generality is indeed implicit in the poem. And it shows that the complexity and ambiguity of the final version were almost certainly deliberately built in to it (witness the line referring to the Church).

It is true that nothing before, after, or alongside a literary work can give complete logical proof of the validity of any interpretation of it. But in the case of this Blake poem the combined evidence of the earlier version, the chimney-sweeper poem, the nature of *Songs of Innocence and Experience* ('Shewing the Two Contrary States of the Human Soul'), and the available knowledge of Blake's opinions and attitudes, gives very strong psychological support to an independent interpretation that is consistent with that evidence.

# 19. W. B. Yeats

## 'An Irish Airman Foresees His Death'

I know that I shall meet my fate
Somewhere among the clouds above;
Those that I fight I do not hate,
Those that I guard I do not love;
My country is Kiltartan Cross,
My countrymen Kiltartan's poor,
No likely end could bring them loss
Or leave them happier than before.
Nor law, nor duty bade me fight,
Nor public men, nor cheering crowds,
A lonely impulse of delight
Drove to this tumult in the clouds;
I balanced all, brought all to mind,
The years to come seemed waste of breath,
A waste of breath the years behind
In balance with this life, this death.

Since what is read thereby becomes a tiny part of one's life, a work of literature that in any way extends one's previous bounds of comprehension effects a transfer from art to life that is not metacritical. Many works, in addition, encourage a less direct transfer through metacriticism — Blake's 'London' being one. Some consideration of the social, political, and psychological issues raised, or at any rate strongly implied, by the poem would seem to follow naturally enough from a critical appreciation of it. Yeats's 'Irish Airman' is in a different, and rarer, category, as the poem itself raises a metacritical issue well *before* the completion of critical appreciation.

It arises because two things become apparent on the most cursory reading. One is that Yeats is adopting a persona that is obviously not simply a replica of himself, the other that his attitudes to his persona and his readers (i.e. the mood and tone of the poem) are not what would be

134

expected of any responsible and intelligent twentieth-century citizen. For here we have no 'hapless Soldier' sent out to kill and die by others, but a mercenary joining in a war that does not concern him ('Those that I fight I do not hate / Those that I guard I do not love') for the pure pleasure of it ('A lonely impulse of delight'). One would have expected the poem to be satirical about such a character, since no possible moral justification can be offered for such an action. But in this dramatic monologue there are no indications that the writer is to be considered as apart from, and disapproving of, his persona (as there are in, say, Browning's 'My Last Duchess'). On the contrary the implied attitude is one of hero-worship (and indeed Major Robert Gregory, on whom the poem was based was one of Yeats's heroes). And great technical brilliance is deployed to ensure that the reader shares that admiration.

Metacritical issues, however, are not the concern of this book. What *is* relevant in this case is the likelihood of a gap in critical appreciation between *what* is said and *how* it is said. It is indeed possible, and proper, for a critic to admire a work as literature while deploring it as opinion, or opinion-forming. In the 'Irish Airman' that gap is likely to be smaller than might have been expected. Smaller, because Yeats does not express any opinion directly; the poem has no theme in the sense of 'message'. In that respect it shares the nature of lyric expression − though its dramatic form, of course, means that it is ostensibly expressing only the feelings of the persona. If such obviously artful elements as the management of rhyme, metre, and antithesis* may be said to infiltrate the author's attitude, they do so very subtly, blending it with the mood of the persona. It is in terms of theme as leitmotif, some constant preoccupation, that the poem offers itself for consideration. And so well does it succeed in conveying the (dangerous) glamour of violence, the romance of (an outdated form of) heroism, that it is only on later reflection that one is likely to be aware of any gap at all − and then mentally add such words as 'dangerous' and 'outdated'. This poem, then, represents a triumph of technique leading through empathy (a non-moral, non-intellectual mode of understanding) to comprehension − if not approval − of a kind of attitude and character that morality and good sense would dismiss out of hand.

The masterplan of that technique is indicated by the twice-repeated 'balance' in the poem's conclusion. A very apt heart to the poem it is, too, since the setting is the cockpit of a World War I plane balancing on its gravitational tightrope in the 'tumult in the clouds'.

Naturally the balance is not regular and mechanical, but rather the swaying balance of constant re-adjustment. Indeed there are several sets of balances measured, as it were, against the fixed landscape of regular rhyme and metre. There is the balance of sense-structure against rhyme-structure, the psychological balancing of possible motives, the balance of two plain statements against each other and against the predominant rhetorical statements, and the various dictional balances of antithesis and parallelism.

Thus the rhymes play over the sense-divisions, acting as a counter-balance; for the sense goes in couplets while the rhyme goes in quatrains. For instance, the poem opens with one of its two plain statements, sober and unrhetorical:

> I know that I shall meet my fate
> Somewhere among the clouds above.

This is balanced against the other plain statement, the explanation of this unreasonable conduct:

> A lonely impulse of delight
> Drove to this tumult in the clouds.

And both are balanced, respectively, with 'this death' (thus beautifully concluding the poem with a return) and 'this life'. However, it may be said also to be less obviously balanced against the persuasive antithetical rhetoric of the next two lines:

> Those that I fight I do not hate,
> Those that I guard I do not love.

Here, then, are two separate sense-blocks which, however, are formally united by the cross-over rhyme. A counterbalancing of sense and form that persists up to the last four lines, when the two come together for the first time to reinforce a ringing conclusion. The balancing of motives, a weighing-up process, is exemplified in 'hate' and 'love' (and of course in the *varying* balances of the next six lines). And the dictional balances are evident throughout. Since the poem gains its conviction from persuasive linguistic devices rather than developed ideas, it may be worth while to give these balances a paragraph to themselves, if only to indicate the subtle variety of their deployment, which both avoids monotony and suits an aerodynamic kind of balancing.

Save for the two plain statements, all the lines contain verbal balances. First, regular repetition ('Those'/'Those') and antithesis ('fight'/'guard', 'hate'/'love'). Then comes the subtly varied parallelism of 'country'/ 'countrymen' and 'Kiltartan'/'Kiltartan's'. Next, the diffused contrast of different ideas, evidenced in purely dictional form only by the blurred contrast of 'loss' and 'happier'. 'Law', 'duty', 'public men', 'cheering crowds' (pivoted on the one verb 'fight') yield yet another kind of balance;

and the last lines another again. Here, balance is at once reinforced by alliteration ('balance', 'brought') and itself counterbalanced by the alliteration and repetition that helps to bring a sense of coming to a conclusion after all the weighing-up (*b*alanced—*w*aste—*b*reath—*w*aste—*b*reath—*b*ehind —*b*alance — itself an elaborately balanced sequence).

A marvellous, reprehensible, Irish poem giving insight into one of the paradoxes of human nature, and being incidentally of some interest in terms of critical theory.

# 20. W. H. Auden

**Sebastian's sestina (from *The Sea and the Mirror*)**

SEBASTIAN

My rioters all disappear, my dream
Where Prudence flirted with a naked sword,
Securely vicious, crumbles; it is day;
Nothing has happened; we are all alive:
I am Sebastian, wicked still, my proof
Of mercy that I wake without a crown.

What sadness signalled to our children's day
Where each believed all wishes wear a crown
And anything pretended is alive,
That one by one we plunged into that dream
Of solitude and silence where no sword
Will ever play once it is called a proof?

The arrant jewel singing in his crown
Persuaded me my brother was a dream
I should not love because I had no proof,
Yet all my honesty assumed a sword;
To think his death I thought myself alive
And stalked infected through the blooming day.

The lie of Nothing is to promise proof
To any shadow that there is no day
Which cannot be extinguished with some sword,
To want and weakness that the ancient crown
Envies the childish head, murder a dream
Wrong only while its victim is alive.

O blessed be bleak Exposure on whose sword,
Caught unawares, we prick ourselves alive!
Shake Failure's bruising fist! Who else would crown
Abominable error with a proof?

I smile because I tremble, glad today
To be ashamed, not anxious, not a dream.

Children are playing, brothers are alive,
And not a heart or stomach asks for proof
That all this dearness is no lovers' dream;
Just Now is what it might be every day,
Right Here is absolute and needs no crown,
Ermine or trumpets, protocol or sword.

In dream all sins are easy, but by day
It is defeat gives proof we are alive;
The sword we suffer is the guarded crown.

If the value of Yeats's 'Irish Airman' lay in its potential extension of the
reader's understanding into an area that would normally be blocked off, so
too, it may be said, does the potential value of Auden's sestina lie in its
departure from current norms. There, however, the similarity ends, for if
Yeats's values are extravagantly pagan and primitive, Auden's are exceed-
ingly Christian and sophisticated. If Yeats laboured to persuade by
physical empathy, Auden labours to persuade by metaphysical abstraction.
If Yeats worked by intensification, Auden does so by amplification. And if
Yeats's technique was so brilliant as to be dangerously effective, Auden's
(it will be argued) is so brilliant as to be irrelevant. Moreover, though both
poems, by their very nature, involve criticism with metacriticism, they do
so in utterly different ways.

*The Sea and the Mirror*, a vast and dazzling display of virtuosity, is sub-
titled 'A Commentary on Shakespeare's *The Tempest*'. In so far as it lives
up to that subtitle, it is a metacritical work of an unusual kind; in so far as
it delights and instructs in its own right it can be seen as a work of art that,
unusually, takes literature for its raw material instead of life. *The Tempest*
certainly invites metacriticism, in that it is clearly meaningful but blatantly
unrealistic. It is also purely dramatic; that is to say it presents itself vividly
without explaining itself: the author does not intrude to tell us how to
interpret it. Most of the interpretations that have been made can be
related to the text, with more or less difficulty; and no doubt there is
something in all of them. What Auden principally concerns himself with
are the relationships between Art and Nature (or, to put it slightly differently, Creativity and Reality) and *their* relationships with metaphysical
Christianity and morality.

Since Prospero can quite plausibly be regarded as a symbol of the artist,
and the artist as a symbol of God creating a world of order and harmony

from primitive chaos, this seems a perfectly legitimate line of metacritical enquiry. However, Auden's ingenuity, his *existentialist* Christianity, and his interest in Freudian psychology, take *The Sea and the Mirror* well beyond the limits of a reasonable metacriticism of *The Tempest* (which is not in fact ever referred to, though its characters appear – often, however, seeming very different from their role in *The Tempest*). It has, therefore, a strong claim to be considered as a work of art in its own right – a work of art about art, and depending for full appreciation on the reader's knowledge of another work of art.

Certainly, Sebastian's sestina is a separable poem. We do not need the rest of *The Sea and the Mirror* in order to appreciate it, though we do need to know of Sebastian's part in the action of *The Tempest* to understand what he is here pondering over. In one way, indeed, we may be better off if we are not familiar with the rest of *The Sea and the Mirror*, as this sestina happens not to involve *art* in its relationships with metaphysics, morality, and reality; and this is the chief concern of the whole work. The other three elements, though, do seem to be crucial to this rather esoteric sestina.

A sestina normally consists of six six-lined stanzas plus an envoy of three lines. The last word of each line of the first stanza must recur as the last word of a line in every other stanza, but the order must differ, according to a regular rule, from stanza to stanza, so as to work through the complete cycle of possibilities (if there were a seventh stanza, that is to say, the line-endings would have the same order as the first). Normally, the word ending the last line of the previous stanza ends the first line of the next, the end of the first line of the previous stanza becomes the end of the second line of the next, the end of the fifth line becomes the third, the end of the second becomes the fourth, the end of the fourth becomes the fifth, and the end of the third the sixth. If we number the end-words of the first stanza as 123456, then the sestina would go as follows: I. 123456, II. 615243, III. 364125, IV. 532614, V. 451362, VI. 246531, envoy – and a seventh stanza would return to 123456. This verse-form is so difficult that few sestinas are in fact written, and those few are usually characterised by a very simple content. Ezra Pound's 'Sestina: Altaforte', for instance, is a straightforward exclamatory expression of war fever: 'Damn it all! all this our South stinks peace / You whoreson dog, Papiols, come! Let's to music!', the last stanza beginning 'Papiols, Papiols, to the music!' Even so, Pound finds himself forced to go wrong in stanza IV (536214 instead of 532614) and therefore has to go wrong again in stanza V in order to get stanza VI back to 246531 which would give 123456 to a seventh stanza; so the reader might have the illusion that the full cycle had been regularly worked through.

In fact a sensitive reader will not have that illusion. If the ear does not detect, on first reading, just where the poem goes wrong it does detect that something has gone wrong somewhere; there is a sense of the permutation not working itself out properly. A bad flaw, since a sestina is very much a poem of imposed form, the perception of whose rolling permutation is an essential part of the literary pleasure. A poet who cannot do it should not try it. If, of course, he can both do it and make it an appropriate form for his content, so much the better. And good sestinas do tend to give a sense of some obsessive mood being worked through, put into order so that it can be released in a dismissive envoy (whose line-endings break with the permutation, before it can begin again). Or there is a sense of a *systematic* unfolding of a mood (or a simple theme, as in Kipling's 'Tramp Royal' sestina), of modulations of the same thing until it has been so fully dealt with that anything further would be plain repetition (123456). But clearly such pleasures of patterning, systematising, permutating, will not come about if there is perceptible cheating. Equally they will not come about if the form is *im*perceptible though properly sustained.

Pound not only sacrifices line-order to the needs of sense but also sacrifices metre to the demands of character. Since formal order — often in tension with unruly feeling — is of the essence of the sestina (or any other obviously difficult imposed form), this seems critically reprehensible. Auden, on the other hand, splendidly assimilates the demands of metre to those of the rhythms of musing inner speech. But alas, one feels, what a mess he has made of the order of line-endings! Understandably, as he is attempting what no man in his right mind would attempt: to analyse an extremely complicated, esoteric line of thought, hovering between psychology and metaphysics, in sestina form! Naturally, then, to say what he wanted to say he has simply had to jettison the proper onward-rolling permutation and repeat end-words anyhow, as the sense required. Surely, he would have been better advised to try an easier form for so difficult a content?

Such is likely to be one's first reaction. Then come doubts. He is managing metre well; and the sense is very clever indeed (right or wrong). Would such a man be fool enough to choose a form he could not manage? Besides, has Auden not written in the equally difficult form of the villa-nelle* with supreme ease? Yet, a second reading, made with the utmost sensitive awareness, alert for patterning, reveals nothing. The end-word ordering still seems more random than systematic. It is only if one abandons the ear for the intelligence that a feat of mind-boggling virtuosity becomes apparent. Considerable arithmetical effort will reveal that Auden has matched a content far more complicated, with a form far more complicated than that of the usual sestina. But the matching seems to have no esthetic value since it is imperceptible to the ear or feelings — and remains so even when it has been laboriously comprehended by the understanding. The feeling remains one not of evolving inevitability but of formal irrelevance: a stupendous technical *tour de force* that does not illuminate, and may obscure the subject-matter.

The stanzas go as follows: I. 123456, II. 364125, III. 615243, IV. 532614, V. 246531, VI. 451362 (plus an envoy which, breaking the pattern, signals the end of a sequence). At first the pattern is unapparent. The first end-word of the second stanza is the third of the first stanza, the end-word of the second line of the second stanza is the sixth of the first stanza, the third end-word of the second stanza is the fourth of the first, the fourth end-word of the second stanza is the first of the first stanza, the fifth end-word of the second the second of the first, and the sixth end-word of the second is the fifth of the first. (Or, starting with the first stanza, we go: third to first, sixth to second, fourth to third, first to fourth, second to fifth, and fifth to sixth.) Thus instead of the normal 123456/615243 we get 123456/364125. Alas, if we apply this more elaborate formula of change to the third stanza it does not work out. What we should have is 451362; what we actually have is 615243. However, if we lay out the sestina horizontally in a column, something turns up to indicate that the changes, after all, may not be random:

```
I.      ⌐123456←
II.      ↳364125  ⟍
III.   ⌐ ↱615243⌐   ⟍
IV.   (  ( 532614⟨    )
V.     ⟍ ↳246531↲   ⟋
VI.      ↳451362⌐
```

The order 451362, which we might have expected for the third stanza, comes up in the sixth stanza — and we find that if we applied the formula 3>1, 6>2, 4>3, 1>4, 2>5, 5>6 to that sixth stanza we should indeed, as in a regular sestina, get back to 123456.

Further investigation reveals that Auden has in fact used his more complex system of changes to operate a rotation of inner and outer wheels. As the arrows indicate, I to II gives the formula and sets the process going, then III gives IV, IV gives V, and V takes us back to III to complete the inner wheel; II (derived from I) gives VI, and VI takes us back to I to complete the outer circle. Dazzlingly clever — but since this form is not even subliminally apprehensible as part of the reading experience and, anyway, is not related to the development of the theme (save that stanza VI does take us back to where we started from, 'Now', 'Here'), it is a pointless cleverness. Nevertheless the poem might still be of worth as an enlightening or stimulating metaphysical speculation that could, and perhaps should, have been cast in some other form. 'Should' is prompted by the fact that though the language is always lucid not every point is easily understood, and it seems at least possible that at least some of the difficulty may have been occasioned by the exigencies of this extraordinary form.

This Sebastian is very different from the Sebastian of the play, who gives little evidence of being prone to metaphysical speculation, but we need to know what that situation was in *The Tempest* which could provide the launching pad for Auden's excursion into a more rarefied and less dramatic realm. We need to know, in fact, that Sebastian, tempted by Antonio, has been prevented (or 'saved') by Ariel from murdering his sleeping brother Alonzo, King of Naples, in order to usurp his crown. The first stanza, which sets the base for Sebastian's exploratory musing, becomes clear enough in this context.

Since there were no rioters and Sebastian was not asleep the opening must be taken to refer metaphorically to a state of mind: the riotous thoughts of a waking nightmare in which, as in real dreams, the speaker was 'not himself'. If coming back to 'day' hints at the idea of 'seeing the light' it does so ironically (as Sebastian is ironic about his 'mercy' in the last line); for the murder has been averted not by pangs of conscience or an accession of good sense but by outside interference. This is 'virtue' by chance, and what Sebastian has awakened to is the daylight of prudence. 'Proof', then, must also be ironic — or at any rate be considered as questioning that part of existentialist doctrine which insists that we *are* what we actually do, not what we allege our motives to be. Such questioning of what he did believe as well as what he did not is by no means uncharacteristic of Auden, whose beliefs, anyway, tended to be a sort of trying-on of ideas to see how they fitted and felt, intellectual curiosity counting for more than emotional commitment.

In detail, the second stanza is much more obscure, though the gist is clear: what is it that, unhappily, separates us from the sharing innocence of childhood? New shades of meaning now attach to the end-words — a very good use of the sestina form, turning repetition into variation. 'Day' now clearly stands for innocence (as opposed both to knowledge and sin). The child is king — in control — in so far as he believes his wishes will be crowned with success and as he can make his own subjects by pretending that objects are alive. Force and the subjection of others are unnecessary to him. The 'dream' that we plunge into, then, must be what would normally be called a realistic or adult attitude — one of 'solitude and silence' because we no longer feel ourselves part of an also-living world. Rather we are a little world to ourselves. From here, it is a short step to a solipsist view: that the only certain reality is our own sense impressions, so that other people and the external world have no more reality than a dream, and indeed may be figments of our imagination, in terms of the strict logic of this intellectual position. But what does Auden mean by saying 'where no sword / Will ever play once it is called a proof'? It seems impossible to make sense of this unless we take 'it' to refer to 'that dream'. Then we can paraphrase like this: since that 'dream' is the contrary of childhood's 'reality' (i.e. since the idea that anything pretended is alive has been turned into the solipsist view that anything alive is 'pretended' — and can therefore be put to the sword without compunction) no sword will ever again be a merely play-sword; it will make real sword-play. The 'proof', on this interpretation, is proof that wishes do *not* wear a crown, reality is *not* an innocent sharing of the world but a separation from it.

This interpretation of a difficult, paradoxically expressed stanza, gets support from stanza three. 'Arrant' is a variant of 'errant'. So again we begin with paradox. The real jewel (more misleading than the jewel of an insubstantial ideal), Sebastian reflects, is what persuaded him into the solipsist belief that his brother was unreal (another shade of meaning for 'dream'). Since there was no logical proof of his independent reality he need not be loved. Yet this intellectual toughness ('honesty') did not extend to taking the sword as unreal or a dream. In this way he came to think himself most alive when actually most corrupted and infected (again, there seems to be an implied criticism of the existentialist idea that choosing and acting creates real humanness, whereas abstaining leads to thingdom).

In the next stanza 'Nothing' presumably refers to materialism, or a valueless world, the world as mere matter. This would tally with the main line of argument of the sestina, with the existentialist view that mere matter is 'nothing' till given form and value by human choice, and with Auden's views elsewhere, especially in 'The History of Truth' which maintains that scientific truth, being merely materialistic, is really 'Some untruth anyone can give the lie to / A nothing no one need believe is there'. This is the 'Nothing' that promises proof to those like Sebastian ('shadows': shallow, wicked men, unreal in proportion as they think themselves the only reality). 'Day' now seems to indicate what is the opposite of 'shadow'; i.e. what does hold values, is enlightened, or is innocent. This is the 'Nothing', too, that offers lying proof to the inferior that murder is merely a *dream* (now, an *illusion*, an *unreal* crime), 'Wrong only while its victim is alive'. Presumably this sardonically implies never wrong – by the standard of the bad principles previously given – for if the victim is unreal before the murder he is not alive, and he is dead afterwards. But what is to be made of 'the ancient crown / Envies the childish head'? Clearly there is a pun on 'crown', so we have an opposition of old head and young head. But clearly both 'ancient' and 'childish' carry overtones beyond the core meanings of 'old' and 'young'. The former, especially in association with the metaphorical meaning of 'crown' as *peak*, suggests wisdom and reverence; it also suggests inherited tradition. The latter suggests pettiness, while also taking us back to the childhood innocence of the first stanza. So now, it would seem, childhood naivety and pretence, though better than the 'childish' adulthood of selfish solipsism that follows it, is not good enough. On the other hand, since it is a 'lie' that the 'ancient crown' envies the childlike, it is evident that Auden (or a 'Sebastian' who is very different from Shakespeare's) is suggesting the need for a supreme traditional wisdom to combat selfishness supported by a false philosophy. The definite article – '*the* ancient crown' indicates some particular crowning wisdom. Which?

From the evidence of stanza five, it can hardly be doubted that it is the 'crowning glory' of Christianity that is implied and, more specifically, that the 'ancient crown' is Christ's crown of thorns, for the stanza goes on to extol the virtue of suffering which is at the basis of Christian doctrine. We are turned from 'shadows' into real people by suffering (by being put to the sword ourselves rather than by putting others to it); so we should bless exposure (Sebastian was in fact spared that humiliation) and shake hands with failure. It is suffering that crowns the error of self-deception, or false philosophising, with 'proof' that people are real and exist in a real world, that the waking 'dream' of the first line of the poem *was* a dream.

The last stanza amplifies this new daylight state in which the existence and love of others is known to be a reality, not a dream, and in which no material crown is needed. There is presumably a pun on both 'Just' and 'Right', and no longer any need for material or logical proof that dearness, justness, and rightness here and now in a real world are what supremely matter. The envoy sums up, with appropriate paradox: we live by defeat (for dream-success is the avoidance of reality) and we are crowned by suffering – and *that* crown is 'guarded', one we cannot be deposed from.

It may be felt that too much time has been devoted to paraphrase, too little to esthetic appreciation. Yet it is arguably the poem itself that is to

145

blame. Both its paradoxes and its complex structure tend to obscure its ideas — and it is very much a poem of *ideas*, despite the presence of these other factors. Hence the overriding need for paraphrase. Such a poem is nothing if it is not understood, in the most literal sense of the word — and once understood it seems rather to invite intellectual discussion than literary appreciation.

In short, the prevalence of paradox and pun (dubious elements in an argument) and the fact that the ideas are by no means self-evidently true strongly indicate the propriety in this case of passing from (mainly paraphrastic) criticism to metacriticism. One might, for instance, wish to dispute the idea that the only alternative to a false philosophy is one that redefines the common idea of truth . . . But metacriticism is not the business of this book. We may rest content with noting that a poem which could be considered as simply a metacriticism of part of *The Tempest*, when considered as a work of art in its own right, returns us — rather more quickly than most poems, and with fewer esthetic rewards by the way — right back to the more abstract realm of metacriticism. In this it is radically different from the next poem to be considered, Auden's 'Lady, Weeping' which, though it has ideas, turns them into vivid experience.

# 21. W. H. Auden

## 'Lady, Weeping at the Crossroads'

Lady, weeping at the crossroads
Would you meet your love
In the twilight with his greyhounds,
And the hawk on his glove?

Bribe the birds then on the branches,
Bribe them to be dumb,
Stare the hot sun out of heaven
That the night may come.

Starless are the nights of travel,
Bleak the winter wind;
Run with terror all before you
And regret behind.

Run until you hear the ocean's
Everlasting cry;
Deep though it may be and bitter
You must drink it dry.

Wear out patience in the lowest
Dungeons of the sea,
Searching through the stranded shipwrecks
For the golden key.

Push on to the world's end, pay the
Dread guard with a kiss;
Cross the rotten bridge that totters
Over the abyss.

There stands the deserted castle
Ready to explore;
Enter, climb the marble staircase
Open the locked door.

Cross the silent empty ballroom,
Doubt and danger past;
Blow the cobwebs from the mirror
See yourself at last.

Put your hand behind the wainscot,
You have done your part;
Find the penknife there and plunge it
Into your false heart.

A first innocent reading of 'Lady, weeping at the crossroads' reveals it as strikingly different from Sebastian's sestina; so different that it might well have come from a different pen. For one thing it is in a very simple verse-form, that of the ballad;[1] for another, it is narrative rather than philosophic, full of exciting atmosphere and incident rather than obscure and rarefied moralising. On reflection, though, some very general similarities do emerge. Neither poem is the expression of purely personal feeling, in the Romantic way; and this is in fact typical of Auden, who believed in writing about a subject or an idea, not about himself. Moreover, the expression 'false heart', given considerable prominence, as the last words of a dramatic twist at the end of the tale, strongly suggests that morality plays an important part in this work too − though what part exactly may not be immediately clear. Again, Sebastian's musings could be construed as a quest for his true self (as against a 'dream' self), and 'Lady, Weeping' is clearly a quest-ballad, reminiscent here and there of Browning's 'Childe Roland' and a number of fairy-stories. It is not, however, immediately apparent just what it is a quest *for*. In spite of the differences − but in view of the similarities − could it be a quest similar to Sebastian's, an *inner* quest? Certainly, the quest theme figures largely in Auden's work, and after 1939 is almost invariably referred to the inner realm of the psyche.

This suggestion gets external support from another angle. Auden generally keeps himself out of his poetry in two ways: either by taking a god's-eye, panoramic view of a subject, abstracting a skeleton of abstract principles from reality's dense body of particulars, or, on the contrary, by telling stories of someone else − such as the 'Lady'. These narrative poems tend to be particularised and dramatic, but also to be just as much concerned with getting at the heart of a matter, with formulating some kind of truth, as the more panoramic, reflective poems are. In short, these poems rely on a mythic method.

1. For very different, but equally apt, uses of the simple ballad form compare critiques 5, 9, and 17.

In France, under the influence of Lévi-Strauss's structuralist anthropology, interest seems to centre on what all myths share, their common structure — a reductive view of mythology that is of little use to the poet. Elsewhere, received opinion seems to be that there is *no* valid general theory of myth, or at any rate no use in any such theory; each myth should be taken on its own merits in its specific local context. An opinion only a little less useless to the poet than the structuralist one, though for the opposite reason: it does not allow for the expression of any general truth through a particular narrative. Until recent years, however, there was an accepted general theory, which placed myth at the meeting point of history, dream, and religion. That is to say, it was a primitive *explanation* of how things had come about in the outer world, or a primitive *expression* of goings-on in the inner world. It differed from history in being *emotionally* believed in, from dream as being true, not merely fantastic (a view near to that of the psycho-analyst), from religion as being also entertaining. Whether explanatory or expressive in mode the myth conveyed knowledge to be *experienced* rather than *understood* — or at any rate to be experienced first, and only later to be understood in paraphrasable form. This idea of myth clearly is of use to poets (and novelists and dramatists), and is in fact the one adopted by Auden, among many other writers.

In Auden's later poetry, then, myth acts as symbolic metaphor extended into narrative, a way of giving vivid form and body to some general truth. Add to this the fact that, whether Marxist or existentialist, atheist or Christian, Auden was always a Freudian, and then consider the poem afresh, and we find everything falls into place.

In any case the poem itself gives us good enough reason for trying out the hypothesis that it is in fact a mythic work, using symbolic narrative to express a truth about some inner quest — perhaps for a true self. As early as the second stanza, for instance, it is made clear that this is not a naturalistic narrative, for a real sun cannot be stared out of heaven and a real night will come anyway, do what we may. And why, in material terms, should anyone wish the night to come, as '[in order] That the night may come' implies? Already, it seems more likely that the night is rather a dark night of the soul, needing purgation (perhaps with the therapeutic help of dream), and the 'hot sun' the pride and egotism that prevents the truth from being acknowledged. The general tone, too, and the nature of the actions demanded (as if by a priest or psychiatrist) are reminiscent of fairy-tales and legends. What is more, the ending, which is dramatic but absurd in realistic terms, becomes perfectly explicable on this hypothesis.

How, then, does it work out as a literary myth, if we look at it stanza by stanza? After all, a narrative poem in particular demands to be appreciated temporally (bit by bit as it happens) more than spatially (as laid out in memory, maplike). It starts with an image of lonely sorrow, and 'crossroads' suggests some crux. There is perhaps a sense of being lost and deserted and not knowing which path to take. This would fit in equally well with a naturalistic or a psychological tale. But the next stanza, both for the reasons given above and because of the odd suggestion that a twilight and with it one's love can be brought about by will, clearly points to the second alternative.

The weighty alliteration gives a sense of effort: *b*ribe—*b*irds—*b*ranches—*b*ribe—*b*e, *d*umb—*th*e—*th*en—*th*em—*th*e—*th*at (plus the less weighty sounds of '*s*tare' and '*s*un', '*h*ot' and '*h*eaven'). Compare the 'open' effect of the third stanza — a matter of sense, of course, as well as the relative sparsity of heavy alliterative effects. Two oddities confirm the idea of reference to an inner realm: the fact of travelling by night (with a faint suggestion of there being no day to travel in) and of running *towards* terror, which one might do in dream (or in psychiatric treatment, concerned with recognising and accepting unpalatable repressed truths) but hardly would in normal life. A moral element is subtly implied by the paradox of 'And regret behind' Why go forward if you regret what you are leaving behind — unless there were something badly wrong with it?

The fourth stanza's exaggeration ('Drink the ocean dry') is rather like the impossible tasks so commonly set in fairy-tales and legends, and thus tends to reinforce the legendary overtones of the setting and detail of stanza one. 'Deep' and 'bitter', then, we must by this time surely take in a personal as well as an oceanic sense. And having done so are likely to be reminded of the sestina's theme of salvation by suffering — a not uncommon theme in myths, and probably the main point of Browning's 'Childe Roland'.

The idea of spiritual testing is carried on in the next stanza, which obviously takes us deep into the world of dream, since real seas have no dungeons, but the sea of the unconscious may; and if Freudian theory is to be believed dreams may provide the key that will release us from imprisoning neurosis. A search among stranded shipwrecks must refer to the result of badly weathered storms in the past, or cowardly scuttlings, and of course it confirms that this is a dream-world not the everyday world. '*The* golden key' suggests one sovereign remedy.

The nightmare, legendary atmosphere is sustained through stanza six, with the 'world's end', 'the dread guard', 'the rotten bridge that totters / Over the abyss' — all standard properties, and reminders that depth-psychology is not without its risks. The 'dread guard' may refer specifically to the Freudian 'Censor' which keeps repressed material from surfacing — though it can be eluded in the disguises of dream; but it is vague enough to have more threatening overtones.

'The deserted castle' of the following stanza may be faintly reminiscent of the story of 'The Sleeping Beauty', but more immediately recalls Freud's view that the self is often figured in dreams by a building. That it is deserted seems to indicate a self rejected long ago, and only now being rediscovered, towards the end of the quest. Since the 'locked door' (a tiny hint at 'Bluebeard' — horrors still to be faced?) can be opened, the golden key has somehow been 'found'. Perhaps the patience, and the courage of the kiss ('Beauty and the Beast'?) and the crossing are themselves the key?

At any rate, the eighth stanza sounds a note of triumph. Doubt and danger are past, the cobwebs are being blown away, as if the castle were about to come to life again, as in 'The Sleeping Beauty'. 'See yourself at last', then — taking 'yourself' almost as two words — implies 'as you really are': the self long ago rejected, imprisoned, and forgotten.

The last stanza continues the note of success: 'You have done your part.' But what sort of success is it that leads to suicide? The answer surely, the twist in the tale, is that it is not suicide but cure. Some emphasis is to fall on 'false'. At last the usurping, false self can be killed off, leaving the way for the *true* heart to flourish and the deserted castle to come to life (again as in 'The Sleeping Beauty': a myth, like this one, ultimately rooted in the age-old fertility cults, based on the vegetation cycle, in which a cutting down, a death, was a necessary precursor to renewal). We may further deduce, in view of the mirror image (and bearing 'Snow White' in mind), that the false self was selfish and self-loving (like Sebastian). Therefore, an extra twist in the tale, 'your love' in stanza one turns out to be the self that is met in the mirror when the (surely symbolic) cobwebs are blown away. A self-love now seen as so hideous as to deserve destruction.

So, a poem in theme not so very different from Auden's sestina, but a world away in its total effect — and a better world, esthetically speaking.

# 22. George Crabbe

### 'Procrastination'

Love will expire — the gay, the happy dream
Will turn to scorn, indiff'rence, or esteem:
Some favour'd pairs, in this exchange, are blest,
Nor sigh for raptures in a state of rest;
Others, ill match'd, with minds unpair'd, repent
At once the deed, and know no more content;
From joy to anguish they, in haste, decline,
And, with their fondness, their esteem resign;
More luckless still their fate, who are the prey
Of long-protracted hope and dull delay:          10
'Mid plans of bliss the heavy hours pass on,
Till love is wither'd, and till joy is gone.

    This gentle flame two youthful hearts possess'd,
The sweet disturber of unenvied rest:
The prudent *Dinah* was the maid beloved,
And the kind *Rupert* was the swain approved:
A wealthy aunt her gentle niece sustain'd,
He, with a father, at his desk remain'd;
The youthful couple, to their vows sincere,
Thus loved expectant; year succeeding year,        20
With pleasant views and hopes, but not a prospect near.
Rupert some comfort in his station saw,
But the poor virgin lived in dread and awe;
Upon her anxious looks the widow smiled,
And bade her wait, 'for she was yet a child.'
She for her neighbour had a due respect,
Nor would his son encourage or reject;
And thus the pair, with expectations vain,
Beheld the seasons change and change again:
Meantime the nymph her tender tales perused,        30

Where cruel aunts impatient girls refused:
While hers, though teasing, boasted to be kind,
And she, resenting, to be all resign'd.

   The dame was sick, and when the youth applied
For her consent, she groan'd, and cough'd and cried,
Talk'd of departing, and again her breath
Drew hard, and cough'd and talk'd again of death:
'Here you may live, my Dinah! here the boy
'And you together my estate enjoy:'
Thus to the lovers was her mind express'd,                    40
Till they forbore to urge the fond request.

   Servant, and nurse, and comforter, and friend,
Dinah had still some duty to attend;
But yet their walk, when Rupert's evening call
Obtain'd an hour, made sweet amends for all;
So long they now each other's thoughts had known,
That nothing seem'd exclusively their own:
But with the common wish, the mutual fear,
They now had travell'd to their thirtieth year.

   At length a prospect open'd — but alas!                    50
Long time must yet, before the union, pass:
Rupert was call'd, in other clime, t' increase
Another's wealth, and toil for future peace.
Loth were the lovers; but the aunt declared
'T was fortune's call, and they must be prepared:
'You now are young, and for this brief delay,
'And Dinah's care, what I bequeath will pay;
'All will be yours; nay, love, suppress that sigh;
'The kind must suffer, and the best must die:'
Then came the cough, and strong the signs it gave            60
Of holding long contention with the grave.

   The lovers parted with a gloomy view,
And little comfort, but that both were true;
He for uncertain duties doom'd to steer,
While hers remain'd too certain and severe.

   Letters arrived, and Rupert fairly told
'His cares were many, and his hopes were cold:
'The view more clouded, that was never fair,

'And love alone preserved him from despair:'
In other letters brighter hopes he drew,                    70
'His friends were kind, and he believed them true.'

When the sage widow Dinah's grief descried,
She wonder'd much why one so happy sigh'd:
Then bade her see how her poor aunt sustain'd
The ills of life, nor murmur'd nor complain'd.
To vary pleasures, from the lady's chest
Were drawn the pearly string and tabby vest;
Beads, jewels, laces, all their value shown,
With the kind notice — 'They will be your own.'

This hope, these comforts, cherish'd day by day,          80
To Dinah's bosom made a gradual way;
Till love of treasure had as large a part,
As love of Rupert, in the virgin's heart.
Whether it be that tender passions fail,
From their own nature, while the strong prevail:
Or whether av'rice, like the poison-tree,
Kills all beside it, and alone will be,
Whatever cause prevail'd, the pleasure grew
In Dinah's soul, — she loved the hoards to view;
With lively joy those comforts she survey'd,             90
And love grew languid in the careful maid.

Now the grave niece partook the widow's cares,
Look'd to the great, and ruled the small affairs:
Saw clean'd the plate, arranged the china-show,
And felt her passion for a shilling grow:
Th' indulgent aunt increased the maid's delight,
By placing tokens of her wealth in sight;
She loved the value of her bonds to tell,
And spake of stocks, and how they rose and fell.

This passion grew, and gain'd at length such sway,      100
That other passions shrank to make it way;
Romantic notions now the heart forsook,
She read but seldom, and she changed her book;
And for the verses she was wont to send,
Short was her prose, and she was Rupert's friend.
Seldom she wrote, and then the widow's cough,
And constant call, excused her breaking off;

Who, now oppress'd, no longer took the air,
But sate and dozed upon an easy chair.
The cautious doctor saw the case was clear,                110
But judged it best to have companions near;
They came, they reason'd, they prescribed, — at last,
Like honest men, they said their hopes were past;
Then came a priest — 't is comfort to reflect
When all is over, there was no neglect:
And all was over — By her husband's bones,
The widow rests beneath the sculptured stones,
That yet record their fondness and their fame,
While all they left, the virgin's care became;
Stock, bonds, and buildings; — it disturb'd her rest,      120
To think what load of troubles she possess'd:
Yet, if a trouble, she resolved to take
Th' important duty for the donor's sake;
She too was heiress to the widow's taste,
Her love of hoarding, and her dread of waste.

Sometimes the past would on her mind intrude,
And then a conflict full of care ensued;
The thoughts of Rupert on her mind would press,
His worth she knew, but doubted his success:
Of old she saw him heedless; what the boy                  130
Forbore to save, the man would not enjoy;
Oft had he lost the chance that care would seize,
Willing to live, but more to live at ease:
Yet could she not a broken vow defend,
And Heav'n, perhaps, might yet enrich her friend.

Month after month was pass'd, and all were spent
In quiet comfort and in rich content:
Miseries there were, and woes the world around,
But these had not her pleasant dwelling found;
She knew that mothers grieved, and widows wept,            140
And she was sorry, said her prayers, and slept:
Thus pass'd the seasons, and to Dinah's board
Gave what the seasons to the rich afford;
For she indulged, nor was her heart so small,
That one strong passion should engross it all.

A love of splendour now with av'rice strove,
And oft appear'd to be the stronger love:

A secret pleasure fill'd the Widow's breast,
When she reflected on the hoards possess'd;
But livelier joy inspired th' ambitious Maid,                           150
When she the purchase of those hoards display'd:
In small but splendid room she loved to see
That all was placed in view and harmony;
There, as with eager glance she look'd around,
She much delight in every object found;
While books devout were near her — to destroy,
Should it arise, an overflow of joy.

Within that fair apartment guests might see
The comforts cull'd for wealth by vanity:
Around the room an Indian paper blazed,                                 160
With lively tint and figures boldly raised;
Silky and soft upon the floor below,
Th' elastic carpet rose with crimson glow;
All things around implied both cost and care,
What met the eye was elegant or rare:
Some curious trifles round the room were laid,
By hope presented to the wealthy Maid;
Within a costly case of varnish'd wood,
In level rows, her polish'd volumes stood;
Shown as a favour to a chosen few,                                      170
To prove what beauty for a book could do:
A silver urn with curious work was fraught;
A silver lamp from Grecian pattern wrought:
Above her head, all gorgeous to behold,
A time-piece stood on feet of burnish'd gold;
A stag's head crest adorn'd the pictured case,
Through the pure crystal shone the enamel'd face;
And while on brilliants moved the hands of steel,
It click'd from pray'r to pray'r, from meal to meal.

Here as the lady sat, a friendly pair                                   180
Stept in t' admire the view, and took their chair:
They then related how the young and gay
Were thoughtless wandering in the broad highway:
How tender damsels sail'd in tilted boats,
And laugh'd with wicked men in scarlet coats;
And how we live in such degen'rate times,
That men conceal their wants, and show their crimes;

While vicious deeds are screen'd by fashion's name,
And what was once our pride is now our shame.

   Dinah was musing, as her friends discoursed,       190
When these last words a sudden entrance forced
Upon her mind, and what was once her pride
And now her shame, some painful views supplied;
Thoughts of the past within her bosom press'd,
And there a change was felt, and was confess'd:
While thus the Virgin strove with secret pain,
Her mind was wandering o'er the troubled main;
Still she was silent, nothing seem'd to see,
But sat and sigh'd in pensive reverie.

   The friends prepared new subjects to begin,       200
When tall Susannah, maiden starch, stalk'd in;
Not in her ancient mode, sedate and slow,
As when she came, the mind she knew, to know;
Nor as, when list'ning half an hour before,
She twice or thrice tapp'd gently at the door;
But, all decorum cast in wrath aside,
'I think the devil's in the man!' she cried;
'A huge tall sailor, with his tawny cheek,
'And pitted face, will with my lady speak;
'He grinn'd an ugly simle, and said he knew,       210
'Please you, my lady, 't would be joy to you:
'What must I answer?' — Trembling and distress'd
Sank the pale Dinah by her fears oppress'd;
When thus alarm'd, and brooking no delay,
Swift to her room the stranger made his way.

   'Revive, my love!' said he, 'I've done thee harm,
'Give me thy pardon,' and he look'd alarm:
Meantime the prudent Dinah had contrived
Her soul to question, and she then revived.

   'See! my good friend,' and then she raised her head,   220
'The bloom of life, the strength of youth is fled;
'Living we die; to us the world is dead;
'We parted bless'd with health, and I am now
'Age-struck and feeble — so I find art thou;
'Thine eye is sunken, furrow'd is thy face,
'And downward look'st thou — so we run our race;

'And happier they whose race is nearly run,
'Their troubles over, and their duties done.'

'True, lady, true — we are not girl and boy,
'But time has left us something to enjoy.'                    230

'What! thou hast learn'd my fortune? — yes, I live
'To feel how poor the comforts wealth can give:
'Thou too perhaps art wealthy; but our fate
'Still mocks our wishes, wealth is come too late.'

'To me nor late nor early; I am come
'Poor as I left thee to my native home:
'Nor yet,' said Rupert, 'will I grieve; 't is mine
'to share thy comforts, and the glory thine;
'For thou wilt gladly take that generous part
'That both exalts and gratifies the heart;                    240
'While mine rejoices' — 'Heavens!' return'd the maid,
'This talk to one so wither'd and decay'd?
'No! all my care is now to fit my mind
'For other spousal, and to die resign'd:
'As friend and neighbour, I shall hope to see
'These noble views, this pious love in thee;
'That we together may the change await,
'Guides and spectators in each other's fate;
'When, fellow-pilgrims, we shall daily crave
'The mutual prayer that arms us for the grave.'               250

Half angry, half in doubt, the lover gazed
On the meek maiden, by her speech amazed;
'Dinah,' said he, 'dost thou respect thy vows?
'What spousal mean'st thou? — thou art Rupert's spouse;
'The chance is mine to take, and thine to give;
'But, trifling this, if we together live:
'Can I believe, that, after all the past,
'Our vows, our loves, thou wilt be false at last?
'Something thou hast — I know not what — in view;
'I find thee pious — let me find thee true.'                  260

'Ah! cruel this; but do, my friend, depart;
'And to its feelings leave my wounded heart.'

'Nay, speak at once; and Dinah, let me know,
'Mean'st thou to take me, now I'm wreck'd, in tow?

'Be fair; nor longer keep me in the dark;
'Am I forsaken for a trimmer spark?
'Heaven's spouse thou art not; nor can I believe
'That God accepts her who will man deceive:
'True I am shatter'd, I have service seen,
'And service done, and have in trouble been;                    270
'My cheek (it shames me not) has lost its red,
'And the brown buff is o'er my features spread;
'Perchance my speech is rude; for I among
'Th' untamed have been, in temper and in tongue;
'Have been trepann'd, have lived in toil and care,
'And wrought for wealth I was not doom'd to share;
'It touch'd me deeply, for I felt a pride
'In gaining riches for my destined bride:
'Speak then my fate; for these my sorrows past,
'Time lost, youth fled, hope wearied, and at last             280
'This doubt of thee — a childish thing to tell,
'But certain truth — my very throat they swell;
'They stop the breath, and but for shame could I
'Give way to weakness, and with passion cry;
'These are unmanly struggles, but I feel
'This hour must end them, and perhaps will heal.' —

Here Dinah sigh'd, as if afraid to speak —
And then repeated — 'They were frail and weak
'His soul she lov'd, and hoped he had the grace
'To fix his thoughts upon a better place.'                     290

She ceased; — with steady glance, as if to see
The very root of this hypocrisy, —
He her small fingers moulded in his hard
And bronzed broad hand; then told her his regard,
His best respect were gone, but love had still
Hold in his heart, and govern'd yet the will —
Or he would curse her: — saying this, he threw
The hand in scorn away, and bade adieu
To every lingering hope, with every care in view.

Proud and indignant, suffering, sick, and poor,               300
He grieved unseen; and spoke of love no more —
Till all he felt in indignation died,
As hers had sunk in avarice and pride.

In health declining, as in mind distress'd,
To some in power his troubles he confess'd,
And shares a parish-gift; — at prayers he sees
The pious Dinah dropp'd upon her knees;
Thence as she walks the street with stately air
As chance directs, oft meet the parted pair;
When he, with thickset coat of badge-man's blue,                310
Moves near her shaded silk of changeful hue;
When his thin locks of grey approach her braid,
A costly purchase made in Beauty's aid;
When his frank air, and his unstudied pace,
Are seen with her soft manner, air, and grace,
And his plain artless look with her sharp meaning face;
It might some wonder in a stranger move,
How these together could have talk'd of love.

Behold them now! — see there a tradesman stands,
And humbly hearkens to some fresh commands;                320
He moves to speak, she interrupts him — 'Stay,'
Her air expresses — 'Hark! to what I say:'
Ten paces off, poor Rupert on a seat
Has taken refuge from the noon-day heat,
His eyes on her intent, as if to find
What were the movements of that subtle mind:
How still! — how earnest is he! — it appears
His thoughts are wand'ring through his earlier years;
Through years of fruitless labour, to the day
When all his earthly prospects died away:                330
'Had I,' he thinks, 'been wealthier of the two,
'Would she have found me so unkind, untrue?
'Or knows not man when poor, what man when rich will do?
'Yes, yes! I feel that I had faithful proved,
'And should have soothed and raised her, bless'd and loved.'

But Dinah moves — she had observed before,
The pensive Rupert at an humble door:
Some thoughts of pity raised by his distress,
Some feeling touch of ancient tenderness;
Religion, duty, urged the maid to speak,                340
In terms of kindness to a man so weak:
But pride forbad, and to return would prove
She felt the shame of his neglected love;

Nor wrapp'd in silence could she pass, afraid
Each eye should see her, and each heart upbraid;
One way remain'd – the way the Levite took,
Who without mercy could on misery look;
(A way perceived by craft, approved by pride),
She cross'd and pass'd him on the other side.

In principle there is no reason why verse should not be used for anything that prose can do, and vice versa, for the only difference between the two is that verse is written in lines and prose is not: too small a difference to give rise to any theoretical reason for restricting the range of either form. In practice, however, novels, plays, and short stories are nowadays always written in prose; with good reason it might seem, since the more obvious artificiality of verse – even free verse – appears to license a density of verbal effects that might seem out of keeping with the prime object of large-scale narratives, namely, telling a story. Certainly all the narratives we have examined so far have been short, and concerned primarily with something other than the story itself, where there was one at all. How unlikely, then, must it seem that Crabbe's heroic couplets should prove to be a suitable medium for a short story – and what is more a short story of a realistic kind.

Yet over the centuries many stories and plays, and a few novels, have in fact been written in formal verse. And of the stories, at least one or two from Chaucer's marriage group could fairly be styled 'realistic' (if we take realism broadly, as the contrary of fantasy). If this paradox is to be resolved it might be as well to probe a little further into the narrative advantages and drawbacks of the couplet, the nature of realism in general, and of Crabbe's realism in particular, before looking into 'Procrastination'.

A major difference between informative writing and fictional is that in the case of the latter, there appears to be no check by external reality. If a historian says that the battle of Waterloo took place in 1816, his information can be checked – and proved wrong. But no such check exists for the date of a scriptwriter's battle between the forces of Robin Hood and the Sheriff of Nottingham. Since this is a fictional battle, a critic would appear foolish indeed who argued for 1215 instead of the writer's 1216. In a fiction what the author says goes. To that extent realism is a literary convention, since the literary work need not correspond to the precise actualities of the real world. The writer can invent people and places not to be found in any parish register or on any map. So it has been argued that realism and fantasy are logically indistinguishable, the only test of validity for each being that of internal consistency. Surely, however, that is not so; consistency, if not correspondence, with the real world outside may be relevant to one type of work and not to another.

Suppose our scriptwriter had indicated that his work purported to be realistic: by, for instance, introducing references to historical characters such as Richard I and King John, by getting details of the laws, dress, customs, and speech of the period right, by developing round rather than flat characters who felt and thought in an unmodern way, then surely we should have had grounds for complaint had he given the date of his battle as 1715, or 1815, or 1915, or indeed as anywhere but the early thirteenth century. For this would be a kind of work in which internal consistency necessarily involved consistency with the outside world of non-literary reality — something not called for by the other kind of work we are roughly styling 'fantasy'. That such works need not correspond with the facts of that world in the way histories must does not absolve them from the requirement of *verisimilitude*, of being very *like* those facts.

It is clear, however, that much depends on what is purported. The writer can establish his own conventions, to a considerable extent, without breaking through such an elastic mode as the 'realistic' altogether. Wordsworth censured Crabbe's tales for being 'mere matters of fact' — surprisingly, perhaps, in view of some inclination of his own in that direction, but in any case wrongly. Anyone who chooses to tell a tale in heroic couplets cannot be *merely* factual. From the beginning the facts of address and dialogue are being subordinated to a convention. For in life nobody reports an event in rhymed verse or has the characters concerned speak in couplets. But that need in no way move the work towards fantasy, or even symbolism. Nothing in this convention need militate against a high degree of verisimilitude in every other respect. And 'Procrastination' does indeed seem to be both internally consistent (in ways other than that of the purely formal consistency imposed by the couplet form) and also consistent with the world of contemporary reality (not to mention the permanent realities of human nature). Still, one may ask, are there any positive advantages to warrant the use of this verse-form rather than prose, which would have reduced the element of literary convention to a minimum — an appropriate aim for realism?

One advantage is the possibility of an esthetically pleasing tension between form and content, or of greater stylistic density than would normally be found in a prose story. Both these advantages are marvellously evident in Pope's *Rape of the Lock*. In that poem, though, story and character are minimal, and its outside reference is to a very limited world. Its virtues lie in its verbal amplification. In brief, it is much nearer to the norms of shorter poems than to those of extended prose narratives.

Crabbe, though often compared with Pope, cannot compete in this field. Another advantage is that verse, especially in the form of rhymed couplets, allows a basically realistic tale more naturally to transcend the limitations of *simple* verisimilitude. It renders more acceptable authorial comment on action and character, and enables it more easily to be made memorably pithy and pointed.

What seems to follow from this is that the writer of extended verse tales should concentrate on stories whose interest lies not in exciting action but rather in matters of mood, tone, character, and the opportunities they provide for pithy comment. Precisely the mode Crabbe adopts.

'Procrastination' comes from *Tales in Verse* (1812). It was written, that is to say, in the heyday of Romanticism; so, though Crabbe is essentially Augustan, it might be expected to differ from something written in the heyday of Augustanism (almost a century earlier); and it does. Crabbe is Augustan[1] in that he is conformist, both in his views and his verse-form, in that his subject-matter is not mainly himself, and in that he 'places' individual behaviour by socially accepted standards, by public rather than private measure. On the other hand, he is just as committed to portraying the humble and the average as is Wordsworth, and like Wordsworth and other Romantics he eschews Augustan poetic diction. Nor does he take the classics as his models as the major Augustans did. Pejoratively speaking, we could say that all this means that formally he is less stylish than they are, and that contentually there is *something* in Wordsworth's jibe about his tales being 'mere matters of fact'. More favourably, we could say that it means he is not so stylish as to blur the narrative line, but is stylish enough to sharpen the points of incidental commentary, and that his factuality creates a sense of authenticity in the whole.

Taken as a whole, the poem is reminiscent of the managerial advice said to have been given to every young music-hall comedian: 'Tell 'em you're going to make a joke, make it, and tell 'em you've made it.' In the opening paragraph of twelve lines Crabbe tells what he is going to say, then he says it at some length in the form of the concrete example that makes up the tale, and he concludes with a moral comment that says, in effect, that he has said it. So this is not a tale that depends on surprise or suspense or plot; nor is the story particularly important; it could be conveyed very briefly. If we are gripped, it is by the unfolding of character and the running comment upon it, explicit or implicit.

In terms of action, the large-scale structure is simple, ordinary, and

1. For other commentary relevant to Augustan and Romantic modes, see pp. 68, note 1 and 93, note 1.

unromantic in every sense of the word. Dinah and Rupert, a humdrum small-town couple, are in love and wish to marry. They postpone their marriage, however, partly out of consideration for the ageing aunt who has looked after Dinah and is now herself looked after by her, and partly out of the prudential consideration of being rewarded with her wealth. Nothing sensational happens. The aunt is not murdered, she does not break her promise to Dinah, making the sacrifice in vain, nor do the lovers have a passionate secret love-life with each other or anyone else. Rupert, finding no advancement at home, goes abroad to seek his fortune (but unlike most fictional heroes does not find it). When he returns, after the aunt's death has left Dinah a well-to-do heiress, she prefers not to share her inheritance with him; and they live once again in the same small town, where they are bound to meet, but now without love or hope.

In terms of tonal and psychological development, however — which is where the verse-form is advantageous — the large-scale structure offers more than the negative satisfaction of the action's deliberate anti-Romanticism or unsensationalism. Many subtleties emerge as the internal tale slowly but economically unfolds. Dinah's original virtue of prudence passes through the stages of esthetic appreciation of valuables, pleasure in business efficiency, insensitivity towards the less fortunate, and pious respectability, before sinking into the vice of 'avarice and pride'. And the reader is left doubtful at the end (to adapt Larkin's phrase) who is the more deceived: Rupert by what she has done to him, or Dinah by what she has done to herself. The tale is not powerful, concentrated, tragic, but muted. Although not long, it is slow; and it is meant to be. It needs the many years of its fictional span to indicate beneath the overt moral theme the psychological leitmotif of Time's gradual, remorseless erosion, shown here in its inward aspect.

Inevitably, however, it is in terms of texture, or small-scale structure that a specifically *verse*-narrative is likely to be justified. Crabbe's qualities may be briefly suggested if we compare the generalisation of his opening couplet with one by the arch-Augustan, Pope. Here is the latter on the subject of marriage:

> Chaste to her husband, frank to all beside,
> A teeming mistress, but a barren bride.

(Moral Essays, Epistle 1)

The victim is spreadeagled, pinned down by brilliant, sharp antitheses. The brilliant management of form and sharp wit arouse admiration and esthetic pleasure, but perhaps leave one wondering if *strict* truth has not been a little subordinated to dazzling effect. Crabbe starts as if he were going to be equally cynical. But not only is his couplet far less packed with matter than Pope's ('the gay, the happy dream' being merely an amplification of 'Love') but also it lacks the pointing-up and pinning-down effect of his antitheses. Instead, we get three possibilities, of which the last changes the suggestion of cynicism into one of realism. If we accept that romantic love *will* inevitably expire eventually, then it seems about right that the chances are one in three that it will turn into something worthwhile, esteem. Indeed Crabbe would probably say, into something better. A plainer verse, in fact, has been preferred as the vehicle of a plain truth. And the same kind of verse – carrying a sense of conviction from its crisp coupletting and clear diction, but abjuring wit and antithesis – carries us through to the end of the introduction, where the fourth and worst possibility – Rupert's fate – is expounded:

> More luckless still their fate, who are the prey
> Of long-protracted hope and dull delay:
> 'Mid plans of bliss the heavy hours pass on,
> Till love is wither'd, and till joy is gone.

Since the title is 'Procrastination' we know in advance what process the tale is to be about.

Not that Crabbe wholly abjures those effects which the obvious artificiality of verse encourages, even in a realistic narrative, more than prose does. Witness, for instance, lines 28 and 29 where the repetition of 'change' formally strengthens what is not fully explicit in the sense, the implied passage of many years:

> And thus the pair, with expectations vain,
> Beheld the seasons change and change again.

Or note the way alliteration links with sardonic effect three key words in lines 90–1:

> With *l*ively joy those comforts she survey'd,
> And *l*ove grew *l*anguid in the careful maid.

Or again, there is the pointing effect of rhyme, so that, for example, we know without italics that 'taste' must be emphasised in line 124:

> She too was heiress to the widow's taste,
> Her love of hoarding, and her dread of waste

(her soul as well as her love has been taken over – but not with conscious malice, and with her own connivance). Sometimes antithesis adds to the sharpening effect of rhyme:

> The thoughts of Rupert on her mind would press,
> His worth she knew, but doubted his success.     (lines 128–9)

But this couplet also serves to remind us that this is a minor element in Crabbe's successful use of rhymed verse for storytelling. For the psychological implication, so crisply conveyed, is what mainly interests us by this time: that Dinah cannily weighed moneymaking against personal worth. Here, of course, we do have a certain wit; the line sums up her state of mind, and its quality, in an epigrammatic way. Moreover, the enforced terseness of a ten-syllable line enables Crabbe plausibly to avoid full explicitness. That we are not *told* which side weighed heavier (though the following lines suggest one) allows us to infer that Dinah does not *consciously* know herself; i.e. to infer unconscious hypocrisy. Similarly, the compressed psychological implications of 'careful' in line 91 probably seem rather more important than those of the alliteration noted. Dinah is careful in that she has cared for the widow, in that she did not take risks with her future or her emotions, and in that she looked after her valuables. Care, in fact, becomes a motif in the poem; witness line 119, where the word means both *responsibility* and (ironically, as the next couplet indicates) *worry*, or line 127 where it introduces a hint of difficult calculation in what ought to have been a state of emotional anguish. Quiet psychological irony, indeed, pervades the poem. It is glimpsed in dialogue:

> 'All will be yours; nay, love, suppress that sigh;
> 'The kind must suffer and the best must die.'     (lines 58–9)

Though less striking than Pope's, this irony has unexpected range. The sigh is clearly for Dinah's postponed marriage, the aunt blackmailingly assumes it to be for her own future decease (thus casting grave doubt on 'kind' and 'best'), and the reader foreknows that Rupert is going to do most of the suffering and sighing. It is glimpsed quite differently in the references to books. First, 'Romantic notions now the heart forsook, / She read but seldom, and she changed her book' (from novels and poems, we may assume, to works of piety, lines 102–3). Then:

> Within a costly case of varnish'd wood,
> In level rows, her polish'd volumes stood;
> Shown as a favour to a chosen few,
> To prove what beauty for a book could do.     (lines 168–71)

Clearly – and this stands as a symbol for her own personality – care for appearances has taken over.

The verse-form also gives an added pungency at key points in the story.

Thus, as Dinah's 'care' is becoming ever more ironically and ambiguously seen, we get these lines:

> Miseries there were, and woes the world around,
> But these had not her pleasant dwelling found;
> She knew that mothers grieved, and widows wept,
> And she was sorry, said her prayers, and slept. (lines 138–41)

Excerpted, it does not have the point and power that Pope may have in quotation, but it is verse sufficiently pointed to add unobtrusively that little extra punch, in its place in the story, that equally plain prose would not. Other, very different, instances are Dinah's hypocritical speech beginning at line 220, where the organised efficiency of the verse-form belies the frailty she alleges; and, following it, Rupert's forthright reply, which must make it impossible for her to deceive herself as to her real motives. Here the verse-form permits us to take the aphoristic clinching lines as perfectly natural, though no one actually speaks in rhymed aphorism:

> 'Something thou hast – I know not what – in view;
> 'I find thee pious – let me find thee true.' (lines 259–60)

> 'Heaven's spouse thou art not; nor can I believe
> 'That God accepts her who will man deceive.' (lines 267–8)

Finally, though the essential tale, the moral–psychological one, is really concluded in the summary couplet 'Till all he felt in indignation died / As hers had sunk in avarice and pride' (lines 302–3), the poem actually ends with a little incident that seems in no way anticlimactic, despite its triviality. The last paragraph, in particular, might well have seemed gratuitous, save for two things. First, the fact that it is entirely composed of authorial comment with a strong moral undertone, nevertheless does not lead to a sense of intrusion; for it fully matches up to realism's demands of external and internal consistency. We do not feel the author is thrusting an arbitrary parable upon us. In the Dinah we have come to know we recognise a human type; and the way she is said, in this paragraph, to think and act is so obviously the way this fictional woman *would* have done that we feel no compulsion to question its relevance. Second, the metre and rhyme give an air of definiteness and clarity to what is in fact a rather subtle psychological analysis, underlining what the tale has already shown of Dinah's development. Thus what might well have seemed trivial and preachy comes over as a conclusive reminder.

# Conclusion

In the preface it was remarked that for literary criticism there was no standard bridge for all crossings; in the introduction, that there were no seven roads to Seven Pillars of Wisdom; and so it has turned out. Following what seemed to be the signposts erected by the poems themselves, we have taken many different paths. Though a number of the poems analysed have been of the same kind – e.g. in being 'Romantic' or 'Augustan' or in being ballads – every treatment has been different. Rightly so, for what is common to different works tends to be commonplace, obvious, or uninteresting; worth comment only as a stage on the way to an appreciation of something richer, each work's individuality.

Sometimes the initial approach was systematic: a preliminary scanning in terms of mode, type, and kind, or form, theme, and background. More often it was not; some particular angle of approach seemed to call for more attention (though never for *exclusive* attention): theme, kind, story, mode, persona, empathetic qualities or intellectual ones, some aspect of the parts-and-whole dilemma, or whatever. Sometimes it seemed useful to compare the poem with another by the same author, or by a different author (or to bring in another critic's views). Sometimes contrast seemed more valuable than comparison – and this accounts for some of the juxtapositions in the ahistorical ordering of the poems. On the other hand, it turned out that many, indeed most of the poems could perfectly well be considered singly. Sometimes social, historical, literary-historical, biographical, or philosophical information in some degree or other seemed highly desirable; at other times it seemed less desirable, or quite unnecessary. Sometimes general considerations seemed to thrust themselves forward as the best starting-place, sometimes details. Sometimes one aspect of theory seemed particularly appropriate for getting the attributes of the poem in the best perspective (say, pondering on the roles of personae, or on imposed versus organic form), sometimes another seemed preferable (say, truth-to versus truth-about, or decorum).

In the course of all this we have run most of the gamut of kinds of

168

poem: lyric, dramatic, narrative; concrete and abstract; personal and impersonal; rhymed and unrhymed; traditional and experimental; metrical, syllabic, and free; fine poems and faulty; those interesting for what was 'of an age' in them, those for what was 'for all time'; and so on. We have also largely covered the gamut of useful points or critical theory: that is to say, those that relate to practical methods of literary appreciation (as against that theory which is devoted to the sociology or the politics of literature in general, or the philosophy of language in general, or which is a branch of ontology – theory that is a handicap rather than a help to criticism; it is theory for metacriticism).

If any absolutely general rule may seem to have emerged, about the relationship of theory and practice, it can only be the rule that for an art so subtle and various as literature any 'rule' should have the status of a tip rather than a dogma. Two rather general principles, however, seem to have emerged: firstly, that one should look and think round a work before coming to conclusions about it, for the interpretation is then more likely to be central than eccentric; secondly that description and descriptive-evaluation should precede approval-evaluation wherever possible.[1] This still leaves, of course, two problems: on what lines does one *start* looking and thinking round, in order to put particulars in perspective or relate them to some generality, and what *sort* of description should come first, for the best result? To these problems no one solution offers itself; there is no substitute for native sense and sensibility as a basis (this indeed is inherent in the idea of theory as tips rather than dogmas). However, in practice, it seems to have worked out that whatever seemed initially striking, or puzzling, or odd in the individual poem proved a more useful starting-place than one derived from some preconceived principle. Clearly this leaves much scope for individuality. Many readers may feel that other ways into these poems would have been preferable for them, and no one could prove them wrong. After all, a poem is like a mountain, in so far as all paths eventually lead to the summit. Provided checks are made, by way of triangulation, classification, and interrelation, to ensure that one is not going wildly astray, the craft of criticism need not be inhibited by guild rules or inflexible methods.

---

1. It is almost always possible to separate literary description from evaluation as the expression of social, moral, or personal approval; but *literary* evaluation is sometimes inseparable from description – especially when criticism passes beyond the elementary – since many descriptive terms are necessarily also evaluative (e.g. 'witty' of a comedy, 'hypocritical' of a character).

# Glossary

*Alienation*. In Marxist theory the supposed sense of separation that a worker in a capitalist society suffers from his work and society and therefore from a part of his true self. Brecht, though a communist, uses the concept more favourably, as that sense of separation from a literary work that enables the reader or hearer to think about its implications rather than simply lose himself in the work. Brecht's own alienation techniques – to remind the audience that it is only a play it is watching, and a play with a message – tend to be cruder than those used in the past: witness the delicacy with which Shakespeare moves the audience further into or out of emotional involvement by modulating from prose or free blank verse to regular blank verse or rhymed verse or song, or by apt references within his plays to the stage and players (e.g. 'All the world's a stage / And all the men and women merely players').

*Allegory*. There is a sense in which all allegories are symbolic, since they are not to be taken literally: one thing stands for another. Hence the two words were often used interchangeably (and to a lesser extent still are). On the other hand, some symbols, simply by standing on their own rather than in line with other symbols, are clearly not allegorical. Hence the tendency to separate *allegory* and *symbolism* – a tendency given considerable impetus by the French *Symboliste* movement of the 1890s (Mallarmé being the most extreme practitioner).

The *symboliste* wishes to dissolve *denotative* meaning (q.v.) into a multiple synesthetic apprehension or into a conglomeration of sound-effects and *connotatory* meanings (q.v.). This almost impossible endeavour follows from Pater's idea that 'all art aspires to the condition of music', but the French symbolists tended to add to that the idea of somehow conveying an occult reality lurking beyond the world of material phenomena. Their work had a big influence on modernist literature – and accounts for some of its obscurities – but English and American modernists more often thought of evoking realities of the subconscious rather than of the occult.

The common element, of course, is *suggestiveness* (as against the definiteness of allegory). (See pp. 120–1.)

There are, however, other differences. An allegory is normally an invented world in which flat cut-out characters and unrealistic items illustrate something in, or alleged to be in, the real world (as, for example, Christian and Giant Despair illustrate, respectively, backsliding and reformation, and the obstacle of depressive failure of will). Symbolism normally uses some item of the real world (e.g. Blake's rose, or James's golden bowl) to suggest something more abstract, or intangible (whether subconscious or supernatural), or indefinite. Allegory is sequential, systematic, and conceptual; symbolism instantaneous, expressive, and intuitive.

But since there are many borderline cases, and there is no word but 'symbol' for the separate elements of an allegory, the critic must rely a good deal on care and context to indicate which meaning of the word is in question.

*Anapaest.* (See *Iambic.*)

*Antithesis.* The technique of contrasting balance, often used for ironic effect. Where there are two contrasting pairs and one is a mirror image of the other we have the form of antithesis known as *chiasmus*. Pope's 'Or stain her honour, or her new brocade / Forget her prayers, or miss a masquerade' gives two plain antitheses. Dr Johnson's remark on Lord Chesterfield is an example of chiasmus: 'This man I thought had been a Lord among wits; but, I find, he is only a wit among Lords.' His epigram: 'Let me smile with the wise, and feed with the rich' indicates why *antithesis* is sometimes used to cover *parallelism* (a balance without contrast) since it *might* be argued that if smiling and feeding are simply two parallel pleasures an ironic contrast is implied by 'wise' and 'rich' (that the wise do not get rich, and the rich are too busy to acquire wisdom). On the other hand, 'wise' and 'rich' could simply be taken along with 'smile' and 'feed'.

*Apollonian.* In *The Birth of Tragedy* (1872) Nietzsche maintained that Greek tragedy was not, as was usually maintained, cool, calm, and collected, but rather an unstable blend of the violent, frenzied passions of the subconscious, represented by Dionysus, and the ordering reason and moderation of the social and conscious mind, represented by Apollo. Hence the 'Apollonian' is often used as more or less equivalent to Classicism or Augustanism, and the 'Dionysian' to Romanticism.

*Art.* This word has been used in so many different senses, with so many contraries (e.g. craft, propaganda, entertainment) that the most useful way of treating it seems to be to make a stipulative definition. Since the commonest use of this word in literary history is in the phrase 'Art for Art's sake' a definition that takes account of the implications of that phrase seems likely to be the most useful. The phrase represents a reaction against Victorian ideas of art for morality's or utility's sake; that is to say art is being strongly associated with the *esthetic* (q.v.). The following definition, then, seems to be as clear and useful a one as is possible in an area where absolute precision is not to be hoped for: *any artefact that is rewarding to purely internal perception is to be considered a work of art*. Works of art, that is to say, are those characterised by a strong esthetic element. It follows that the property of being 'art' need not be a work's most important property. This seems particularly true of the novel, where such properties as excitement, humour, psychological insight, perceptive moral comment, and so on may make the work worthwhile as literature though its esthetic element might be slight. Thus limited, 'art' may become more useful as a critical term than it has been.

**Blank verse.** Unrhymed iambic pentameter (see *Iambic*). The standard form for Elizabethan and Jacobean plays, but also commonly used then, and later, for non-dramatic poetry — Milton's *Paradise Lost* being the most eminent example.

**Biographical fallacy.** Basically the assumption that a writer's life gives a measuring-rod for the assessment of his work. The term is also used to cover what is often distinguished as the *Romantic fallacy*: the assumption that a work is valuable in the degree to which it gives insight into the heart of the writer. Objections to the first are that we often do not know the author's life, and that if we did it would most likely be quite irrelevant to the assessment of the qualities of any kind of work except the self-expressive. Objections to the second, the Romantic fallacy, are again that we may not know about the writer's life and are therefore simply talking in an obscure way about the qualities of the work when we allege what it reveals of the life, and that such revelations anyway are irrelevant to the qualities of works on some other subject. The following passage from one of Coleridge's lectures implies, without bluntly stating, both fallacies (in reverse order):

> No one can rise from a perusal of this immortal poem without a deep sense of the grandeur and purity of Milton's soul, or without feeling how susceptible of domestic enjoyments he really was, notwithstanding the discomforts which actually resulted from an unhappy marriage. He was, as every great poet has been, a good man; but finding it impossible to realize his own aspirations, either in religion, or politics, or society, he gave up his heart to the living

spirit and light within him, and avenged himself on the world by enriching it with this record of his own transcendent ideal.

*Carpe diem.* (Latin: 'seize the day' — or in modern parlance 'live now, pay later.') The phrase goes back to Horace, the kind of poem even further. In English this kind of poem — urging people, usually maidens, to make the most of their youth — is most commonly found in the sixteenth and seventeenth centuries; the best-known example probably being that quoted in critique 3, Herrick's 'To the Virgins, to Make Much of Time'.

*Connotation.* For literary critics the connotation of a word is the suggestions and associations it has, and the *denotation* is its central, or dictionary meaning. The former, then, is roughly the emotive meaning, the latter the cognitive meaning. Thus 'shade' and 'shadow' have very similar denotatory meanings (a patch of darkness, in a brighter area, caused by the interception of light-rays), but the connotations of 'shade' are favourable, those of 'shadow' unfavourable as a rule. Philosophers use the terms differently.

*Dadaism.* The precursor of Surrealism. The Dada movement began in Zurich in 1916 as an anarchic reaction to the monstrosity of World War I. All traditional forms of art were subverted (e.g. poems were created by drawing words at random out of a hat, music by throwing metal pots and pans downstairs). In 1922 it was superseded by the somewhat more purposeful surrealist movement, which — drawing on Freud — maintained that the subconscious had a reality of its own that was superior to that perceived by consciousness. They aimed at a revolution in consciousness that would change the world; and much to Stalin's annoyance tried to associate themselves with the Communist Party. Both movements have had an enormous influence on the avant-garde, but less on literature (since words are essentially carriers of meaning) than on the visual arts and music. Several explanations of the word *dada* have been given, but it was probably chosen as a nonsense-word.

*Denotation.* (See *Connotation.*)

*Dionysian.* (See *Apollonian.*)

*Dramatic.* (See *Type.*)

*Empathy.* Feeling in, as against *sympathy*, feeling with. If Keats had written 'The petals of sweet peas, like butterflies . . . ' that would have been a straightforward simile. What he actually wrote, 'Sweet peas, on tiptoe for a flight', is an example of empathy, for the image draws in the reader to share the sense of muscular tension, of incipient lift-off. In Burns's 'Wee, sleekit cowrin' timorous beastie' we have an example of sympathy.

*Esthetic.* Esthetics (or aesthetics), usually defined as the study of the beautiful, has developed into a very formidable subject. But the essence of the esthetic is the idea of *disinterested* pleasure. Pleasure, that is to say, unrelated to any moral or practical benefit. The object, whether a work of nature or art, is regarded and appreciated for itself; it is an end in itself and not a means to some other end. Esthetic appreciation, then, involves a state of being comparable to that involved in genuine moral decisions – a state in which one is temporarily freed from the tyranny of the self. According to Kant, in any given case the esthetic state should be potentially universal. Thus, though it is a subjective state, it is derived from real qualities in the object perceived – therefore potentially perceptible by others – and is not merely personal and illusory. This means that esthetic appreciation is dependent on the perception of formal qualities: appreciation derived from a perception of the relations of parts with parts and parts with the whole, or of form with content (where there is a 'content').

Esthetic *appreciation* presupposes esthetic *attention.* For unless a work is regarded in the way indicated – for what it is, not for what it is up to – its esthetic qualities are likely to go unnoticed.

We may distinguish three kinds of esthesis (a blend of esthetic pleasure and critical appreciation): *esthesis of composition*, resulting from purely formal relations (and therefore more characteristic of the fine arts than literature); *esthesis of complementarity*, resulting from the relations of form and content; and *esthesis of condensation*, resulting from the critically appreciative perception of esthetic qualities in part of a work only (strictly speaking, a minimal instance of either of the other two modes). Since the esthetic is the purest of the literary pleasures, the one least exposed to bias from outside the work, it seems the most suitable for defining 'art' (see *Art*). But it by no means follows that this need be the work's most important or valuable quality – only that which defines it as a work of *art.*

*Form.* A word often used to refer to literary kinds or genres; but since we already have those terms it seems better to take form as what contrasts with paraphrasable content, as the *way* something is said as against *what* is said. The word 'paraphrasable' is important since in literary works the way of saying alters the total effect to a greater or lesser degree according as there is more or less reliance on *connotation* (q.v.).

Form is often felt to be *organic* or *imposed*, but the distinction is not always easy to make, nor of great critical relevance. A 'given pattern', such as a sonnet, must in some sense count as imposed form, but in some cases one may feel that though the form came first it suits the content just as well as if the form had grown out of the content – and in that sense it would be a case of organic form. Contrariwise, in a free-verse poem, where the content has not had to be adapted to a pre-set form, content and form may nevertheless seem inadequately matched — thus giving a vague sense in which this would be a case of imposed form. In short, this is more a psychological distinction than a technical one, and is therefore imprecise enough to require some care in use.

Whether organic or imposed, form must be either *structural* or *textural*, the one being large-scale (a matter of arrangement), the other small-scale (a matter of immediate impression). Structural form is a matter of memory, textural form of sensibility. Structure at its most obvious (plot, story, argument) may be said to be the skeleton of the work, texture (diction, rhythms, imagery, syntax) the skin. Some elements are comparable to muscles; a *motif*, for instance, in so far as it is apprehended as a chain of similar images (such as those of darkness and light in *Macbeth*), is structural. In so far as the impact of each image is apprehended as it occurs, it is textural. (And, of course, in so far as it implies a theme, it passes out of the area of form and into that of paraphrasable content.)

In terms of time-arrangement, structure may be *linear* (as in life: a, b, c, d . . . ) or *fugal* (counterpointed for ironic or other effects: d, a, c, b . . . ).

*Given pattern.* (See *Form.*)

*Iambic.* The most common of the metrical forms used in English verse, the other commonly used forms being the *trochaic*, the *anapaestic*, and the *dactylic*. An iambic foot consists of a relatively unstressed syllable followed by a relatively stressed one. ('Relatively', because what matters is not the actual amount of breath used but the amount in relation to the next syllable; so an unstressed syllable in one part of a line might require more effort than a stressed one somewhere else but would still count as unstressed if the following syllable required still more emphasis.) 'The cúr/fĕw tólls/the knell/ŏf pár/tĭng dáy' is a perfect example of the commonest metrical form in English poetry, the iambic pentameter (a line consisting of five iambs). A *trochee* is the reverse of an *iamb* (DUM-di, instead of di-DUM). An *anapaest* is like an iamb with an extra unstressed syllable (di-di-DUM) and a *dactyl* is the reverse (DUM-di-di).

The art of good metrical composition is to adapt metre to the demands of sense and speech-rhythm without losing it altogether or lapsing into doggerel. So, normally one has in a good poem the sense of a solid metrical base but relatively few perfectly metrical lines.

*Implication.* (See *Purport.*)

*Imposed form.* (See *Form.*)

*Intentional fallacy.* Intentionalism is the idea that a literary work can be

175

judged successful in the degree to which it corresponds to the intention of the author. There are, however, several reasons for supposing such a standard of judgement fallacious:

(1) We usually do not know the author's intention, and if he is dead have few ways of finding it out. All anonymous works would be in principle unassessable.

(2) Scholarship, designed to show what the author's intention was likely to have been, can never be conclusive; an author might on occasion act out of character, or just for once write against the political party or church he normally favoured.

(3) Even if we do know the author's conscious intention, the work may well have been influenced by an unconscious intention — whether for good or ill being a matter of literary judgement.

(4) The intention might be foolish or trivial or otherwise reprehensible. Are we to rate a work that perfectly realises such an intention above one that does not quite perfectly realise a clever or profound or noble one?

(5) Suppose a computer were to be programmed with the syntactical rules and the vocabulary of Shakespeare's sonnets and set to work at random. Eventually, by chance, it would turn out an exact replica of one of the sonnets. By the intentional theory we should be obliged to say — logically, but nonsensically — when faced with two identical sheets of printed paper that one, written with an intention, displayed a fine poem, the other, written by a machine, a meaningless one — but we could not say which was which!

(6) Just as a writer can deliberately say what he does not mean (believe) so he can accidentally not mean (intend) what he does say. In each case, whether what he says is meaningful or not is determined by publicly agreed dictional usage and rules of grammar. Whether it is *valuably* meaningful is to be decided by any number of standards (degree of interest, wit, subtlety, insight); in *fictions* the author's intention or sincerity will not be among them.

(7) If it is said that, *faute de mieux*, we can deduce the writer's intention from the work itself, we have of course implicitly acknowledged that we do not need the intention in order to perceive the meaning and qualities of the work.

The prevalence of intentionalism in criticism is probably due to confusion between *external* intention (derived direct from the author or from scholarship) which is irrelevant (see 1 to 7 above) and *internal* intention (implied by the work itself) which is essential to critical appreciation. Since the distinction is so vital it seems sensible to use different words.

That is why *Purport* (q.v.) has been introduced in this book. (See also *Meaning* and *Mode.*)

*Interpretation.* The investigation and exposition of meaning (including the emotional as well as the cognitive). In personal intercourse this *will* involve the speaker's intention, in so far as practical consequences may follow from an utterance. Literary interpretation, however, for the reasons given under *Intention* and *Purport*, is normally better if it confines itself to meaning considered as a property of word-sequences rather than as personal utterance; that is, of what is actually said or implied rather than what might have been in the writer's mind.

Since writing cannot partake in the question-and-answer cycle of spoken communication, the main tool of interpretation is analysis. When interpretation passes over to evaluation (passing, that is, from considering what the work is, to what it is worth) then analysis may well profitably yield to comparison – though this is not invariably the case.

Literary appreciation is not the *product* of interpretation but a *process* that includes it. Degree of interest, for instance, may be part of it; but that belongs more to evaluation than interpretation. Both are necessary to the critical process. Interpretation, in short, is a necessary condition for literary appreciation but not a sufficient one, and should if possible be related to the *whole* process.

*Intrinsic criticism.* The term intrinsic has been used to denote criticism limited to stylistic competence, or, somewhat more widely, to interpretation without evaluation (see *Interpretation*). The former of these usages would exclude reference to any of the 'background' matters covered by 'scholarship' (see the introduction), which would count as being *ex*trinsic. It seems much more useful, however, to have the terms *intrinsic* and *extrinsic* denote different directions of critical interest (i.e. to be synonymous with what we have called *literary* criticism and *meta*criticism). If the critic is primarily concerned to grasp the work's inherent meaning, its identity, to comprehend what it is, then (by our definition) he is doing *intrinsic* criticism, no matter how much background information he finds it necessary to use in order to arrive at that comprehension. He is using that information for the sake of the poem, so to speak, to move inwards to its heart. If, on the other hand, he is concerned to grasp the work's extraneous meaning, its relationship to something else, to comprehend what it is unwittingly a *sign of*, then he is doing extrinsic criticism. He is using the poem for the sake of something else. As was argued in the introduction there are good reasons why intrinsic criticism should precede extrinsic. This is no way prejudges the relative importance of the two.

**Kind.** The words *genre* and *kind* have been used to classify literary works according to any sort of similarity: by form, e.g. sonnet, ballad, ballade; by subject-matter, e.g. war-poem, love-lyric, social novel; by type, drama, epic, lyric; by purport, e.g. satire, parody; by mode, e.g. realism, comedy; and so on. To make the term practically useful it is here regarded as a sub-species of a *type* (q.v.). Thus as *kinds* of the *dramatic* type we would have: play (stage, radio), filmscript (cinema, TV), monologue (ritual, recitation); as kinds of the *narrative* type, ballad, short story, novel, etc.; of the *lyric*, song, elegy, ode, etc.

This definition of *kind*, therefore, is mainly technical (from the differing structural and authorial characteristics of the three types), but partly psychological, from *purport* (q.v.).

**Literature.** The word is most commonly used in three ways. Firstly, to refer to any written material; secondly, to refer to any creative writing or oral compositions (songs, poems, plays, novels, good, bad or indifferent); and thirdly, to refer to highly regarded creative work.

Between the first and the second usage little confusion is likely to arise, as the context will usually indicate whether factual or informative writing is in question, or, on the other hand, imaginative writing. In case of doubt, anyway, the latter can always be distinguished by prefixing 'literature' with the word 'creative'. In this book 'literature' is always used in the second sense: to refer to verbal compositions, written or oral, that are primarily imaginative rather than factual or informative. In short, it is a general term covering lyric, narrative, and dramatic compositions (see *Type*).

Between the second and third usage a good deal of confusion commonly arises. Since no useful purpose is normally served by making 'literature' generally evaluative instead of generally descriptive — it simply encourages a lazy evasion of the critical job of teasing out *why* a work should be highly regarded — there seems good reason for discouraging the third usage. On the rare occasions when a general evaluative statement seems required the established phrase 'classic literature' adequately distinguishes this sense from the (second) descriptive sense.

**Lyric.** (See *Type*.)

**Meaning.** An inherently ambiguous word, for not only are there emotive and cognitive meanings, and meanings supported or not supported by logic or fact (two very different supports), but also a man 'may not mean what he says' in two ways: he may be attempting to deceive or he may incompetently be saying something other than he intended (see *Intentional fallacy*). In common parlance, too, it is often equated with *significance* (q.v.). The only solution to the difficulties of meaning in critical

178

practice is to be careful and explanatory about one's meaning of 'meaning'.

In particular it is especially necessary to be aware not only of the differences but also of the overlapping of three meanings of 'meaning' that constantly crop up in critical discussion:

(1) What the author meant (intended).

(2) What the text says.

(3) What the facts support.

The problem is that (1) and (2) usually overlap, and so do (2) and (3). Naturally, what the author intended to say will usually have a considerable (and often a total) correspondence with what the text actually does say; and what the text does say will similarly overlap with what the facts it refers to support. But there is no *necessary* correspondence. An author might intend to write about a Jacobin but mistakenly refer to him throughout the novel as a Jacobite. If the novel were set in the period of the French Revolution and the character was a Frenchman the facts would not tend to support what the text actually said. On the other hand, if he were a Scot whose father had gone into exile in France after the 1745 rebellion, one set of facts might support the idea that he was a misdescribed Jacobin, another that he was in fact a Jacobite; and a good deal of judicial weighing up might be required. Few cases so crude are likely to be found but many subtler ones, similar in principle, are.

*Metacriticism.* (See *Intrinsic criticism.*)

*Metaphor.* Roughly definable by contrast with *simile*. A simile says something is like something else ('My love is like a red, red rose'), a metaphor equates the two ('My love is a rose'). And perhaps one should stop at that, for metaphor is so important to literature and so integral to language itself that further discussion could well reach book-length. Still, something more may be worthwhile if not adequate.

I.A. Richards's terms, *tenor* and *vehicle*, are now normally used to distinguish the different elements conjoined in a metaphor: *tenor* for the abstract or literal meaning, *vehicle* for the concrete or figurative one. Thus in the example above the rose is the vehicle and the idea 'My love is sweet, natural, and beautiful' the tenor. The vehicle, of course, does more than illustrate the tenor; it gives it body. But the *ideas* that the vehicle conveys are more important than the particular image it happens to conjure up (for these will differ from reader to reader — for one perhaps the texture of rose petals would predominate over their scent, for another the rose's subtleties of form; but all these things should embody the ideas of the natural and the beautiful). Where it is difficult to distinguish tenor and vehicle the metaphor is on the verge of being a *symbol* (q.v.). At the other end of the spectrum metaphor may merge with literal usage (as in 'table leg', 'the foot of a mountain', or 'head of state').

Since human thought seems to progress by using the concrete as a step to the abstract, the language is full of *dead metaphors*; that is, metaphors in which the figurative element has been lost sight of. Almost all the abstract terms of literary criticism, for instance, are of this kind. 'Metaphor' itself is metaphorical (lit. 'a carrying over'), so is 'abstract' ('to draw out of') and 'express' ('to press out'). Creative literature is characterised by a higher proportion of live metaphor than normal speech. Since an element of unlikeness between tenor and vehicle is essential to a successful metaphor most could be styled 'mixed', but the term *mixed metaphor* is normally used only when the vehicle conjures up images quite incongruous with the tenor — as the idiotic domestic activity of 'let us iron out this bottleneck' is incongruous with the tenor of efficient reordering and speeding up.

**Metre.** The regular alternation of stressed and unstressed syllables in some set pattern (see *Iambic*). Where it is difficult to say whether a syllable is stressed or not it is usual to speak of a hovering stress; where two stressed syllables come together we have a spondee (e.g. farewéll). Metre, like *rhyme* (q.v.), tends to act in the same way as a frame for a picture, setting it apart from the practical world as an object for contemplation. It also acts as a base against which effects of speech-rhythms may show up more sharply or significantly. Or, for good or ill, it may induce a state of slight hypnosis.

**Mimetic.** (Greek: *mimesis*, imitation.) Since 'imitation' is useful as a term for pieces of writing that loosely copy other literature, 'mimesis' is better reserved for writing that tries to imitate, or recreate in verbal form, a three-dimensional world. This is not to limit the mimetic to *realistic* writing. It is to be contrasted rather with the *didactic* or the *emblematic*. Thus a round character would be mimetic, even if he appeared in a romance or fantasy, whereas a flat character standing for some quality (like Jonson's Volpone, the Fox) would be both didactic and emblematic, even if he appeared in an otherwise realistic work. Mimesis is much more characteristic of works striving for verisimilitude (truth-to) than works striving for elucidation (truth-about). Mimetic writing tries to 'prove on the pulses', the didactic tends to rely on argument, and the emblematic is akin to ritual (graphic heightening of what is already accepted). 'The Twa Corbies', in this book, provides an example of a work which is to a considerable degree mimetic but cannot be described as fully realistic (since crows do not talk).

**Mode.** A concept closely allied with those of *kind* (q.v.) and *purport* (q.v.).

Roughly it might be said that if a work turns out in fact to be the kind of work it purports to be at first sight then that is its mode. But the matter is more complicated than that, for the concept of mode is a very general one that cannot claim absolute validity but only critical usefulness – and its usefulness lies precisely in the flexible generality which leads the critic into more refined areas.

A work's mode, let us say, is whatever it is in its most general aspect. But that leads us into the parts-and-whole dilemma: the fact that we often cannot interpret the parts properly without knowing what sort of whole they are parts of, but can only build up that idea of the whole bit by bit from the parts. A tacking progress is required: checking some parts against a preliminary idea of the whole, seeing if that idea illuminates other more tricky parts, revising the hypothesis if it does not, and so on. In this way a consideration of mode leads into matters of *mood* (q.v.), *tone* (q.v.), *type* (q.v.), and *kind* (q.v.), and thus provides variables for triangulation. Moreover, what *is* most general may depend in part on our special concerns. If we are concerned, say, with 'the ballad', then it would be useful to take as 'mode' what we would more usually call a kind. For, firstly, we wish to sort out everything that would count as 'ballad', we want the most general characteristics; only then can we go on to consider *kinds* of ballad. On the other hand, were we interested in narrative poetry, we should first have to sort out the narrative mode – of which the ballad would be one kind. With this reservation in mind, mode may be defined as follows: basic genre-name denoting the nature of literary works in their most general aspect or effect (a psychological conclusion, rather than a logical one, derived from a consideration of all elements in the work – unless the mode has been predetermined by some special interest). Examples of modal aspects, running from the more to the less exclusive – the last being interchangeable with 'kinds' – could go as follows:

(1) Fictional/non-fictional.

(2) Realism, fantasy.

(3) Mimetic, metaphoric, rhetorical/factual, abstract, controversial.

(4) Mythic, Romantic, Augustan.

(5) Tragedy, comedy, tragi-comedy, farce, meditation, sentimental work, celebration, thriller.

The merit of asking after mode is not that of establishing the obvious but rather that of drawing attention to *various* general aspects of the work (which may then lead to more particular ones). Thus (1) would draw attention to the fact that there is a base of real (though mixed-up) history in *Macbeth*; (2) that there is much realism (especially of a psychological kind) alongside the obvious fantasy; (3) that though the play is largely metaphoric (especially of light-and-darkness) it is often mimetic and contains passages of rhetoric; and so on.

*Modernism.* The term is commonly used to cover all kinds of experimentalism in the period *c.* 1910–50. But it is more usefully restricted to writing like that of Joyce, Eliot, Pound, or Virginia Woolf that abandons or distorts traditional forms in order to convey a new vision of the nature of reality. Experimentalism that consists of novelty for novelty's sake or for the sake of annoying the bourgeoisie is better distinguished as avant-garde. The age of *Modernism*, so restricted, seems to have passed (so the term is unfortunate; today's writing has to be distinguished as 'contemporary'). The avant-garde is still with us but seems to be ailing, Dada and Surrealism, the main movements, being mere shadows of what they once were.

Though Modernism started before World War I that conflict rendered it acceptable to a much wider public and stimulated its output. The great period of modernist literature comes in fact between the wars.

*Mood.* (See *Tone.*)

*Neo-Dadaism.* (See *Dadaism.*) That development of Dada which is known as concrete poetry, or shape poetry and sound poetry. At its most extreme, shape poetry, so called, becomes a form of sub-art, since it consists of shapes made not with words but with letters or even bits of letters, and thus abandons meaning, of any sort, altogether; and sound poetry, so called, becomes a form of sub-music, since it consists of tape-recorded whistlings, hissings, spittings, gruntings and the like, sometimes speeded up or played backwards, with or without the accompaniment of the original tape, and thus also abandons meaning.

*Narrative.* (See *Type.*)

*Objective.* (See *Subjective.*)

*Organic form.* (See *Form.*)

*Pantheism.* The identification of God with nature as a whole.

*Persona.* Literally the mask worn by actors in Greek and Roman drama. Now applied to the *voice* or *mask* of a literary work. Since we cannot ever be sure that an author is speaking in his own person it is probably better, in strict theory, always to speak of the persona rather than the poet or the novelist — though in many cases we may feel it highly probable that the mask is exactly like the face. In cases where it is obviously not, we may have to assume a double persona. For example the duke whose monologue makes up Browning's 'My Last Duchess' is so clearly not Browning, and not meant to be identified with him, that we have to assume a ghostly Browningesque persona subtly tipping us off about the duke. On the other

182

hand, there seems to be no other persona lurking behind Defoe's Moll Flanders, guiding our attitude to her. Sometimes we are for her, sometimes against her, but not under any consistent guidance; so she seems to reflect mixed attitudes in the author himself. Sometimes, as in 'The Twa Corbies' (q.v.), we have not an ostensible and implied persona (as in 'My Last Duchess') but a primary and secondary one.

**Petrarchan sonnet.** Named after the Italian poet Petrarch (1304–74) who was noted for his elegantly extravagant and idealistic love poems. By no means all his sonnets were in fact in the form now known as *Petrarchan* (as distinguished from the *Shakespearian*).

In both forms the metre is iambic pentameter (see *Iambic*), but the Petrarchan sonnet is divided into two parts, an octave (or octet) and a sestet; the Shakespearian into four parts, three quatrains and a concluding couplet. A Petrarchan sonnet normally rhymes *abbaabba cdecde* (though some latitude is permitted for the sestet), a Shakespearian, *abab cdcd efef dd*. Thus the one form is particularly suitable for an example and a reflection upon it (or vice versa) and the other for a progressive argument and a summing up, or for showing three aspects plus a concluding comment (or twist in the tail). But in fact all kinds of content have been expressed in both forms.

**Plot.** According to E.M. Forster, the grammar of *story* is 'And then . . . ' while that of *plot* is 'And therefore . . . ' Story, we may say, is sequential, plot is consequential. 'The queen died, and then the king died', Forster says, is story. 'The queen died, and then the king died *of grief*' is plot. In the present work 'The Twa Corbies' and 'Lady, weeping' are examples of narrative poems with *plots*, of action and psychology respectively. 'The Draft Horse' and 'Procrastination', examples of narrative poems with *stories*, of symbolic action and moral psychology respectively.

Plot, the later development in literary history, is usually regarded as superior to story, but in many novels depth of character-study and plausibility of action may be sacrificed to the demands of plot, as they need not have been to the lesser ones of story.

**Pointillisme.** From the French *pointiller*, to dot. The term is primarily associated with the practice of the neo-impressionist painters of the late nineteenth century who evolved the technique of rendering objects *as seen in a certain light or atmosphere*, conveying colour not as a wash of that particular shade but as a varying mixture of tiny dots of different (mainly complementary) colours. Since the dots are not seen as such, unless one peers closely at the canvas, but do contribute to a total effect not obtainable otherwise, the term can be used in literary criticism for tiny, even subliminal, effects which nevertheless contribute subtly to the poetic total.

*Prose.* A word responsible for a good deal of confusion, largely because it is taken to be the contrary of two other words, often but not always regarded as referring to different things, namely, *poetry* and *verse*. If 'poetry' is taken in an evaluative sense rather than a descriptive one, we can get the paradoxes of 'prose poetry' and 'prosy verse', which do not aid clear critical discussion. The existence of 'free' verse, having neither rhyme nor metrical or syllabic patterning, complicates the matter still further. It might seem sensible to drop the word 'poetry' altogether, in favour of 'verse'; but the word is so well-established that this is likely to prove impracticable, and anyway the word 'poem' is certainly needed, since there is no parallel, for verse compositions, to 'novel', 'short story', or 'essay' for those in prose; it would be tedious indeed always to have to speak of 'a complete set of verses' instead of a 'poem'. The answer seems to be to remove the evaluative element from 'poetry' and 'poem' (the search for an intangible 'poetic' quality or essence having, in any case, produced mountains of inevitably useless and fruitless argument). So, we might define 'verse' as any writing in which line-length is part of the expressive form; 'prose' as any writing in which it is not. A 'poem' would be any complete structure of verses; 'poetry' a complete body of poems (as in 'eighteenth-century poetry' or 'ballad poetry').

*Purport.* Briefly, *purport* distinguishes the internal 'intention' of the work – a necessity for adequate criticism – from the intention deduced from external evidence, which is irrelevant – at any rate in logical, if not always in psychological terms (see *Intentional fallacy*). It is closely connected with *mode* (q.v.) and *kind* (q.v.). Indeed, it might be argued that the term is not really needed, since if we discern a work's purport rightly then that is what the work *is*, as a whole, taken generally: i.e. that is its mode. So, for instance, the evidence showing that a work purported to be didactic would also be evidence showing it *was* didactic. There is a good deal of truth in this, for in the nature of things what a work purports to be will often coincide with what it actually is – and both of them probably with what the author intended. Even if this were *always* the case, however, there would be some sense in having both terms; the concept of 'purport' introduces a beneficial element of preliminary uncertainty. We are asking 'What does this mean to mean?' before jumping to a conclusion about what it does mean. But it is not always the case. What a work signals it means to be may not, on closer examination, tally with what it actually turns out to be – in which case purport will not coincide with mode; indeed, the discrepancy may be such that we need to speak of an ostensible purport disguising the real mode (e.g. in cases of clever propaganda). For those cases in which the writer unconsciously departs from his purport we need the term *implication*. For instance, Milton's *Paradise Lost* certainly purports to be on God's side, indeed specifically to be justifying the ways of God to Man. And everything we know of Milton's life and opinions suggests that such a purport represents his conscious intention. Yet Blake held that he was on the Devil's side without knowing it, and Shelley thought he was deliberately attacking Christianity under the guise of defending it. And it is at least arguable that as a defeated rebel, cast (doubly) into darkness. Milton had a subconscious sympathy with Satan that caused a discrepancy (especially in the early books) between purport and mode — the discrepancy itself being the implication glimpsed in tone, mood, and matters of diction.

The concept of purport, like that of mode or kind, is needed because a work cannot be sensibly criticised without some idea of what *sort* of work it is. There is no point, for instance, in blaming a poem that means to be light and amusing for lack of high seriousness (see the Sedley poem in the introduction) — though metacritically the whole genre of light verse might be argued against quite legitimately. Again, the parts making up the poem as a whole cannot be interpreted correctly unless we know what sort of whole they are parts of (e.g. parodic, symbolic, fantastic, say, rather than serious, didactic, or realistic). But as it is only from the parts that our idea of the whole is built we may need several hypotheses, each corrected in the light of the evidence of later parts, before we arrive at the idea of a modal whole. That is to say, the purport may turn out to be more complex than it first appeared (or more confused, by implication). In either case, consideration of this concept will have led us towards many aspects of the poem, and helped to encourage looking round before leaping to a conclusion.

Many critical terms — especially perhaps 'structure', 'texture', and 'form' — tend to suggest that the work is an *object*, 'Purport' acts as a useful corrective to this tendency, reminding us that literary works are essentially interior *actions* (see the introduction).

*Referent.* The non-verbal reality words may refer to. For example, the referent of the word 'wasp' is the striped, stinging, winged insect that gives the word its meaning, as a referential noun.

*Rhythm.* If *metre* (q.v.) is rhythm formalised, conversely *rhythm* could be described as metre liberalised, so that the stresses are not pre-set but organised within groups of words so as to bring out the appropriate sense and tone. Thus we saw, in Ransom's 'Piazza Piece', that the technically iambic line 'Ĭ ám/ă lád/y̆ yoúng/ĭn beáu/ty̆ wáit/ĭng' could be read in two, rhythmically different ways, giving different implications of meaning and tone:

Ĭ aɱ ă lădy/yoúng iň béautў/wăitiñg

Or:

Ĭ aɱ ă ládў yoŭng/iň beăutў wáitiñg

It could also be read *un*rhythmically, i.e. so as to make the worst of sense and tone, and not to sound like natural pleasing English speech, e.g. 'Ĭ aɱ á/ládў yoŭng iń béau/tў wáitiñg (see critique 6).

*Rhyme, feminine.* A rhyme is masculine when the final syllables are stressed, as in 'sigh' and 'die'; it is feminine when the stressed syllable is followed by an unstressed one, as in 'sighing' and 'dying'. When the rhyme is less than exact in one way or another, as in 'sing' and 'rang' or 'will' and 'well', the term half-rhyme is usually used (or sometimes 'para-rhyme' or 'near-rhyme').

Rhyme helps to set a piece of writing apart as clearly an object for contemplation, to bind a poem together even though it may lack an argument, to emphasise thrust and parry in the content, to point up key concepts, to give a sense of pattern or irrevocable predestination, or just to satisfy the primitive delight in similar sounds evidenced by small children's nonsense rhyming.

*Significance.* In normal usage often more or less equivalent to '*meaning*' (q.v.) but usefully distinguished by E.D. Hirsch, *Validity in Interpretation* (Yale University Press, 1967) as a technical term (roughly equivalent to 'extrinsic' and 'metacritical' as used in this book). Meaning, that is to say, is what the work says in its own created context; *significance* is the meaning of that meaning in a wider context. The pursuit of meaning is the main part of the practice of literary, or *intrinsic* (q.v.), criticism; the pursuit of significance, the practice of metacriticism. The endeavour of the former is to lead to a grasp of the work's identity, to what it *is*; the endeavour of the latter to lead to an understanding of what it is (usually unwittingly) a *sign of*. To pursue meaning is to investigate the poem as poem; to pursue significance is to treat the poem as *document* in some field other than that of literary criticism. Thus the meaning of Shakespeare's Sonnet 138 (q.v.) is all that it reveals of the emotional and cognitive complications in the relationship of an older man and an unfaithful younger woman, plus the tonal effect of the inversion of the conventional use of the sonnet for love poetry. If, however, the reader were to take the persona as Shakespeare himself, and be primarily interested in what the sonnet revealed of his love life – as *his* – then he would be concerned with the poem's significance. For whether he knew it or not he would be using the work as a document in the service of biography. Similarly a Marxist critic who saw the poem, say, as revealing the corruption of early capitalist society and the decadence of bourgeois relationships, in contrast to an

ideal communist society where the sexual relationships of comrades would
be honest and uncomplicated, would be using the poem as a document in
the service of political theory; and again, in so far as he was elucidating
what the poem's significance was, what it was a sign of, would be doing
metacriticism. It seems evident that metacriticism should be preceded by
criticism proper, since the meaning of the work is the only valid evidence
for its alleged significance (see the introduction). To put it logically, one
must have the meaning before one can have the meaning of the meaning,
i.e. its significance.

**Spondee.** (See *Metre.*)

**Stanza.** A group of formally similar lines of verse, making up a unit which
is repeated throughout a poem. It is often called 'a verse'; but a verse
(Latin: *furrow* or *turning*) is strictly speaking a *line* of poetry (see *Prose*).
The strict use of 'verse', of course, accords with such usages as 'blank
verse', 'rhymed verse', or 'free verse'. To speak of a group of verses as 'a
verse' is not logical, so *stanza* is to be preferred.

**Story.** (See *Plot.*)

**Structuralism, structuralist.** French Structuralism (now fashionable also in
America) is neither a simple nor a single system of thought. Nor does it
always go under the same name. In sociology, the method tends to be
known as 'semiology' or 'theory', in literary studies it often goes under the
name of 'deconstruction'. Two basic things, however, can be said of all its
varieties: firstly, that it is a kind of semiotics (the study of signs); secondly,
that it is based on the belief that the methods of Ferdinand de Saussure's
structural linguistics can profitably be applied to all other disciplines.
Thus, in spite of many references to *meaning*, structuralists are in fact
largely concerned only with what our introduction distinguishes as *significance*; and literature has no more importance in principle than advertisements or wrestling matches — which also, when interpreted in terms of
linguistic models, may be seen as unwitting signs of social, economic,
political, or psychological structures.

Philosophically speaking, Structuralism is a form of metaphysical
scepticism. That is why it is known also as 'deconstructive' criticism when
wearing its literary hat. Its two chief theorists, Jacques Derrida and Roland
Barthes — in so far as their jungles of jargon are penetrable — seem to
maintain that the whole Western intellectual tradition is wrong. Words do
*not* refer to the world or its inhabitants. Indeed people themselves are *not*
personalities, but spaces where various currents of convention cross. They
are merely signs of hidden structural forces — and so is the world that each
is in fact constructing for himself under the influence of these structures.
The world is *not* an objective fact. It then follows: that literature can never

be about the world or people, though it has always seemed to be; that it derives not from them but from other literature; and that we are free to read texts as mere *play*, with verbal counters, without feeling any responsibility (e.g. for the iniquities of concentration camps, the deplorableness of greed or whatever, that a novelist might imagine he was revealing through his fiction). Writing that seems to reflect, or reflect upon, reality or human experience is taken by the structuralist to be a trick of language and of preconceptions brought to the text by the reader. (No non-structuralist critic, of course, has ever doubted that language *can* falsify reality or that preconceptions *may* influence a reading; but he has taken it to be the critic's job to distinguish false from valid writing, and to give aid in allowing for preconceptions.)

Since there are no meaningful texts for the structuralist (only signifying ones), Structuralism is open to the logical objection that all the structuralist works that say this must themselves be meaningless, and Structuralism itself be merely another 'sign', another mere expression of structural forces under the surface. But there are more empirical objections.

For instance, it seems inherently improbable that new methods of grammar should turn out to be a key to all other subjects — though the attempt to apply them elsewhere might be stimulating to begin with. Little more than this can be said, for example, in favour of the idea of interpreting whole *novels* as if they were single *sentences* (see Barthes, 'Structuralist Analysis of Narratives', *Image–Music–Text*, trans. Stephen Heath; Fontana, 1977). It is possible but not profitable to do so. The end-result is in fact less illuminating than that of standard critical procedures, for the text tends to be reduced to a skeleton, its structural 'grammar'. Reductiveness is indeed characteristic of the very little actual literary criticism produced by structuralist theorists. The influence of linguistics tends to push back studies already limited by structuralists' own preconceptions (about reality and personality) into the study of language as a general system of signs. The predominant sociological, or otherwise metacritical, concern (for whatever works are signs of) tends to push investigation towards what is common to all works of a kind rather than to the detail and variety that distinguishes one work from another. Indeed Tzvetar Todorov argues that the real business of Structuralism, when it concerns itself with literature, is with 'the system of literary discourse in so far as this is the generative principle behind any and every text'.

Occasionally Structuralism appears to support certain of the more 'advanced' concepts of normal modern criticism. In particular, when Barthes says that it is the reader who is the source of a text's interpretation, not the author (see *ibid.*, 'The Death of the Author') it might seem that he was in accord with the *intentional fallacy* (q.v.). Not so. Critics who uphold the intentional fallacy do not deny that an author does purvey a meaning, or try to. They merely maintain that either it is there in the text or it is not; and since an author may not manage to say what he meant, his alleged intention will not affect what the text actually *does* say. Barthes is maintaining that there is no real author (as there are no real persons) and no meaning — and 'Once the Author is removed, the claim to decipher a text becomes quite futile' (*ibid.*, p. 147). This is almost the opposite of the idea behind the intentional fallacy, the idea of deciphering what a text actually does mean.

In short, Structuralism seems more useful to sociology than to literary criticism, though not all sociologists would agree. It has, however, interestingly extended metacriticism (particularly on advertisements), and stimulated a renewed interest in purely formal intrinsic criticism. But in general it has to be said, in spite of its air of epoch-making discovery, that Structuralism seems, where new, not to be true, where true, not to be new.

**Structure.** (See *Form.*)

**Subjective.** The terms *subjective* and *objective* are sometimes used to distinguish writers who create their works out of their own personality from those who annihilate their personality in that they subordinate it to their subject. In this book, however, such writers have been distinguished as personal, Romantic, or Dionysian (according to the kind of subjectivity displayed) or impersonal, Augustan, or Apollonian, 'subjective' and 'objective' being reserved for kinds of judgement.

As is argued in the introduction objectivity in literary criticism is more akin to that of the law court than that of the laboratory. An objective judgement in science is based on inductive (experimental) evidence which leads to a general theory which in turn enables predictions to be made. A literary judgement is not based on inductive experimental evidence (for literary works are not essentially material things, but mental recreations of the reader), and it cannot be used to predict the nature or quality of future literary works. As Kant long ago pointed out the objectivity of a literary judgement consists in the fact that other readers *ought* to agree with it if they are reasonable, sensitive, and intelligent beings. It is 'objective', in short, by being fair and reasonable rather than eccentric or biassed, and by appealing to evidence — and deduction from it — rather than relying on purely personal impression (i.e. being subjective).

This means that the concept of objectivity in arts, though so different from that in science, does presuppose the existence of a common world independent of the perceiver. It also presupposes that all people of normal senses and sensibilities perceive it in roughly the same way, unless their

189

perceptions have been distorted by extreme cultural pressures. To justify subjectivism in criticism these assumptions would have to be denied. However, since cognition and emotion and feeling derived from the meanings of words are all internal and intangible rather than external and material an element of subjectivity is a necessary part of objective literary criticism. Hence the argument for subjective objectivity in the introduction.

The benefits of objective criticism, as against the purely subjective, seem to be these:

Firstly, it enables us to read out of the work whatever it has to offer, which may well be something we were not already familiar with, rather than reading into it what was already within us – a common habit of the subjectivist. Secondly, it provides valid specialised evidence for any meta-critical excursions we might wish to make. Thirdly, if we are criticising for others, the appeal to common evidence gives us a claim on their consideration, which is not inherent in an unsupported opinion, however striking or sensitive it may be.

*Symbolism, symboliste.* (See *Allegory.*)

*Texture.* (See *Form.*)

*Theme.* Used in two senses: (1) for the paraphrasable or explicitly stated message of a work, and (2) for the main preoccupation of the work in sensory or emotional terms (rather than the cognitive terms of theme (1)). Thus theme (1) in *Macbeth* (see critique 14) might be given as: 'Vaulting ambition o'erleaps itself'; theme (2) (or 'leitmotif') as: 'The conflict of good and evil in the human psyche, as revealed by the succession of scenes and images involving light and dark.' That one word is commonly used for both ideas is due to the fact that repetition of sensory or emotional items is likely to lead to an abstractable idea about them.

*Tone.* Refers to the modulations and inflexions of the voice that indicate a speaker's attitude. But as the 'voice' in a literary work has to be conveyed through print, the *tone* is the result of various devices of intensification, association, or convention (often played *against*) which indicate to the reader how he should read the work if reading aloud.

If the tone of a work may be said to indicate the persona's attitude to the reader, the *mood* (similarly the result of various literary factors) indicates the attitude to the subject. In parodies, for instance, the *mood* will always be mocking (though perhaps with a touch of suppressed envy or admiration) while the tone will always be one of connivance, since the reader is expected to share the joke. Often, however, tone and mood are almost indistinguishable – though the attempt to distinguish them may produce a beneficial spin-off in terms of critical refinement. Sometimes the two are interconnected: witness 'The Twa Corbies' (q.v.) where the neutral tone of the narrator, in an area where we should expect moral indignation, is one of the main elements producing the sardonic mood of the poem.

*Truth.* Even outside the realm of fiction the concept of truth is more likely to lead to confusion than clarification, since it is used differently in logical, empirical, and emotional contexts. The risk of confusion increases when we extend its use to fictional ones; so there is a case for using it sparingly in criticism. Yet there is no necessary contradiction in using 'truth' in connection with admitted fictions (and not all literary works *are* admitted fictions: witness, for example, purportedly autobiographical, or moral, or descriptive poems – or the new 'factional' novels). The opposite of 'true' is 'false', the opposite of 'fiction' is 'fact', so it is logically possible for the concept of truth to be meaningfully applied to admitted fictions. In this book we have distinguished two such usages: *truth-to*, and *truth-about*.

The former implies a correspondence theory of truth: what is true is what seems to correspond to our experience, psychological or social; it is connected with *mimesis* (q.v.) or 'proving on the pulses'. The latter implies a logical or cognitive theory of truth: what is true is what follows from certain assumptions; it is connected with propositional statement or argument. There is also the matter of a work's being true to itself. But as all three categories are rather broad and, for the reason given, potentially misleading, it is probably better to use more specific words and phrases: e.g. common experience, psychological insight, reportage, verisimilitude; value judgement, logical insight, moral wisdom, didactic implication; or consistency, unity, coherence, composition, complementarity; respectively.

*Type.* A basic genre-classification defining the general nature of all literary *kinds* (q.v.) in terms of the way they are presented:

(1) *Dramatic.* The author typically disappears behind his characters. Usually entirely in dialogue, occasionally monologue. The author's relationship with the audience is indirect. (Most typical kind, the play.)

(2) *Narrative.* The author usually mixes narration and dialogue. His relationship with the audience is mediate, as he or his persona is partly visible. (Most typical kind, the tale.)

(3) *Lyric.* The author's relationship with his audience is direct; he speaks for, or as if for (persona) himself. A subjective utterance, giving a sense that it is *confessed* or *overheard*, where narrative is *listened to*. (Most typical kind, the expressive poem.)

*Verse.* (See *Prose.*)

*Villanelle.* A poem in five tercets (three-line stanzas) plus a quatrain. It is entirely on two rhymes, the one in the middle of each tercet, the other everywhere else. The whole of the first line must be repeated as the third line of the second and fourth tercet, the whole of the third as the third of the third and fifth tercets; and the quatrain ends with the first and third lines, in that order.